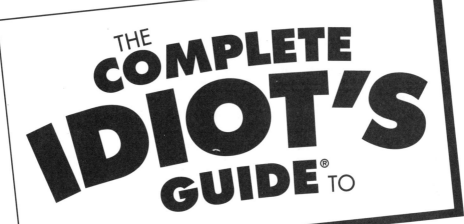

THE COMPLETE IDIOT'S GUIDE® TO

# Macintosh OS 8.5

*Todd Stauffer*

201 West 103rd Street, Indianapolis, IN 46290

# The Complete Idiot's Guide to Macintosh OS 8.5

## Trademarks

## Warning and Disclaimer

**Executive Editor**
*Jeff Koch*

**Acquisitions Editor**
*Mark Cierzniak*

**Development Editor**
*Jane Brownlow*

**Project Editor**
*Kevin Laseau*

**Copy Editor**
*Anne Owen*

**Indexer**
*Heather Goens*

**Proofreader**
*Jennifer Earhart*

**Technical Editor**
*Lisa Lee*

**Illustrator**
*Judd Winnick*

**Interior Design**
*Nathan Clement*

**Cover Design**
*Maureen McCarty*

**Layout Technicians**
*Staci Somers*
*Timothy Osborn*
*Mark Walchle*

# Contents at a Glance

# Contents

## Part 4 The Internet and Other Computers          231

# About the Author

**Todd Stauffer** is the author of more than a dozen computer books, including *Using Your Mac* and *Using the Internet with Your Mac* for MCP. He's also the author of *Macworld Mac Upgrade and Repair Bible* for IDG Books and is the co-author of *PC Upgrade and Repair Answers!* for Osborne/McGraw Hill.

Aside from writing computer books, Todd is co-host of *Disk Doctors,* an Emmy-nominated, nationally televised show on JEC Knowledge TV (http://www.knowledgetv.com). He's also online editor for *NetProfessional Magazine* and a writer for a number of Web sites and publications including CMP's Techweb, The Mac Report, Inside Line, Inside Mac Games, and Webintosh.

Todd is the Mac Chat columnist for *Peak Computing Magazine* and has hosted regional computing radio shows in Denver and Colorado Springs. He publishes a number of Web sites and acts as a Web consultant for print newspapers and publications. Since graduation from Texas A&M University with a degree in English literature, Todd has worked as a magazine editor, advertising writer, and technical writer all in computing fields.

You can reach Todd at **tstauffer@aol.com** or through his site at http://www.shutup101.com/todd/ on the World Wide Web.

# Tell Us What You Think!

As the reader of this book, *you* are our most important critic and commentator. We value your opinion and want to know what we're doing right, what we could do better, what areas you'd like to see us publish in, and any other words of wisdom you're willing to pass our way.

As the Executive Editor for the operating systems team at Macmillan Computer Publishing, I welcome your comments. You can fax, e-mail, or write me directly to let me know what you did or didn't like about this book—as well as what we can do to make our books stronger.

*Please note that I cannot help you with technical problems related to the topic of this book, and that due to the high volume of mail I receive, I might not be able to reply to every message.*

When you write, please be sure to include this book's title and author as well as your name and phone or fax number. I will carefully review your comments and share them with the author and editors who worked on the book.

Fax:     317-817-7070

E-mail:  **opsys@mcp.com**

Mail:    Executive Editor
         Operating Systems
         Macmillan Computer Publishing
         201 West 103rd Street
         Indianapolis, IN 46290 USA

# Introduction

People generally turn to the Macintosh—and therefore the Macintosh operating system, or Mac OS—for one of two reasons. Either they like the Mac OS's ease of use, or they like its built-in tools for creative computer users. Some Mac users are even the sort who appreciate a combination of the two.

If either or both of these reasons are true for you, then rest assured that Mac OS 8.5, the latest version of the Mac's operating system, has both sides covered. It remains easy to use but offers even more features for intermediate users and creative users who want unprecedented control over their computers.

The Macintosh operating system—the computer software that gives a Macintosh computer its own unique personality—keeps making impressive strides and improvements. Now, with Mac OS 8.5, we're seeing some significant changes that represent Apple's vision for the future of the Macintosh. This book covers those changes, while making sure to catch all the tried-and-true features and methods found in older versions of the Mac OS.

Whether you're upgrading or starting fresh with computing, you'll find that *The Complete Idiot's Guide to Macintosh OS 8.5* is an easy-to-digest and enjoyable trip through the world of the Mac OS. By the time you're done, you'll have all the bases covered—from basic mousing all the way up to getting on the Internet and creating your own World Wide Web sites.

Thanks for choosing this book; I hope your experience with the book and your Mac prove pleasing and productive. Let me know if you have any problems or concerns. You can find contact information at this end of this introduction. Best of luck!

## How This Book Works

You'll find that this book really isn't a radical departure from similar books; it offers pages, printed and bound in ascending order (if all goes well), with page numbers, punctuation, and all the goodies you would expect from a book. If anything at all is different, you'll find that the cover is a slightly different color from many other publications.

Best of all, this book takes an incredibly simple approach, eschewing technical terminology in favor of words that have been in dictionaries for 15 years or longer. If you do come across a technical term, I'll thoroughly define and humiliate it before moving forward.

Otherwise, you need to realize and remember only a few basic points:

➤ First, **bold text** is liberally shaken onto the pages of this book and is meant to represent anything you select, type, click, or press, as well as anything you see on the screen.

**Check This Out**

This sort of note will be scattered all over the text, pointing you to more advanced features, shortcuts, different ways of doing things, or other interesting tidbits. You should probably read all of them because they're usually full of advice, information, and useful warnings. Plus, I spent days of effort to make one or two of them witty.

**Techno Talk**

Although I'll stray from long-winded definitions of technical terms, occasionally I'm simply too impressed with my own knowledge to skip offering you some geeky tidbits. You can probably skip these notes if you feel like it. Better yet, though, soak them all up and then regurgitate them in your next job interview. Might not get you the job, but I'll think you're pretty cool.

➤ You'll occasionally encounter a way to accomplish some task that requires you to hold down more than one key on the keyboard at a time. These keypresses are called keyboard shortcuts, and they're usually accomplished by holding down some combination of the oddly named keys toward the bottom of your keyboard. For instance, you'll often be asked to hold down the Command key ([cmd]) along with other keys such as Option and Control (Ctrl). Instead of writing out "hold down the **Command** key while pressing the **Shift** key and **Delete**," I'll often use a plus sign to join together keys that should be held down at the same time, as in **[cmd]+Shift+Del**. You'll know that you should press all three at the same time to invoke a particular command.

➤ *Italic text* is used for words being defined, new words, interesting words, or words that like to draw attention to themselves.

Aside from these conventions, you'll encounter a few marginal notes that are designed to add to, detract from, or otherwise emotionally affect the regular text.

# Feedback and Questions

Nothing helps me more than getting questions, answers, and the occasional correction from an interested and caring reader. If you happen to be one of that sort, please feel free to get ahold of me with your issue in hand. You can find me through Macmillan.

If you have Internet access, feel free to visit me directly on the World Wide Web at `http://www.shutup101.com/todd/`, where you'll find answers to questions, errata, and other important issues as they come up. You'll also find help there for sending me questions or comments via e-mail.

Please check my Web site before writing directly, as many Frequently Asked Questions (FAQs) will be answered there, and I would rather you get the answer immediately than be forced to wait on my personal answer, which can sometimes be delayed for many days.

If you don't have Web access or if you just need to write me directly, feel free. Send an e-mail message without attachments to **tstauffer@aol.com**. Please try to make the subject line as meaningful as possible (not just "Question" or "Hi"). An approximate date by which you need an answer can be helpful, too, as in "2 Days: Error on Page 53." I'll get back to you as quickly as possible.

**Cross Reference**

Often topics will build upon previous material. Even though this book is surely a page-turner in the best traditions of movie novelizations and Harlequin romances, you may feel the need to skip around to different parts of the book. If you do—and you might have missed something in another chapter—I'll try to anticipate such a scenario and point you in the right direction.

# Part 1
# Get Started with Mac

*The Mac OS is pretty easy to learn, as long as you aren't allergic to metaphors. Fire up your Mac and you'll be looking at a desktop, complete with trash cans, folders, pieces of paper, and drawers full of tools. Sort of; actually, you'll be looking at a computer monitor. But the pictures on the screen are metaphorically representing a real-world desktop so that you might feel more comfortable working with your Mac. Rather thoughtful pictures, aren't they?*

*In these chapters you'll learn the ins and outs, and ups and downs of the Mac OS. If you're persistent, you'll even get to meet parts of the OS like Sherlock, Balloon Help and the Chooser. My favorite chapter is Chapter 7, "Mac OS Walkthrough," where you get hands-on with the Mac OS, in a one-on-one bout to the finish.*

# Chapter 1

# Meet the Mac OS

---

### In This Chapter

➤ What the Mac OS is, and why you might care

➤ What's new in Mac OS 8.5?

➤ Can your Mac use Mac OS 8.5?

➤ The ideal upgrade scenario

---

A lot of people at Apple Computer spend a lot of time coming up with exciting new things to do to the Macintosh operating system—the Mac OS— to encourage us all to run out and buy new copies. These people are called software engineers, and they get paid a lot of money to attend Star Trek conventions, design T-shirts, fire off angry e-mail messages to soft drink companies, and, sometimes, to write the computer-language codes that make the wheels of global commerce spin.

Try not to be too afraid.

These same engineers designed and wrote the Mac OS, which in turn is responsible for making sure all the windows, icons, menus, printers, control panels, and the other stuff on your Mac's screen work when you need them to. You'd think this is the sort of thing that could have been mastered years ago, and no additional upgrade versions would be required.

Well, there's an argument for that point of view; I know plenty of folks who compute along just fine without the latest version of the Mac OS. Then again, those Mac OS engineers are pretty bright folks, and they've come up with great stuff in the last few years that makes using a current version of the Mac OS very different from the Mac experience of just a few years ago.

I'll cover some of that in this chapter. If you've never used the Mac OS—or if you're using an older version—be prepared to be wowed. There are a lot of things in Mac OS 8.5 that make computing that much more fun and powerful. And the best part? With most Mac models, all you have to do is install the Mac OS 8.5 software to get all these new features.

# What Is the Mac OS?

Before I get too far ahead of myself, let's backtrack for a moment and take a look at this "OS" lingo. An *OS*, or *operating system*, is really a simple concept: It's a collection of computer commands that tell the computer's hardware how to communicate with its human user and its input/output devices, like printers and keyboards. The Macintosh OS, then, is a particular one of these collections: It's the OS sold by Apple Computer that makes a computer look and feel uniquely like a Macintosh.

If you've used Microsoft Windows, DOS, OS/2, UNIX, or even VMS, you've used an operating system. (In fact, if you've used an Automated Teller Machine to get some Quick Cash, you've used an operating system.) OSes are designed for any number of different uses, from allowing the foreman to control machines on a factory floor to allowing the airflow-to-gasoline ratios to change in an automobile engine.

In the case of personal computers, the OSes tend to be a bit more generalized. The Mac OS, as with other desktop computer OSes like Microsoft Windows, is designed to allow you to accomplish any number of tasks when used in combination with applications. Applications are programs that help you do things: write documents, design pages, create graphics, play games. The applications have to work in conjunction with the OS because the OS is managing the user-to-computer relationship.

Applications like ClarisWorks rely on the Mac OS to interpret the mouse, let it know when a key has been pressed, and even help it print to a connected printer. Here's a scenario: You've launched Microsoft Word, and you want to begin typing a memo. For this to happen, you might think you just press a key on the keyboard, and Word would put the corresponding letter on the page. Well, yes and no. You do press the letter, and Word does put the letter in the memo, but the Mac OS acts as a go-between the entire time. What actually happens is a bit more complicated.

It goes something like this:

```
Mac OS: Okay, Word. You are primary in our sights and go for
processing, over.
Word: Roger, OS. Awaiting data redirection. Over.
Mac OS: We have a confirmed key hit. That's a confirmed key hit, the
letter 'A.' Redirecting data your way, Word.
Word: Roger, OS, data received. The letter 'A' is posted...we have a
```

confirmed visual. I gotta tell ya, that's a beautiful sight. Over.
Mac OS: Roger that, Word. Good job up there.

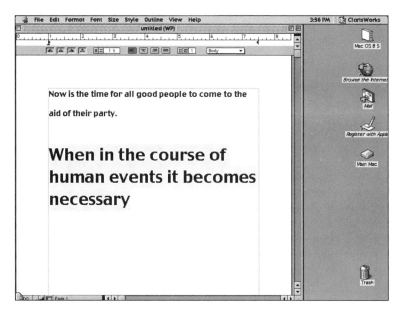

*ClarisWorks works in conjunction with the Mac OS.*

The difference, of course, is that the OS and application communicate using a slightly less jargon-riddled computer language that also happens to be a lot less fun to write.

## Mac OS: Duty, Honor, Service

So why would we want to have the Mac OS as this go-between for applications? Because it allows everybody to work together more happily. It's the same reason that Windows is popular in the PC world: At one time, they had MS-DOS to contend with, which was another thing entirely.

Did you ever use that text-based version of WordPerfect that was so popular on IBM PCs in the 1980s? It ran on MS-DOS, as did all of those old-style, pre-mouse computer applications. It was a good program, especially if you learned all the hidden keystrokes for high-end features like spell-checking, formatting, and printing. It took a while (in fact, there were entire magazines dedicated to WordPerfect—a single application!), but eventually you became an expert. WordPerfect itself had to be expert in something, too: printing. Because it ran on top of MS-DOS, which didn't work like our modern Windows and Mac OSes, WordPerfect actually had to know how to talk to just about any individual printer that might be hooked up to a PC. If the software for your particular printer wasn't built into WordPerfect, you'd have to call the printer manufacturer and ask for a WordPerfect add-on you could install from disk. If the manufacturer hadn't yet written the printer software, you were out of luck.

**9**

It was exactly this sort of problem that advanced operating systems like the Mac OS were originally designed to address. Instead of forcing applications to be responsible for recognizing keystrokes, noticing that you've inserted a new disk, or printing to a connected printer, the Mac OS acts as a knowledgeable middleman that can respond to standard requests from the application and allow it to communicate with the Mac's external devices—including you. (Hey, you're the ultimate external Macintosh device. And you thought your life had no real purpose.)

This separation of duties offers two advantages. First, it allows application developers to focus on creating an interesting application, not the mundane aspects of making a computer work. For instance, Microsoft can focus on making it easier to create charts and add images to documents in Word, instead of figuring out the differences between an Epson inkjet printer and a Hewlett-Packard laser printer. Word just says, "Mac OS, print this letter on whatever printer the user has selected," to which the Mac OS replies, "Aye, aye, Cap'n!"

The second thing this separation of duties does is it allows you to add new features to your entire Mac (applications and all) by upgrading the Mac OS version. For instance, in Mac OS 7.6, Apple added a feature called Desktop Printing. This put a little icon on the Mac's desktop that made it easier to see what's going on with your printer. The best part, though, is that Word, Appleworks, and other programs *don't care*. It simply doesn't matter to them, as long as the standard "print this document" command continues to work. You get a better user-to-computer experience, but the applications don't have to learn any new tricks.

### Know Your Naval

Notice that the phrase "Aye, aye" should always be followed by either a salutation or the rank of the officer (or non–commissioned officer) giving the order. Also, "Aye, aye" is meant specifically as an affirmative response to a direct order, as in, "Well, jump in after him, ensign!," to which you would reply, "Aye, aye, sir!" You only use "Yes, sir" if you happen to be answering a question, as in, "Did Brinkley just fall in the blasted ocean, ensign?" to which you would reply, "Yes, sir!" (Believe it or not, I don't know this because I spent a long stint in the Navy. In fact, I wasn't in the Navy at all. I do, however, catch more than my share of those early-morning fishing shows on ESPN 2.)

## *Making Serious Improvements*

By allowing the Mac OS to control tasks at this level, a number of other things become possible. Not only is it easier for each one of your applications to perform basic tasks like reacting to the keyboard, printing, accepting a scanned image, or dealing with data from the Internet, this control also allows the Mac OS to perform some near magic, like allowing more than one application to be running at the same time.

*The Mac OS allows you to run more than one program at a time and switch between them. They can also keep running "in the background" without your input.*

You've probably heard the term "multitasking"—well, this is what we're talking about. A multitasking OS, like the Mac OS, will actually allow more than one program to be running and active at the same time. You can transfer a file to your Mac across the Internet, for instance, while typing away in Word. The file transfer can be going on in the background (without your being forced to watch over it) because the Mac OS is capable of acting as a go-between for both applications.

And that's just the tip of the iceberg. Because the Mac OS requires application programs to follow certain rules when asking to perform a certain task, newer versions can anticipate those commands and substitute more advanced responses. For instance, when an application says to the Mac, "I'd like a new window, please," the Mac OS will respond by popping a new window up on the screen. But in Mac OS 8.5, that window is popped up in a completely different way from past Mac OSes, because now the Mac OS has its new Appearance technology built in. Every single window on the Mac can be universally changed making it look wacky, futuristic, or just a little more 3D. Regardless of which you choose, the applications doesn't care because the standard New Window command still works just fine.

# What's New in Mac OS 8.5?

So what sort of changes does Mac OS 8.5 have in store for you?

Any sort of Mac OS upgrade is going to feature two basic types of changes to the computer code: things you'll see and things you won't see. For minor updates—upgrading from version Mac OS 7.5.3 to version Mac OS 7.5.5, for instance—nearly every change is something that's going on behind the scenes. Maintenance updates—upgrading Mac OS 8.0 to Mac OS 8.1, for instance—tend to offer mostly behind-the-scenes fixes, with perhaps a few new technologies supported or cosmetic differences. It's the major changes—like the recent one from Mac OS 8.1 to Mac OS 8.5—that introduce new features. While Mac OS 8.5 certainly has some bug fixes and new underlying technology,

**11**

it also offers some fairly dramatic changes to how you communicate with the computer. And there are some major new technologies designed to support new peripherals, run new software, or make things easier.

So, what's new with Mac OS 8.5? Quite a bit, actually.

## It Works Better

Certainly many of the changes in Mac OS 8.5 are really designed to fix or slightly improve upon things that already existed in Mac OS 8.1 but, for whatever reason, could use a little tweaking. This includes USB (Universal Serial Bus) support, for instance, which was brand new in certain distributions of Mac OS 8.1. There are more drivers, better support, and more bug-free code in the Mac OS 8.5 for dealing with USB if your Mac happens to have USB ports.

That's the sort of thing that goes a long way to making the Mac OS more reliable: fixes to its core technologies, better handling of errors, and more awareness of new technologies and the factors involved in getting them to work right. And that's just within the Mac OS's programming own codes.

Other fixes involve the Mac OS's dealing with other applications, like word processors, photo editors, and Web browsers. You'll find that each iteration will fix quite a few "known issues" or conflicts that crop up between the Mac OS and popular applications.

Mac OS 8.5 also focuses on speed in a number of different areas, most of which is accomplished through the writing of more efficient underlying computer coding. In fact, there's one way in particular that the Mac OS continues to accomplish speed gains as it's rewritten for upgrades—through the use of "native" PowerPC code.

### Version Numbers

These Mac OS version numbering schemes tend to make sense, by the way. For the most part, Mac OS versions that don't change anything about the way the Mac OS looks or underlying technology will have a number added to the thousandths place: 7.5 to 7.5.1, for instance. Version upgrades that add technologies or new capabilities but don't really alter the user experience generally merit a single addition to the tenths place: 8.0 to 8.1. A more significant update usually merits either a full half a point (from Mac OS 8.0/8.1 to OS 8.5) or a full point, although full points are often used for marketing reasons, as in the upcoming Mac OS X (ten), which is meant to suggest quite a jump from the current Mac OS. One other difference? Minor updates are usually free or can be had for shipping and handling; major releases are usually retail purchases.

Mac OS 8.5 is actually a pretty significant upgrade in this respect. It's been updated for better speed in many different areas, including the networking protocols, a completely native implementation of AppleScript, and speedups for things like the Mac OS help system and faster graphics on some Mac models.

### Minitower of Babel

When Apple decided to transition from its older Mac processors—the Motorola 68000 series—to the PowerPC processor (this happened right at the beginning of 1994), they were faced with an interesting dilemma. Much of the Mac OS had actually been written specifically to run on 68000 series processors—I mean, *really* written for them specifically. If the 68000 processors spoke English and the PowerPC processor spoke French, then the Mac OS was definitely written in English. As with many Americans educated in the U.S., the Mac OS spoke a lot of programming languages, but not many foreign tongues.

So when the French introduced their processor (try to keep in mind that it's not actually speaking French; I'll try to do the same), the PowerPC, suddenly we had a problem. The Mac OS was not a native language for the PowerPC processor. But because the PowerPC processor was European (it's actually Asian, but bear with me), it was adept at languages and able to adapt. So this native French speaker (PowerPC) was taught a little English (the Mac OS).

But it still thinks in French. (Let's start calling "French" the "PowerPC instruction set.") Because the PowerPC thinks in its own instruction set, any commands that occur in English (that is, the "68000 series instruction set") have to be translated first. The PowerPC can do this because it's somewhat adept at translating languages (or "emulating instruction sets") but this still slows it down a bit.

You can witness the phenomenon in actual French people who say "Uh" and "Umm" a lot when speaking English. They're not speaking their native tongue.

So how do you speed up the Mac OS when it's running on a PowerPC processor? Rewrite emulated code so that it's in the PowerPC native instruction set. It's that simple. Since 1994, the Mac OS team has slowly rewritten parts of the Mac OS—very complex parts—using more and more native code. The more native code, the faster each new iteration of the Mac OS.

## New Stuff to Play With

What's probably most exciting for all of us Mac users, though, are changes in the way the Mac OS actually operates or the addition of new features and capabilities. There are a number of both of these sorts of changes in Mac OS 8.5.

### Read Who?

To learn about all of the fixes that Mac OS 8.5 includes, check out the Read Me documents (SimpleText files) that Mac OS 8.5 installs in the folder Mac OS Read Me Files found on your hard drive.

One big change you'll run across is the look and feel of the Mac OS—the Mac OS has been upgraded with a new Appearance Manager that gives it the capability to take on many different forms, colors, sounds, gizmos, and other personality traits. For the first time ever, really, you can make the Mac OS truly your own.

The Appearance Manager is quite a coup, even if it seems like more flash than substance. This allows the Mac OS to focus even more on the individual than ever before, allowing you a unique and personal interface for your Mac.

*Mac OS 8.5, in fact, gives you the freedom to get a little too carried away with creative interface building.*

Other feature improvements include an updated and altered help system that focuses on using industry standard HTML (the language of the World Wide Web) to make using the Mac's help files just like browsing in a Web browser. Other aspects of this are the new Assistants, mini-applications that help you do things like set up your Mac on the Internet, get it ready for a Mac network, or get the color-matching information correct so that your Mac and your color printer agree on what exactly Red is.

Another new feature? The Network Browser. If you've used the Chooser before to find other Macs that are connected to your Mac network, you know that the Chooser is about as much fun as drawing straws to pick a prom date. The Network Browser is much cooler, making it a simple matter to find connected Macs, log into them, and start passing illicit notes and documents among your nearest and dearest coworkers.

# Can You Use Mac OS 8.5?

I don't know, *can* you?

Actually, the correct phrasing is: *May* you use Mac OS 8.5? And the answer is: No, you may not. At least, not if you have a Mac that isn't based on the PowerPC processor. Mac OS 8.5 doesn't support any earlier Mac models at all.

There are a few other factors: Mac OS 8.5 can take up 100 MB of hard drive space or more, so you'll need to have about that much free for a full installation. If you install fewer of the Mac OS's features, it'll require less hard drive space. You'll also need about 32 MB of RAM (random access memory). While 16 MB is the stated minimum, at least 32 MB is necessary, in my opinion, for decent performance. Even more RAM is a great idea.

Otherwise, you're home free. My only other advice is to check carefully with the companies that wrote or made the software or products that you rely heavily on when using your Mac. If they're not compatible with Mac OS 8.5 for some reason, you might want to find out why and wait until they are—or shop for new, compatible products—before upgrading to Mac OS 8.5.

**Talkin' Interfaces**

Just a quickie, because we'll be talking about it a lot. When I say "interface" all I really mean is how the Mac OS desktop, picture icons, menus, and windows appear on the screen. You can say something has a good or useful interface when it's a bit more intuitive or helpful—for instance, it uses little buttons or icons that make sense when you first look at them, instead of cryptic commands that are tough to decipher. In talking about the interface, I'll also mention the "look and feel" by which I'm simply referring to the colors, textures, and other elements that make the interface garish, boring, or something in between.

# How to Upgrade to Mac OS 8.5

Before installing the Mac OS, there are a couple of important things you need to concern yourself with. First, you need to back up your Mac's hard drive. I know, I know—backing up is too hard, and you're just upgrading the OS, so what's the big deal?

If backing up seems hard now, wait until your novel, your thesis, your big presentation to the board of directors, or your entire brochure layout is gone—thanks to some act of nature, major computer crash, or a power failure. That lost work will be very hard to back up. You *must* have a backup plan. (Chapter 6 will help you come up with one.)

If you have Web access, you should also head over to Apple's Support Web site at `http://www.apple.com/support` in your Web browser. This is a good idea because it's there that you'll read about any critical support issues that could affect your upgrade to Mac OS 8.5. (Also, read those Read Me files you'll find on the Mac OS installation CD-ROM.)

**15**

The other part of the equation is deciding what sort of installation you're going to perform. If you're upgrading from an older version of the Mac OS, you really have two choices:

➤ *Upgrade installation.* This will install Mac OS 8.5 over any Mac OS that's already on your startup drive. You'll likely be able to keep the same settings and preferences, although you may lose a few things in the translation. This also won't solve any troubleshooting problems you're having with the older Mac OS version.

➤ *Clean installation.* In this case, you create an entirely new System Folder with the Mac OS 8.5 files in it. That allows you to upgrade to a clean version of the Mac OS 8.5, but you won't have all your old settings, third-party control panels, and so on. Instead, you'll have to drag them from the previous System Folder manually. This one is a bit more for experts but a good idea if you're having trouble with your older Mac OS version.

## The Least You Need to Know

The Mac OS is the computer code that controls a Macintosh computer, giving it that unique look and feel of a Macintosh while helping application programs communicate with you, the user. This frees up an application, like Microsoft Word, to focus on their unique tasks instead of being forced to re-invent the wheel every time it needs to do something basic like interpret a keystroke or print one of its documents.

If you have a Mac that uses a PowerPC processor, you can upgrade to Mac OS 8.5. This version includes many exciting new features, including a new Appearance Manager, Network Browser, and features that make it easier to get on the Internet, get help, and work with peripheral devices.

When you're ready to upgrade, back up the files on your Mac, and then choose if you'll perform a regular installation or a clean installation.

# Chapter 2

# Moving Around the Desktop

## In This Chapter

➤ Secrets of the Desktop revealed

➤ Why rodents are involved

➤ Iconically speaking

➤ Working through windows

➤ Mousing up the menus and commands

When you first start up a Macintosh computer, you're greeted with a little smiley Macintosh, followed by the words "Welcome to Mac OS." If you power down your computer every day, starting again with that smiley Mac can be a welcome sight, ushering in a new day of pleasing productivity. Of course, you may not like your job much. Or maybe you're using the Mac at home, and most of what you do is enter stuff in your checkbook program, and you find that disheartening.

At least you get to use a Mac, right?

Actually the "Welcome to Mac OS" message tells you something pretty interesting about your Macintosh: The startup process has just been handed over to the Mac OS when you see that message. (Before that, the computer is self testing, using instructions stored on a special memory chip.) From there on, the Mac OS is in control, loading itself, and preparing for action up until the Finder has completed loading, and activity seems to cease. Now, the Mac is waiting for you.

What you're looking at is the Desktop.

# What Is the Desktop?

At its most basic, the *Desktop* is the solid color or pattern that's behind everything else on your Macintosh's display. That's why it's called the Desktop: It's what you put all your stuff on. Everything else (like folders, the menu bar, and the Trash) is on top of the Desktop.

If you think of the Desktop just as you would a standard desk at the office, you can start to see the parallels. *Icons* (little pictures) represent storage spaces, in-boxes, and tools like a calculator or address book. *Menus* (little words at the top of the screen) are a little like the drawers in your desk: They're what you open when you need a new type of pen, a stapler, or some scissors. And *windows* are like pieces of paper—for writing, reading reports, or drawing. Windows can be stacked one on top of the other, so, for instance, you can address an envelope with the letter beneath it.

*A real-world desktop is represented by pictures on the Mac's screen.*

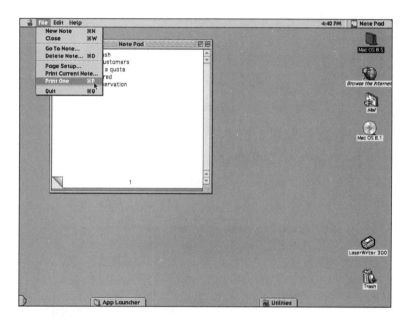

In the real world, all these pens, pieces of paper, and in-boxes are kept on your desk. On the Mac, all your icons, menus, and windows are kept on the Desktop, too. Of course, the difference is, in the real world, you can use your hands to manipulate things. Because you can't reach into your Mac's monitor without causing unnecessary damage, you're forced to rely on yet another metaphoric little device that acts as an extension of your hand into the world of your Mac: the mouse.

That's why the Mac OS has icons. Icons are basically little pictures or symbols on your computer screen that let you see and manipulate things onscreen with a mouse. The Trash, for instance, is an icon. So is the little picture with the words "Macintosh HD."

Menus and windows are designed to work with a mouse, too. The menus act like virtual desk drawers you can open and close by clicking on them. Windows, likewise, can be manipulated onscreen, allowing you to open, close, and move them about using a mouse.

More on the mouse in a moment; let's take a quick look at what else is on the Desktop.

## What's "Macintosh HD?"

The *Macintosh HD icon* represents the internal hard disk. (This disk is an actual, physical box inside your computer that contains rotating, magnetic platters that store data files for later use.) Try thinking of this as a filing cabinet because it's where you'll keep stuff, including folders, documents, and the applications you'll use to get things done.

The Macintosh HD icon isn't always named "Macintosh HD," by the way; it's named that when the Mac is first taken out of the box, but it can be renamed by users. The Macintosh HD icon is always in the top-right corner of the desktop (below the menu bar) right after you power up your Mac.

## What Are the Words at the Top of the Screen?

If the Macintosh HD icon is the main filing cabinet, then what are those words at the top of your screen? They're the drawers in your desk. It's called *menu bar*, and it's where you tell the Mac what you want to do and what tools you want to use. To open a desk drawer, move the mouse pointer to the word in the menu bar by physically moving your Mac's mouse, and then click the mouse button. When you open the File "drawer," you get selections like *Open*, *Close*, and *Quit*.

### What's the Finder?

In this chapter, I'm discussing elements that are common to all Macintosh applications: icons, windows, and menus. In the process, I'll probably mention the *Finder* once or twice; the Finder is a special application that, like all others, features icons, windows, and menus. The difference is that the Finder is *always* loaded, and it's the part of your Mac that allows you to find, manipulate, and file away your documents, applications, and other computer files. It works very closely with the Desktop, although the two are slightly different. We'll discuss the Finder specifically in Chapter 3, "Finder Basics."

What you're choosing on the menu bar are *commands*, or instructions for the Mac. If you select New Folder, for instance, your Mac will create a new folder (called "Untitled Folder") and drop it on the Desktop. If you tell the Macintosh to open that folder (**File**, **Open**), that's what will happen. Then you can see and manipulate the contents of that folder.

*The menu items act like drawers in your Mac's desktop: They give you access to all your tools.*

Menu items⌐

Mouse pointer⌐

## The Trash: You Guessed It

The easiest thing to recognize on the Desktop is the *Trash*. The Trash is significant because it's the only way you can throw things away on a Mac. Why is that? Because if you have to do it deliberately, consciously, and the same way every time, you are not likely to throw something away by accident. How do you throw something away? You point the mouse pointer at the file or folder, click and hold the mouse button. Now, drag the item to the trash can icon. When it changes color (it will flash a darker gray) let go of the mouse button. The trash icon will change to show that it has something in it.

The Mac OS's Trash works very much like any real trash can. Throw something away, and, if you absolutely have to, you can dig it back out. Empty the Trash, however, and it's gone for good. (There's no "dumpster" to go digging through on the Mac.) The Trash also has a cute way of telling you it's got something in it: Its sides bulge out to indicate that it's waiting to be emptied.

### Mouse Practice

Want to practice using the mouse a bit, but afraid to choose a bunch of menu commands? Go up to the little Apple icon in the top-left corner and click it once. Now, find the Puzzle command and click it once. This will bring up the Puzzle game, which is a great way to become a bit more dextrous with you click, drag and drop, and perform other mousing tasks.

The Trash is also, unfortunately, one way to eject floppy disks, Zip disks, and other storage icons that appear on your hard drive. It can be a little unnerving when you first drag a floppy disk to the Trash, but it won't be erased; it'll just pop out of your Mac. I promise.

# Rules Your Mouse Lives By

Using a mouse to manipulate data on a computer screen has become so commonplace that most people, by now, have some experience doing it. If you've never used a mouse before, here are a few of the basics:

1. The point of the mouse is to put it in the palm of your hand and roll it around on your desktop. (You'll probably want to roll it around on a mouse pad, which will keep the mouse a bit cleaner and offer more precise movements.)

2. It's called a mouse because it's sort of moused-sized and has a little tail. Clever, eh? It's also called a "pointing device" by geeky types (like me).

3. The reason you're rolling it around is that your movements correspond to the movement of the mouse *pointer*, which is a small arrow on the Mac screen you use for selecting items like menu commands and icons.

4. Once you've positioned the mouse pointer on the screen (by pointing it at an icon, window, or menu that interests you), you'll use the button on the mouse to click once or twice in rapid succession to make things happen.

### Gone for Good

It's worth making this point twice. When you drag a file or folder to the Trash, it's almost always retrievable: You can double-click the Trash icon to open it and drag files back out. But once you select the Special, Empty Trash command, those files will be gone for good. So think twice before throwing stuff away and never store important files in the Trash, even temporarily.

### Secret Life of the Pointer

The mouse pointer we've been talking about has its secret: It can change to mean different things. When the pointer looks like an arrow, that means you can select things and work with the mouse. When it turns into a rotating beach ball, though, that means the Mac is currently busy and may not respond to you immediately. It's busy thinking. The pointer can turn into other things, too, depending on the application.

And there's another pointer-like thing to worry about, called the *insertion point*. This is the little blinking line that appears when you need to type something. It tells you where text and images will be placed in a document if you type or invoke some other sort of command. You move it around by using the arrow keys on your keyboard or by clicking the mouse once elsewhere in a document.

But even if you've held a mouse, dragged it across the screen, and clicked its buttons before, you may not realize that—on a Macintosh—the mouse adheres to some pretty strict rules.

Here, then, are some of the common moves you can make with a mouse:

➤ *Select something.* To select something onscreen, move the mouse so that the mouse pointer is touching that item, usually an icon, and then click—press quickly—the mouse button once. This also works for menus: You click once on the text item in the menu bar at the top of the screen, and then you click again on one of the items in the menu that appears to invoke that command. A selected item usually responds by becoming highlighted.

➤ *Select a group of things.* There are two ways to select multiple items. If you're selecting icons, you can begin just outside the first icon and drag a box around all the icons you want to select; release the mouse button, and they'll all be highlighted. You can also hold down the Shift key and click an item in the Finder in order to add it to the previously selected items. You can highlight text and images in your applications the same way. Start at the beginning of a line of text, hold down the mouse button, and drag to the end of that selection of text. The text will be highlighted, waiting for your next move. Often, your next move will be a menu command—like changing the text font by choosing Edit, Copy—or typing, which would replace the highlighted text.

➤ *Respond to a question.* This is the same as a selection—point and click once—but under different circumstances. A response is required when the Mac OS or an application displays a dialog box: It's asking you a question like "Do you want to save?" or "Are you ready to quit?" When you answer a question by clicking on an OK, Cancel, or No button, you move the mouse pointer to that button and click the mouse button once.

➤ *Open something.* To open something—whether it's a folder icon an application icon, or a document, you point the mouse at the icon in question, and then double-click the mouse button (click it twice in rapid succession).

➤ *Drag something across the screen.* This movement is used to select more than one item on the screen. Basically, *dragging* is accomplished by pointing to an item with the mouse, and then holding down the mouse button (instead of simply clicking the mouse button).

➤ *Drag and drop.* This movement is used to move things from one place on the screen to another. It's similar to dragging except, in this instance, you point the mouse directly at the item you want to move. This is like a selection, except you don't just click: You hold the mouse button down. Now the item moves around on the screen along with your mouse pointer. When you get to the final destination for the item, release the mouse button. This *drops* the item, leaving it where the mouse was last pointing. If you have more than one item selected, you can drag them all by simply pointing to one of the items highlighted and dragging it. The rest will come along for the ride.

> ➤ *Drag and drop on.* You can drag and drop icons on other icons, too, in which case the receiving icon will become highlighted—it'll usually appear darker in color—meaning it's okay to drop the icon. In this same way, you can even drag highlighted text from one document window to another.

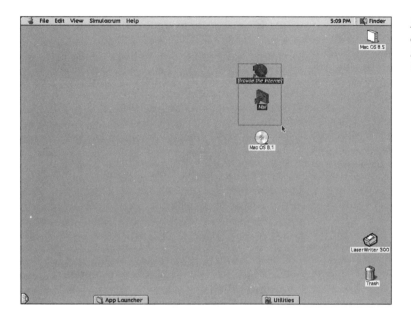

*Dragging is the most efficient way to select many but not all of a particular item on the screen.*

So that's the extent of the more basic movements. You'll find in other parts of the book that the mouse can be used in other ways to perform some interesting tasks, usually in conjunction with keystrokes. (Mouse movements performed in conjunction with backrubs and chiropractic adjustments are also highly recommended.) We'll discuss those keystroke combos as they come up.

# What Are Icons For?

You already know that icons are just pictures that represent things on the Desktop. What things? Well, there are four basic elements that can be represented by icons: *disks*, *folders*, *applications*, and *documents*. (Actually, icons can represent other things, too. For instance, in applications—like Microsoft Word—icons can represent toolbar commands that let you open files and change font styles. For now, however, we're discussing *Desktop icons*.)

Icons can also occasionally represent ancient gods, baseball players, and lost youth. But we're not really talking about those sorts of icons.

### Ctrl+Click

Actually, let's discuss one quick one now. In recent Mac versions, a somewhat new feature has been added to the mouse's repertoire: Ctrl+Click. In this movement, you hold down the Ctrl key on the Mac's keyboard while you click anywhere onscreen. This brings up a *contextual menu*, which is Apple's fancy way of saying a menu that shows only relevant commands. (You can then release the Ctrl key and select a menu item with a single mouse click as usual. To get rid of the menu, click elsewhere on the screen.) Not all applications support contextual menus, but many do, including contextual menus that appear when you Ctrl+Click an icon, window, or the Desktop itself. (Microsoft Windows users might recognize this as similar to "right-clicking" on objects in Windows 95/98.)

## Types of Icons

So let's look at what each sort of icon represents:

➤ *Disks.* Remember the Macintosh HD icon? It's the perfect example of a disk icon where you store files, documents, applications, and all that other stuff. There are different types of disks, including hard disks, floppy disks, and CD-ROMs. When the Mac recognizes a new disk (like when you put a floppy disk in the floppy drive), a new icon shows up on the Desktop automatically.

➤ *Folders.* Folders are icons that can be used to store other icons—whether those other icons represent more folders (usually called subfolders), documents, or applications. Like file folders in a physical filing cabinet, these folders are simply designed to help you organize all the different files (represented by icons) stored on your disks.

➤ *Applications.* Icons are also used to represent the programs, called applications, that help you get something done. On a typical, physical desktop—straight from the Oak Furniture Outlet—there's nothing that will help you get work done. You need to supply the pens, paper, calculator, reports, and research text. In the world of the Mac OS, that's what applications are for: They're the tools that help you get work done.

➤ *Documents.* This final sort of icon is used to represent work you've accomplished in an application. Most of the time when you're working in one of your applications, it's important to save that work so it can be stored, filed for future reference, or opened later and worked on some more. When you save your work, it's represented by a document icon.

*The Mac OS tried to help you determine what each sort of icon represents by matching it visually with its purpose; document icons look like little pieces of paper, usually, and folders look like filing folders, for instance.*

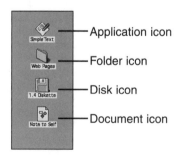

Application icon

Folder icon

Disk icon

Document icon

# What About These Windows?

As mentioned previously, windows are like pieces of paper you use to work on at any given time when you're using your Macintosh. They represent different workspaces that can be stacked on one another, rearranged, or closed to get them out of the way. You can even drag folder windows down to the bottom of the screen to create a *tabbed window* so you can remember it's open but clear your desktop space for something else.

Windows are used to let you see *into* just about anything; any time you open something, whether it's an application, a document, or a folder, you'll see a window. It's inside a window where you'll accomplish just about anything you set out to do with your Mac, whether it's typing a document, manipulating a photo, or browsing the Internet.

## *Window Bits*

Just like certain laws, statutes and common sense dictate that there be a somewhat standard interface for cars built in Detroit—a steering wheel, certain pedals, controls for the turn signals—the Mac OS imposes similar standards on applications. Specifically, applications have to have standard windows, menus, icons, and so forth. Their behavior needs to be consistent with other applications.

So Mac windows in Mac applications will all have the same parts. If you've ever used another windows-based OS (like Microsoft Windows, UNIX X Window, or IBM OS/2), some of these elements will be familiar. Of course, just like the way that every single car stereo's radio presets are handled in a *completely* different way from any other car stereo's presets, you'll find that Mac windows act slightly differently from their counterparts in other OSes. It's called choice, I guess.

These choices include:

➤ Close box: When you're done with the window, you can click here to get rid of it.

➤ Title bar: Point and drag here to move the window around the screen; release the mouse button when you've gotten the window where you want it.

➤ Zoom box: This causes the window to expand to its largest possible size (sometimes it expands it to the default size dictated by the application).

➤ Windowshade (minimize) control box: Click here to shrink the window so that only the title bar shows. This can allow you to quickly look at what's behind the window.

➤ Scroll bars: Using the arrows, you can scroll the window up or down to see any of its contents that currently fit in the window. You can also drag the small scroll box up and down to see parts of the window's contents.

➤ Size box: Click and drag here to change the size of the window manually. When you release the mouse button, the window will snap to its new size.

➤ Window sides: Like the title bar, the sizes of a window can also be used to drag it around.

➤ Tabbed window: drag the window (by its title bar) all the way to the bottom of the screen, and it turns into a tabbed window. You can click the tab to see the window's contents, or drag an icon onto the tab to reveal the window.

➤ Minimized window: This window, behind the current window, has been "windowshaded" so that only its title bar appears.

*Elements of the Mac's standard window interface.*

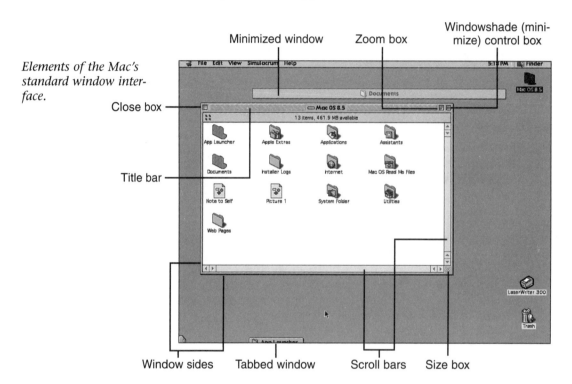

Again, as with a car stereo, you might find that the best way to learn about windows is to simply play with the dials and knobs a bit if you haven't already had the chance. (Just remember to keep your eyes on the road.) You can open a few windows by double-clicking your Mac's hard drive icon, and then double-clicking some of the folders that appear in the Macintosh HD window. From there, you can practice moving windows, turning them into tabbed windows, and using the windowshade control to make the windows appear or disappear from view (except for the title bar).

## Getting a Window's Attention

After you've gotten a couple of windows on the screen, you're going to immediately run into an interesting issue: window focus. While this sounds like something that can be easily solved with an ammonia-based cleaning solution, we're talking about something else: getting windows to stack up the way you want them.

You'll notice that the windows appear to stack on top of one another when you open more than one of them at a time. The top window is the one that has focus; it's the *active* window. There are two ways you can tell that: One, it's completely unobscured, and, two, its title bar and scroll bars show detail. Note that the windows in the background—those that don't currently have focus—are grayer in appearance with less detail.

### Tabbed Finder windows

You may get frustrated if you try to turn any non-Finder windows into tabbed windows—this only works in the Finder. The point is to place often used folder windows at the bottom of the screen for easy access. It won't work in applications other than the Finder.

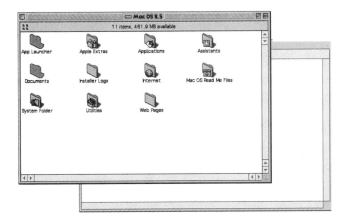

*Windows in the background have less detail, so you can tell which window has focus.*

So how do you change the focus? Simply point the mouse at the window you'd like to give your attention to, and then **click once** with the mouse. That should bring that window to the front. Notice that if the window you select happens to be part of a different application, that entire application will come to the front along with the window.

### Swicheroo

For more on switching between applications, see Chapter 3.

## *This Window Is in the Wrong Place!*

Easily rectified. Simply move the mouse pointer so that it's hovering over the window's title bar or one of the side edges of the window, and then hold down the

**mouse button** and **drag** the window along. When you get it to its destination, release the mouse button to drop the window in its new position. Note that you can drag the window all the way to the bottom of the screen to create a tabbed window.

Is the window in the background? (That is, do you want to move a window that isn't currently the active window?) There's a really cool way to move such windows, as long as the background window you're trying to move is part of the same application as the focus window. (This trick should impress your friends, too.) Just hold down the **Command** key, and then point to the background window in question and **drag** it across the screen as usual. It'll move, but it won't become the focus window.

## This Window Is the Wrong Size!

The size problem has two basic solutions. You can try clicking the **zoom box** to see if that changes the window to a size that's more pleasing—sometimes it will, sometimes it won't. Ideally, the zoom box will change the windows to the largest possible size to fill the screen, but that isn't always the case. Its actual behavior is a bit more complicated.

When you first open the window, the zoom box will often either resize the window to a full-screen window, or it will simply size the window to the *default* size—that is, the size that's been predetermined as optimal by the application's programmers. You may not agree with this, but there's not much you can do short of writing the application programmers a nasty letter. (If you do this, don't forget that the most effective nasty letters also have something nice to say, too, if only for contrast. And there's really no need to mention my name.)

The other thing the zoom box does is switch between the default size and the last position you've chosen using the size box (discussed next). That way, you can resize the window, and then click the zoom box over and over again to switch between the two different views. It's not as much fun as it sounds, but it's not the worst way to kill a rainy Saturday afternoon.

To change the size in an arbitrary way, you just point your mouse at the **size box** in the lower-right corner of the window and drag away until you've changed the size of the window. Release the mouse button, and the window will snap to its new size.

## Close That Window

Feeling a bit drafty? (Sorry, that's an obvious joke, but I couldn't help myself. I can hear you saying, "Try, Todd. Try.") If you're ready to close a window, the easiest way is to point the mouse to the **close box** in the upper-left corner of the window and click once. This will exit the window from existence, as it becomes a fading memory in your waning attention span, as well.

Actually, the window might not leave without a fight. Instead, the Mac OS pretty much requires applications to take care of any unfinished business before banishing the window —things like making sure you really don't want the window anymore and that you've saved any changes you made in that window's document. It'll do that by presenting you with a dialog box.

And here's a little trick. If you want to close all open windows in a given application (like the Finder), hold down the **Option** key while clicking the **close box**. They'll all close at once.

## Carrying on a Dialog

Usually content to sit in the background and quietly mock you, every once in a while the Mac OS or a particular application will need to ask you a direct question. Whether it's in response to a command on your part or due to an error, your Mac will sometimes encounter a situation where it needs more information or it needs a decision from you. In those cases, you'll likely see a dialog box.

The most common sort of dialog box is actually an *alert* box; this sort usually offers a chance to say either "Cancel" or "OK," and it pops up in direct reference to an issue that the Mac OS or the program wants you to be absolutely sure of something you're about to do—like closing an unsaved document or throwing away files that have been put in the Trash. An alert dialog box gives you one last chance to pull yourself back from the precipice while choking up the expletive, "Goodness, man, get a hold of yourself!" (An odd thing to say if you're female, incidentally.)

**Closing, Not Quitting**

In many Mac OS programs, there's a distinct difference between closing a document window and quitting the application. In a word processor, for instance, you can close all of the word processor's open windows and still leave the application open—so you can begin another document, for instance. So remember to choose File, Quit if you want to completely quit an application. Don't make the mistake of thinking you're done after you've closed the window.

These dialog boxes generally won't let you move on with answering the question by selecting one of the options.

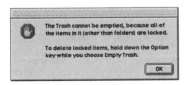

*Alert dialog boxes often include an "!" (exclamation point) or a "Halt!" hand icon to indicate the severity of the problem.*

But alerts aren't the only sort of dialog boxes you'll come across. Preferences (or settings) dialog boxes will pop up from time to time, too, usually in response to your choice of a command from the menu bar. (In particular, commands with ellipses after them tend to pop up preference dialog boxes, as discussed in the next section of this chapter.) These sorts of dialog boxes often act a little more like windows: You can move them around the screen, for instance. In some cases, you can even move back and forth between the dialog box and the document you're working on that's immediately behind the dialog box.

*Some preference dialog boxes act a lot like alerts, but they just need more information before they can move on. Eventually, though, you'll click OK or Cancel.*

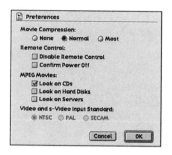

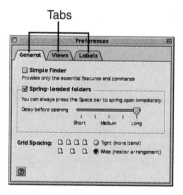

*In some other cases, you'll have more answers to give, though. In this tabbed dialog box, more options appear depending on which tab you click.*

By the time you finish reading this book, you'll have encountered quite a few dialog boxes, including some that are governed by the Mac OS, so they appear as standard in nearly every Mac application. For now, just realize that a dialog box needs an answer, usually to a very specific question, before the Mac OS or a particular application can get on with its business.

# Make It So! Menus and Commands

At the heart of all Macintosh programs is the *menu bar*. The menu bar is where you decide what to do and how you want to do it. In the case of the Finder, it's how you manage your files and applications. In other applications, it might be where you decide what font to use, when to print, or what formula to use in a spreadsheet.

Because the Macintosh is designed so programs look and work alike, the menu bar generally acts the same in every application. You'll notice that when you switch from one application to another, the menu bar switches to represent the commands available in that new application. And whether it's the Finder or Microsoft Word, you choose menu items the same way.

## How Do I Select from a Menu?

*Click, move, and click.*

The menu bar uses a system *pull-down menus* (sometimes called *drop-down menus*) that's a lot like opening a drawer in your desk. The menu item (or drawer) labeled File, for instance, pulls down a menu of commands (stuff in that drawer) that enable you to create new documents, save them, and print them. And opening that drawer is easy.

Let's try it with the File menu in the Finder.

1. **Click** the mouse button with the mouse pointer on the word *File*. Its pull-down menu appears.
2. **Move** the highlight bar (by moving the mouse) until you get to what you want to do, like Find**.**
3. **Click** the button. The highlight bar blinks a few times to let you know it's executing that command.

## Why Are Some Options Black and Others Gray?

All commands are not equal. In the Finder and many applications, you will sometimes find that a command is *grayed*, or appears lighter than the other commands. This is the Macintosh way of telling you that there's no reason to select this command now. A good example of this is if you try to choose Print before you've opened a document in your word processor. The Print command will be gray until you open up a document or start a new one. If you don't have a document open, you can't print, so you can't choose the command.

## What Does the ... Mean?

You'll notice that many pull-down menu items are followed by an *ellipsis* (...). The ellipsis means "more to come." It's the Mac's way of telling you that if you select this command, a dialog box will appear asking you for more information. If you select the File, Find... command, for example, a dialog box will appear asking you to type in the name of the file you want to find.

## What Are the Little Symbols on Each Menu?

Another thing you might have noticed in the typical pull-down menu is that many commands have symbols and letters next to them. For instance, the Finder's File pull-down menu has **New Folder ⌘N** as one of its commands. The ⌘N means that pressing these keys simultaneously on your keyboard while working in the Finder allows you to create a new folder without touching the mouse. See the sidebar "Save Time and Wrists!" for more information on keyboard shortcuts.

### Save Time and Wrists!

Going to the mouse every time you want to get something done is a little like getting up and walking across the room every time you want to change the channel on your TV. The Macintosh provides you with a few "remote control" buttons that allow you to keep working with your hands on the keyboard. Get to know a few of the more important keyboard shortcuts, and you'll have much more productive sessions at the Macintosh. The cool thing is that these shortcuts work in nearly every Macintosh program! What are the top five most useful? Depends on how you use your Mac, but try these for starters:

⌘+Q        Quit a program

⌘+S        Save a document

⌘+C        Copy to clipboard

⌘+V        Paste into document

⌘+P        Print

## The Most Basic Commands

When you go to the menu bar in just about every single Mac application ever written, you'll see some very common commands. In fact, as a rule Mac applications always have the same two menus in the menu bar: the File and Edit menus. And those menus are usually pretty similar; you'll find the same basic commands in most of them.

Here's a quick list of the commands you can expect to find in Mac applications (they're covered in more depth in upcoming chapters):

➤ **File, New.** This command is used to create a new document in most applications; in the Finder, it's used to create a new folder.

➤ **File, Open.** This is the command you use within an application to open an existing document; in the Finder, it opens the selected folder.

➤ **File, Close.** Works just like the close box on the window itself. In the Finder, it closes the current window.

➤ **File, Print.** Need a hard copy of the active window? Choose File, Print in almost any application.

➤ **File, Quit.** Use this command to close any documents and quit using the application. Can't be used in the Finder.

➤ **Edit, Cut.** Cuts the highlighted text or images from the document and places them on the clipboard. This clipboard is a special file on the Mac used to store temporary text or images.

➤ **Edit, Copy.** Places a copy of the highlighted text or images on the clipboard but doesn't delete them from the document.

➤ **Edit, Paste.** Takes whatever is on the clipboard and places it in the active window, usually where the insertion point currently is in the active document window.

# The Least You Need to Know

In this chapter, you learn the basics of moving around in the Mac OS and in most any application written to work with the Mac OS. The Mac OS presents you with a desktop metaphor that, for better or worse, is the basis for how you interact with the computer. Using icons, windows, and menus, you're able to accomplish just about anything by rolling the mouse around and selecting, dragging, or double-clicking.

Everything on your Mac's virtual desktop is represented by an icon: a little picture that can be manipulated in order to get at a particular file, application, or folder. The meaning of the icon is usually made clear by its appearance: Folder icons look like folders, document icons look like pieces of paper, and disk icons often look little floppy disks or hard drives.

Double-click an icon, and you're presented with the basic workspace for any Mac application: a window. These windows roughly approximate electronic pieces of paper that allow you to have different tasks going on at once and to shuffle the tasks by focusing on one at a time, with the rest of the tasks stacked beneath the current one. Each window has standard controls for changing its size, position, and appearance. A special sort of mini-window, called a dialog box, used with the computer has a specific question or otherwise needs more information about a task you're trying to complete.

While you're working in windows, the menu bar is where you find the tools you need to accomplish the tasks that are possible in that particular application. You can pull down these menus and execute individual commands to accomplish anything in the application.

# Chapter 3

# Finder Basics

## In This Chapter

➤ The most important application

➤ Filing files, electronically

➤ Learning about trash cans

➤ Other finder commands and controls

➤ Special menus and the Chooser

In this chapter, I discuss one of the single most important applications included with the Mac OS: the Jigsaw Puzzle. Right there on the Apple Menu is one of the longest-lasting applications ever written for the Mac OS, with nary an update or addition made to it since for a number of years, and yet it continues to be a paragon of usefulness. Not only is the puzzle a wonderful diversion, a welcome companion, and a devoted friend, it's also believed to be completely Year 2000 compliant. Score another one for Apple!

Okay, I'm joking about the Jigsaw Puzzle. The most important Apple-written application is actually the *Finder*. It is the heart and soul of your Mac, making it possible for you to copy and organize your folders, documents, and applications. Sure, maybe it's not as fun as the Jigsaw Puzzle, but the Finder is important, nonetheless.

# What's the Finder?

The Finder, like the Jigsaw Puzzle, is an application. But it's a very special application that's an important part of how the Mac OS works. The Finder is automatically launched as the Mac starts up—in fact, it's a part of the startup process. After it's launched, it becomes mission control for your Mac; you'll manage everything from the Finder.

The Finder is where you'll launch your applications, create folders, and maintain your Mac. While other applications—like word processors and Web browsers—are designed for getting stuff done, the Finder is a little different, because it's all about getting your Mac configured and organized. Plus, it's special in another way: You can't easily quit the Finder. You'll notice that there's no File, Quit command if you ever go looking for it in the Finder.

In fact, the Finder's menu bar is somewhat out of the ordinary. It offers some commands that other applications don't, particularly those found under the Special menu that allow you to deal with disks, shut down the Mac, restart the Mac, and put the Mac to sleep. These commands are part of what make the Finder unique.

The Finder is basically responsible for displaying all the icons that represent files on your Mac's hard drives, floppy disks, and any removable disks that you insert into a drive on your Mac. (A removable disk is like a floppy disk but usually a little bigger and capable of storing much more data. Instead of saving just a few files like a floppy does, a removable disk can store a lot of data—sometimes equal to an internal hard drive. You may have heard of the "Zip" disk or Syquest cartridges; both of these are examples of removable disks.)

The Finder gives you access to these files by displaying icons that represent each disk—like the Macintosh HD icon that appears in the top-right corner of the Desktop.

I said back in Chapter 2, "Moving Around the Desktop," that the Finder and Desktop are closely related, and now you can see why. Even though the Desktop is always back there, it's up to the Finder to put the first layer of basic tools—like the Macintosh HD icon, the Trash, and other icons—on the Desktop. Those tools can then be used to organize your other files, and even to launch applications.

If you think of the Mac's desktop metaphor again, the Finder is what gives you tools like staplers, markers, folders, and paper clips. In a real office, you'd create new file folders, organize your files, and "launch" your brain on a new document: writing, editing, and revising. With the Finder, you have the "virtual" tools on your Mac to create new folders, organize your files, and launch applications that help you create and edit documents. It's the same thing, just on the computer screen.

# Working with Folders and Files

So the bottom line is that the Finder allows you to work with your files. What can you do with them? You can launch applications, open documents for editing, rename, delete, and get more information about your files. The Finder is the heart of file management on your Mac.

Here are a few of the things you'll accomplish from the Finder:

➤ *Create folders.* Using the File menu in the Finder, you can create folders for organizing your files.

➤ *Move, duplicate, rename, and delete files.* Whether they're documents, applications, or utilities, you can organize, store, or get rid of all your stored files using the Finder.

➤ *Get information about files.* Every Macintosh file includes special information you can access through the Finder, including the size of the file, the author of the file, and other tidbits.

➤ *Create aliases.* Aliases are special icons whose soul purpose is to act as a copy of the original file's *icon*; you can then use that icon as you would the original file (you can duplicate it, double-click it, and so on). In the real world, you might put a notecard in a file folder saying "Find the Hughes file stored under 'C' for 'Current.'") An alias allows you to do the same thing on your Mac: It points back to the original file, but the alias doesn't take up as much storage space.

### The Finder Doesn't Find

The Finder's name is interesting in that it doesn't actually help you find things in an automated, computer sort of sense. It's more like a library's card catalog system: The Finder helps you organize and manipulate your file icons, but you need to manually hunt for a particular icon by opening various folders before you can find it. For an automated searching system, you'll access a different program called Sherlock. This works more like a computer-based library search: You enter keywords or parts of a filename, and it's automatically located for you. Sherlock is discussed in more depth in Chapter 4, "Actually, Uh, Finding Things."

➤ *Launch applications.* By double-clicking application icons, you can launch them to begin your work.

➤ *Erase and format disks.* Disks—whether hard drives, removable disks, or floppy disk—must be specially formatted before they can be used to store Mac files. Formatting a disk erases all previous information from the disk, and then overlays the necessary structure for storing new Mac files. The Finder gives you the ability to quickly format a disk, when necessary.

➤ *Restart or shut down your Mac.* The Finder features the special commands that allow you to restart your Mac or shut it down.

➤ *Sleep.* If your Mac supports the command, the Finder allows you to put the Mac to sleep, which allows it to spin down the hard drive, dim the monitor, and take up less electricity until a key is pressed, and the Mac is awakened.

You may notice that the Finder doesn't allow you to create new files. The reasoning for that is pretty simple: You should be creating most of your other documents and files in applications, not in the Finder. Instead, the Finder will help you locate, manipulate, and manage those documents after you've created them elsewhere.

## What's on That Disk?

You need to open up your filing cabinet if you're going to get a look at your files—the same goes for your hard disk icon in the Finder. To start, you'll want to open up your hard drive icon and take a look at the folders and files you have stored there.

Point your mouse at the icon, double-click, and a new window will appear, showing you the contents of that drive. To look inside one of the folders, just point to that folder and double-click again. You'll get another window that shows you the contents of that folder.

*Looking at a drive's or folder's contents is easy. But it's clear already that you'll want to be pretty organized, or you'll be doing a lot of double-clicking.*

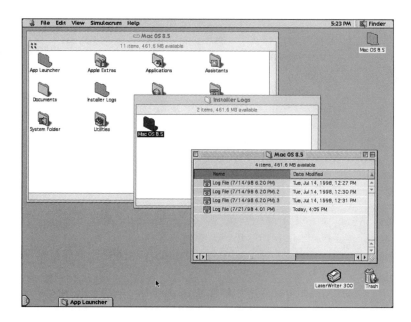

## Create Your Own Folders

After you've opened the filing cabinet, you might want to create some new folders to help you organize things a bit. In the Finder, creating a folder is simple. You need to make sure the window in which you want the new folder to appear is the active window: click it once to make sure its topmost and ready for the new folder. (If you create a folder with no windows open, the folder will appear on the Desktop.)

Now choose File, New Folder to create the folder. A new folder called "Untitled Folder" will appear in the chosen window. If you begin typing immediately (before clicking the mouse again), you can change the name of the folder to something else. If you click the mouse on another part of the screen, you can go back to the Untitled Folder and rename it.

Did the folder disappear after you named it? You might have that particular window set to a List view or a similar alphabetical listing. If so, the folder will move to its proper place in alphabetical order when you change its name.

## I'm Icon, You're Icon

In Chapter 2, you read about some of the most common mouse movements. One of the more sophisticated of them, drag-and-drop, is the method you can use to move icons around in the Finder. In fact, drag-and-drop is a big part of using the Finder: Not only can you move folders around, but you can drag documents onto folders to move them, you can highlight text and drag it around to move it within document windows, and you can even drag a document icon from the Desktop to an application window to open it. In other words, get used to dragging and dropping.

**Folder Open Trick**

You already know how to open a folder, right? Just double-click its icon. But what if that folder is in another folder's window, and you'd like to close the original folder window behind you? Hold down the **Option** key while double-clicking the new folder's icon. The new folder window will appear just as the old folder window is closing.

At its most basic, drag-and-drop allows you to pick up an icon, move it across the screen, and drop it somewhere else. This is a great way to arrange things. You can drag files from one window to another window or from the Desktop to an open window to move the file around in the folder hierarchy on your disks.

But what if you drop one icon on another icon? You will get a reaction, but what happens depends on what each icon is.

## Move Files (or Folders) to a New Folder

This follows the desktop metaphor very nicely. If you were going to move physical documents between two filing folders, you'd have to pick the documents up and drop them in the new folder, right? Same thing with your Mac.

If there's any difference at all, it's the fact that you don't necessarily have to have the destination folder's window *open* in order to drag the document to it; you can just as easily drop the document on the folder's icon, and the document will be stored inside the folder. (In real life, if you drop a document on the outside of a folder, you'll get worse results.) Of course, you can also drag the document into an open folder window. The choice is yours.

To move a file, locate it, and then point to its icon with the mouse and drag the file from the original folder's window to the destination folder icon or window. After you've got the files hovering over the new folder (the folder should become highlighted), release the mouse button. Remember, by "file" I mean any sort of computer file—a document, an application, a utility, even an alias. as long as it has an icon, it can probably be moved into a folder.

### Drop on Top

Here's an interesting problem. What if you already have something in that new folder? Say you're dragging a document—it's a listing of all your LP record albums—from the Desktop to a folder called Household. Within the Household folder, you have a subfolder called Fish. Unfortunately, every time you go to drop the album document on the Household folder, you end up dropping it on the Fish subfolder, and the Finder thinks you want to store the document in the Fish folder. What to do?

Drop the icon not in the window itself, but at the top of the window where the column names appear (not on the title bar, but just below that). This tells the Finder that you want the file stored in that window's folder, not one of its subfolders.

Want to move a folder so that it becomes a subfolder of another folder? Easily done. Just drag and drop the folder onto its destination folder (either its open window or its icon) as if it were a document or similar file. Now the dragged folder appears as a subfolder of the destination folder.

# Advanced Drag-and-Drop

The Finder offers another interesting way to put stuff into folders through another approach called "spring-loaded" folders. In essence, this allows a folder to jump open without requiring you to double-click on it. It only works when you drag and drop.

For instance, say you have a document on the Desktop that you want to put in the Sales Presentation folder that's inside your Documents folder, but you don't have any of those folders open. Well, no worries. Here's how to do it with spring-loaded folders:

1. Drag the document to the Macintosh HD icon. Place it directly on top of the icon but don't drop the document. Just wait a few seconds.

2. The Macintosh HD icon should pop open to reveal the hard drive's window. Locate the Documents folder. (If you need to scroll the window to find the folder you're looking for, just drag the document icon to the bottom edge of the open window, and it should scroll automatically.)

3. Drag the document to the Documents folder and leave it hovering over the folder again for a few seconds. The Documents folder will spring open.

4. Find the Sales Presentation folder until the folder is highlighted, and then drop the document icon on top of that folder. The document should now be stored

in the folder. In the meantime, all but the Sales Presentation folder will close themselves automatically.

Pretty cool, huh? There's more! Mac OS 8.5 adds another cool advanced drag-and-drop feature. For instance, in the folder window, notice that there's a little icon next to the folder's name in the title bar. Want to move this folder without closing the folder window? You can drag that icon from the title bar to the folder's new destination in the Finder.

## Drag-and-Drop III: Tabbed Folder

There's one more cool addition to the Mac OS that I want to cover. In the Finder, you can take any open window and drag it all the way to the bottom of the screen, where it becomes a tabbed folder. All you'll see of the window is a little tab sticking up from the bottom of the screen. Click that tab, and the window pops open, revealing its contents.

With one of these tabbed folders at the ready, you can drag and drop other icons into the folder. Just drag the icon until it's hovering over the tab, and the window should pop open. Drop the icon, and it's securely within the confines of that folder.

## Renaming Files and Folders

Spend enough time working on your Mac, and you'll probably experience two different issues related to what I call *file sprawl*. First, you'll end up with a ton of files named Untitled 1, Untitled 2, Untitled 3, and so on. Second, you'll probably come up with some doozies when you're naming your files that you later learn to regret, names like "Report Sam Ver. 4 Revised" or something equally meaningless—at least, it becomes meaningless after you've forgotten the clever little code you were using to create the names in the first place.

In this case, it's time to rename some of those files. Fortunately, it's pretty easy to do. In the Finder, locate the icon you want to rename (this can be a folder, a file, an application, or most anything else). Now, click once on the name of the icon and wait a few seconds. (If the icon is already selected, you can also press the Return key to rename it.) After a slight delay, the name becomes highlighted, and a blinking cursor appears. Now you can type to change the name of the icon. When you're done, press Return or press the mouse button to exit the editing mode.

*Click, wait a second, and you're ready to type a new name for your icon.*

## Get Info About a File

When you first start using a Mac, you probably get to know your files and documents fairly intimately. After all, you're just getting acquainted; everything seems so fresh and new, and you have no idea how you'll ever get sick of creating new documents, moving them around, and classifying them in folders.

Eventually, the romance will wear off, and you'll be stuck with thousands upon thousands of files you couldn't care less about. Even worse, you may not remember what the file is for, how big it is, or what application was used to create it. (Or what software author created it if it happens to be an application.) In that case, you'll want to get some info on the file.

That's easily accomplished. In the Finder, select the icon about which you need more information. Now choose **File**, **Get Info** (or ⌘**+I**) to bring up the Information window. Now you can see everything you've ever wanted to know about this file. You can even rename it. Just click the file's name to edit it to taste. Click the window's close box to dismiss it.

You can use the Get Info window for one fun trick—change this document or folder's icon. You do that by highlighting an icon or picture somewhere else (in the Finder or in another application) and choosing Edit, Copy to copy the new image for the icon. Then, select the file whose icon you want to change and choose File, Get Info. Now, select the icon in the Information window, then choose Edit, Paste. That will change the icon to the new, copied image.

### The Get Info Window

You may notice that, at least for certain sorts of files, there are some other fun things you can do in the Get Info window. If you're interested in locking files, see Chapter 10, "Let's Get This Mac Organized." And Chapter 11, "Change Settings for Better Performance," will tell you how to change the memory partition granted to an application through its Get Info window. Hey, this is one busy little command.

To get rid of a custom icon, select the icon in the Information window and press the delete key on your keyboard.

## Move It or Dupe It

You may notice that sometimes when you drag a file around the Finder, you move the file to the new location. Other times, though, you create a duplicate of the file. Why? Because any time you drag a file from one disk to another disk (instead of simply to another folder on the same disk), the Finder decides to duplicate the file.

But what if you want to create a duplicate of the file on the *same* drive? You can do that in one of two ways. First, the easier way: Select the file and choose the **File**, **Duplicate** or ⌘**+D** command. A duplicate (complete with the word *copy* appended to the name) appears in that same window, right next to the original.

Your other option? Hold down the **Option** key while dragging the file to it its new destination. When you release the mouse button, a duplicate of the file will be created (without the word *copy* appended) instead of the original file moving to the new location.

## Creating an Alias

An *alias* in real life is an alternative way of referring to a particular individual, usually for the sake of adding cadence to the lines spoken by a TV detective. "Be on the lookout for a man by the name of John Henry, alias, Quincy Adams, alias, Douglas Adams, alias Quincy Jones. He's armed and dangerous." It just sort of rolls off the tongue.

On your Mac, an *alias* is an alternative way of referring to a particular file. The alias can be given another name, it can be stored in a different location, and it can be placed on a drop-down menu. (Especially using the Apple Menu, as discussed in Chapter 10, "Let's Get This Mac Organized.")

When you double-click an alias, it's like you're double-clicking the original. But when you move an alias—even to the Trash—it won't affect the location of the original. It's safe, wherever it is.

In the meantime, the alias is designed to stand out a bit. While it has the same icon as the original file, its name will always appear in italics. Also, it can be renamed like any other icon, but it will continue to refer to the original file.

To create an alias, select in the Finder the icon you want an alias of. Then choose **File**, **Make Alias** or ⌘**+M**. An alias appears onscreen next to the original. You can also create an alias while dragging a file. Hold down the **Option+cmd** keys while dragging a file, and, when you release the mouse button, you'll create an alias instead of moving or copying of the original.

## Find the Original

Other times you'll be in the Finder, and you'll need to work backward: You'll be looking right at an alias, but you need to find the original file. You can do that by using the alias. First, select the alias's icon. Then use the **File, Find Original** command to find the original on which this alias is based. The original will pop up in the Finder, and you can go to work.

## Put Away

Consider that you're dealing with a computer, and that computers are stupid. In that light, I think it's really pretty cool that the Mac OS includes a file command that's as simple as Put Away.

You can use this command in two different situations. First, you can use the Put Away command whenever you want to eject a floppy disk or removable media disk (CD,

Zip, and so on), and you don't want to drag it to the Trash. (That's the customary way, but it makes some people uncomfortable.) Instead, highlight the disk icon and choose **File**, **Put Away** or ⌘**+Y**. The disk should eject almost immediately.

In other cases, you can use the Put Away command to send a file—like a document, an application, or a data file—back to where you last dragged it from. For instance, if you have a document called Memo #4578 and you drag it from the Documents folder to the Desktop to work with it, you can later select the icon and choose **File**, **Put Away** or ⌘**+Y** to send it back to the Documents folder. This works fine with files that have been moved for other reasons—to the Trash, for instance.

# Trash: The Inside Scoop

Gotta file that's simply rubbing you the wrong way? You know the kind: beady eyes, sweaty palms, a squeaky voice. The kinda file you feel like taking out just because you're not thrilled with the way it's *lookin' atcha*. Well, there's a way to do just that: drag that Edsel of a file over to the Trash can, and then bid him a fond farewell.

Deleting a file, for all practical purposes, causes it to leave the Finder completely. Its icon is gone, and it can't be retrieved without special utilities. For all practical purposes, a deleted file is lost to you forever. (That's one good reason you should always have a backup copy of your important documents.)

So seriously, why would you delete a file? Usually it's because you don't want to continue to keep the file in your organization system, and you want the hard drive space back so you can store something else. Remember, just like a physical filing cabinet, your hard drive can eventually get full of documents. If you find some files you no longer need, it's best to delete them and clear up the space.

But just putting a file in the Trash doesn't delete it—just like putting something in a regular trash can in your office doesn't cause that item to be lost to you forever. You could still go digging through the Trash on your Mac, just as you could in your cubicle at work or in the wastebasket near your Mac at home.

## *Trashing Something*

It used to be there was one and only one way to throw something away. Apple's engineers liked it that way because it meant you had to be very deliberate in what you were doing. You had to grab the mouse, drag the file you want to delete to the Trash icon, and then let go. That put the file in the Trash. (You can also select multiple files and drag them all to the Trash at once.)

*The Trash bulges a bit to let you know it's got something in it.*

These days, though, Apple has relented and will now allow you to use a keystroke combination to throw things away. Select the files in the Finder, and then choose ⌘+**Delete** to toss them in the Trash. Fortunately, the files still aren't deleted immediately—instead, they're placed in the Trash where they then wait to be thrown out.

You can also select the files and choose **File, Move to Trash** to accomplish the same thing.

## Digging in the Trash

Did you toss something you didn't mean to get rid of? You can get it back *if you haven't emptied the Trash yet.* In this respect, the Trash works just like any other folder. Double-click the Trash icon, and a window opens showing you the Trash's contents. To get something out of the Trash, just drag it to the Desktop or to another folder.

Note that you can't launch applications or load documents that are still in the Trash. The Mac insists that you move them out of the Trash before using them. (This is for your own good. It wouldn't be right to empty the Trash while it contained a document you were working on, would it?)

## Emptying the Trash

Here's the moment we've all been waiting for: emptying the Trash. Because files dragged to the Trash are left there for a while, they're still taking up space on your hard drive. They haven't actually been deleted. To do that, you have to empty the Trash. That's done with the **Special, Empty Trash** command in the Finder.

Choosing this command generally results in a dialog box that tells you how many items are to be deleted, how much space they consume, and asks you whether or not you really want to delete the files. (Recognizing, of course, that they won't be retrievable.) If you really want to delete the files, click **OK**.

*Be really sure that you want to delete all the files in the Trash before you click OK in this dialog box.*

Your Mac will then proceed to delete all the files in the Trash. And, nine times out of ten, it works just fine. There are two exceptions, though. First, the Trash won't delete a *locked* file without encouragement. There are two ways to get that file deleted if that's what you really want to do. The first way is to select the file in the Finder and choose **Get Info**, and then click the check mark you'll find next to the Locked option at the bottom of the window. Close the Get Info window, and the file is now no longer locked.

The second way is to hold down the **Option** key while choosing the **Special, Empty Trash** command. This will cause any locked files to be deleted without warning.

The second exception: Files currently in use will not be deleted by the Mac OS, even if they've since been moved to the Trash. You'll need to close the file (it's probably open in one of your applications) or close the application or utility if that's what you're trying to delete.

**Double-Dare**

Are you the sort of person who doesn't ever have to think twice about any of your actions? Apple knows your type only too well. They've actually made it possible for you to empty the Trash without first being forced to read some wimpy (your word, not mine) confirmation dialog box. Here's how: Get Info. Select the Trash icon, choose **File**, **Get Info**, and uncheck the box that says "**Warn Before Emptying**." Now you can delete files without a safety net.

# Isn't That Special?

So what about all those hidden, secret commands on the menu bar in the Finder? Don't let them worry you. With the proper training, you'll master them in only a few weeks or months, if not in seconds. And if you never do master them, just ignore them. That's my solution for just about any problem that doesn't work itself out quickly.

On tap in the Special menu are a few important commands, including Restart, Shut Down, and Sleep. Surprisingly, these are all commands that have nothing to do with your Mac; they're only intended as magic hotspots for parents of young children to use in case of emergency. Similarly, the Erase Disk command is reserved for use by chiropractors only.

## *Restart and Shut Down*

Actually, these are pretty important commands; they're how you tell the Mac that you're either done for the day or you'd like the Mac to reset itself, go through the initialization process again, and present you with a fresh screen as if the day were just dawning.

Choose the **Special**, **Shut Down** command, and the Mac goes through a sequence of events before it shuts down the Mac completely (so you can leave the office and catch the last few minutes of "Jeopardy," for instance). It will close all applications that are still running and ask you if you want to save any documents that have been left open. After Mac has closed all applications but the Finder, the Shut Down sequence performs some last-minute administrative tasks. Then it turns off the computer. (Most of the time. With some Macs, you may still need to throw a power switch.)

It's important to shut down your Mac in this fashion; otherwise, you may lose data—even if you've closed your applications. Shutting down a Mac without using this command (for example, by pulling the power plug or flipping the switch on a surge protector) could cause important System Folder items to become corrupt or cause other problems.

**Special, Restart** is similar to the Shut Down command, except that the Mac never gets completely turned off: After it goes through the Shut Down sequence, it immediately begins the startup sequence again. This is a good idea if you've just witnessed a crashed application or if you're seeing a lot of problems or errors reported with your Mac's main memory. A quick restart won't hurt anything (even data on a RAM disk, explained in Chapter 11, "Change Settings for Better Performance," is preserved), and it can solve some annoying little problems.

## Sleep, Perchance Too Green

The Sleep command should appear only if your Mac is capable of taking advantage of it. What Sleep does is put your Mac in a state of suspended animation, so to speak. The monitor is powered down, the processor works only at a trickle, and even the internal hard drive spins down so that it's not wasting energy. Your Mac is still consuming electricity, but just barely.

After you've invoked the **Special**, **Sleep** command, it shouldn't take more than a single keypress to wake it up and let you start working again. In the meantime, all your applications stay open, and your data should be intact.

## Achieving Full Erasure

The Special menu has one other command worth checking out: the Erase Disk command. This is really a command for *formatting* a disk or turning it into a disk that's capable of being used by a Macintosh computer. You see, just because a floppy disk or a hard drive is being used with a Mac doesn't mean it was initially designed for a Mac. In most cases, hard drives, floppies, and other disks can be used with all sorts of computers, even those running Windows, DOS, and UNIX.

The difference is that each operating system has its own format scheme for disks. For the Macintosh to save a file to a disk, the disk doesn't have to be manufactured in some special way; it just needs to be formatted as Mac-compatible. That's done (if necessary) with the Erase Disk command.

### Sleep Offline

When you put a Mac to sleep, it's a good idea to log-off of any modem-based online services and make sure the Mac isn't expected to act as a server of some sort—whether for sharing files with other Macs or allowing other Macs to print. This won't always cause problems, but it's best to put an "offline" Mac to sleep, so that nothing unexpected wakes it up or, even worse, crashes the Mac while it's in a low-power mode.

You can also run the Erase Disk command on a disk that's already been formatted as Mac-compatible. In that case, the entire disk is erased and formatted again, so you can start over as if it were brand new.

Note that the Erase Disk command should not be invoked lightly. You'll lose *all of the data* that's currently on a disk if you erase and format it. And the data will be basically irretrievable. Instead, this command should be used only when you know for a fact that you have a new floppy or other removable disk that needs to be formatted for Mac-compatibility, or you're absolutely sure you're doing the right thing by reformatting another sort of disk.

1. To erase and reformat a disk, select it in the **Finder** (after careful consideration), and then choose the **Special**, **Erase Disk** command.
2. A dialog box will appear, asking you to enter a name for the disk and choose which sort of format you'd like to use for this disk. (Most likely, you'll choose **Mac OS Standard**.)
3. Then click **Erase**.

That's it. I hope you didn't make a mistake and accidentally select a disk that you didn't want to format, because the Mac OS will begin erasing and formatting the disk immediately. Use caution around this command.

# Other Finder and Mac OS Stuff

Although these other elements of the Mac OS interface—the Application menu, the Apple menu, and the Chooser—aren't strictly part of the Finder, they still deserve a quick introduction here. They'll be discussed elsewhere in the book, too, especially when their particular specialties pop up. But here's the quickie *high-school-reunion-this-is-my-third-husband*-type introduction.

➤ *The Application menu.* Discussed in-depth in Chapter 5, "Getting Things Done," the Application menu is at the top-right corner of the Mac's screen, located on the menu bar. It's always there, allowing you to pick which application will be frontmost, so you can work with it. It's through this menu that you can *multitask*, running more than one program at the same time.

➤ *The Apple menu.* In the top-left corner of the menu bar, the Apple menu is a convenient way to launch applications, load documents, and access special parts of your Mac, like the control panels and the Chooser. The Apple Menu is discussed in Chapter 5, and again in Chapter 10.

➤ *The Chooser.* The Chooser (located on and launched from the Apple Menu) is one of the ways you choose printers, set up your network connections, and access remote computers over networking cable. In Mac OS 8.5, you have a couple of other ways to do these things, too, so you probably won't see too much of the Chooser, which is really a holdover from older versions of the Mac OS. Still we'll talk about it a bit in Chapter 15, "Getting Your Stuff Printed" and Chapter 17, "Networking Macs."

# The Least You Need to Know

The Finder is file-management central. It is the base of operations you'll use to give some discipline to the files you create, install, or delete on your Mac. In fact, it's the headquarters for a number of important tactical commands that are used to manage your Mac's resources: shut down the Mac, and erase and format disks for utilization with the Mac OS.

Basically, if there's a military-esque metaphor to be used, you'll use it in reference to the Finder. It's *ground zero* for disk-related maintenance.

Most of file management is drag-and-drop: You can drag files into new folders, drag them to the Trash; you can even drag files and hold down the **Option** key to create duplicates or hold down the **Option+⌘** keys to create an alias. You can use other file commands by selecting the file and choosing a command in the Finder's menu bar. These commands include **File**, **Get Info** (for learning more about a particular file); **File**, **Duplicate**; **File**, **Make Alias**; **File**, **Move to Trash**. Each of these commands also has keyboard combination equivalents to make them a bit easier for the Finder expert.

The Finder also has some special capabilities, including shutting down the Mac, restarting it, putting the Mac to sleep, and erasing any disks that are connected to the Mac. These commands need to be used carefully and under particular circumstances. They do have one thing in common: They're found on the Special menu in the Finder.

Finally, the Finder has some kissing cousins that are always around on your Mac's menu bar: the Application Menu, the Apple Menu, and the Chooser. Each of these is designed to make things a little more convenient, completing your F-16 fighter jet-like cockpit of controls that reach into the Mac OS. If there's something you need to do, you can accomplish it by using one of these tools, the Finder, or both together.

# Chapter 4

# Actually, Uh, Finding Things

---

## In This Chapter

➤ Starting Up Sherlock

➤ Finding files

➤ Searching through documents

➤ Finding stuff on the Net

---

While the Finder is certainly an interesting and impressive way to get around a computer, there's something specific it lacks. Considering it's called the Finder, it's not actually that great at helping you automatically search for things. The Finder is really more about helping you organize your folders and dig around for files by double-clicking on icons. For more automated searches, you'll have better luck with the Find command.

In fact, the Finder is nicely complemented by a new addition to Mac OS 8.5, Sherlock. This update to the original Find command (itself a small application) now does some amazing things besides just finding files, although it's still really good at that. How does searching *through* all of your Mac's documents for certain text sound? Huh? Now what would you pay?

Or how about searching the Internet directly from the Finder? That's pretty cool, too, and there's still no extra charge for this feature. All you need to know are the secrets to this wonderful Find command. Let's play ball!

# Starting Up Sherlock

First of all, a little confusion-dissolution. Sherlock is the name for the small application that pops up when you invoke the Find command in the Finder's menus. They are one and the same. You may also hear Sherlock called Find File or Find 2.0.

You can start up Sherlock in a number of different ways, so that you can pretty much always get to it, even if you're not currently in the Finder. Be careful, though; some applications have their own "find" commands, and they can sometimes be launched in the same way that Sherlock is launched (especially using keyboard commands like ⌘+**F**). If you're in an application other than the Finder, the best way to launch Sherlock is through the Apple menu.

Here, then, are the different ways to launch Find:

➤ *The Finder menu.* With the Finder active, choose **File, Find** from the menu bar.

➤ *Finder keystrokes.* You can also use the keyboard command ⌘+**F** to launch Sherlock.

➤ *Apple menu.* From any application, including the Finder, you can head to the **Apple** menu and select the Sherlock item.

After you've launched Sherlock, you're switched to the Sherlock window, complete with tabs for the different sort of searching you can do, along with a number of different options. Sherlock opens, by default, to the Find File tab.

*The Sherlock window is a compact but complete interface for finding things on your Mac and on the Internet.*

Click to search for text within documents

Click to search the Internet

The Find File tab

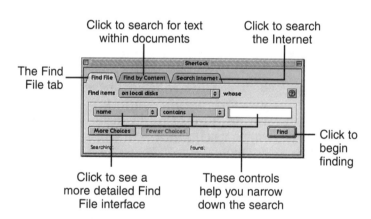

Click to see a more detailed Find File interface

These controls help you narrow down the search

Click to begin finding

For the rest of this chapter, we'll take individual looks at the different types of searches you can do. If you'd like to perform a particular type of search, turn to that section in this chapter for a complete rundown.

# Find That File!

If you know the name of the files you're looking for—or if you know just about anything else about them—you'll want to use the controls found on the Find File tab in

Sherlock. These allow you to search by any number of criteria, including the name of the file, the size of the file, the date it was created, and any number of other options.

Note that this doesn't mean you need to know the exact name, date, and so on. You can also search for ranges; if it's a name that you're searching for, then entering the keyword **simple** might bring back results like SimpleText, SimpleSound, and SimpleText Preferences. If you're searching for a date, you can search a range of dates to find, for instance, files created or changed in the past week or month.

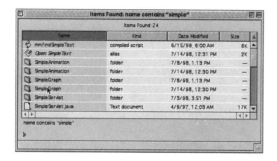

*The results of a search using the word "simple" include many files that have "simple" as only part of their names.*

In fact, the Find File portion of Sherlock is particularly adept at helping you find *more than one* file that fits certain criteria. This is great, for instance, if you want to gather all files that meet certain requisites and then copy them to another disk or transfer them through e-mail.

## Heeeere File, File, File!

There are two basic things you need to decide when you set about trying to find a file. First, where among your Mac's various disk drives do you want Sherlock to look? In the Sherlock window, the **Find** items pull-down menu allows you to select where the search will take place.

You might notice, at this point, that the Find File tab's window really looks uncomfortably like a sentence being diagrammed in a grade-school Language Arts textbook or, perhaps, one of those Mad Libs fill-in-the-word joke books. That's how you tell Find to search for a file: You fill in the sentence so that it knows where to look, and then what to look for.

In the "where to look" pull-down menu, you can choose how, if at all, the search should be limited. Your options include:

➤ *on all disks*. This means Sherlock will search all disks that this Mac has access to, including any that are on a network.

➤ *on local disks*. In this case, the search takes place only on disks that are physically connected to the Mac, including CD-ROMs and floppies.

➤ *on local disks, except CD-ROMs*. Same as above, excluding CD-ROM drives.

➤ *on mounted servers*. This option causes Sherlock to search only on networked drives that currently appear on the desktop.

➤ *on the Desktop*. Searches only on the Desktop.

➤ *in the Finder selection*. This searches any Finder window or icon that had focus before Sherlock was launched. It allows you to look in a particular folder, more than one folder, or more than one drive by simply selecting them in the Finder.

Once you've chosen where to look, the second step is to enter criteria that represent what to look for. You begin by using the pull-down menu that defaults to **name**. In this menu, you'll find a lot of different ways you can search for files aside from simply by name.

*The Find File tab features a number of menus that are used to build a Mad Libs-style sentence.*

The "where to look" menu

The "what, exactly, to find" entry

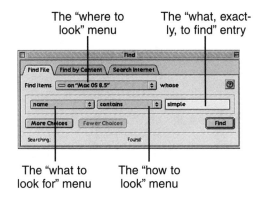

The "what to look for" menu

The "how to look" menu

The options in the "what to look for" menu are fairly self-explanatory; you should experiment with them a bit to see what sort of result you can get. Much of the time you'll simply search by name, but it's nice to know you have other options available.

You'll also notice something else about those options. Change the type of search so that you're searching for, say, a date instead of a name. When you do that, the subsequent menus change. Instead of **contains** as an option in the "how to look" menu, you'll now have a different set of options that make more sense for dates.

Finally, you enter the "what, exactly, to look for" information. With this one entry, most of the time you'll actually need to type something. If you're searching for a name, remember that you don't have to type the whole name and that capitalization doesn't matter.

The last step in setting up the search is: Click the **Find** button. The Sherlock program takes over and begins searching the specified drives and folders for the files you're seeking.

## *Your Items Are Served*

If Sherlock comes across any of the files using the criteria you've specified, it responds in a dignified and appropriate manner by popping up an Items Found window. This window is not only attractive, but functional, giving you a number of ways to access to files that have been located.

### Pile 'em on

You might be looking down the list of possible search types thinking to yourself, "Why would I want to search a whole drive to find out which has a locked attribute of 'locked'?" You probably wouldn't want to do that. But what if you could use that criteria in conjunction with a date or a name search, so that you're searching for all files named "letter" created in the past month that are locked? That would be a more useful search. Just click the **More Choices** button to get a chance to enter extra criteria for this search. Each time you click the button, you get to add another variable to the equation.

The Items Found window is made up of two different panes. In the top window pane, every instance of a matching file is displayed. In the bottom pane, you can see the hierarchy of folders that shows where, exactly, you will find the file in the Finder.

Single-click a file to select it; double-click the file to launch it

Top pane shows found items

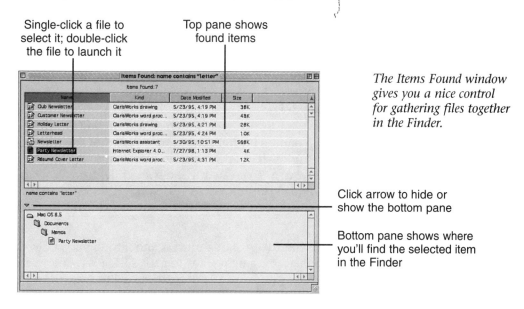

*The Items Found window gives you a nice control for gathering files together in the Finder.*

Click arrow to hide or show the bottom pane

Bottom pane shows where you'll find the selected item in the Finder

Fortunately, you don't need to dive into the Finder to work with one of the found files. If you like, you can doble-click to launch the file directly from the top pane of the Find window. Similarly, you can single-click to select the file and choose **File, Open** or ⌘**+O** to launch it.

If you'd rather move the file, you can do that, too, simply by dragging its icon from the top pane to the Desktop or to an open folder (or a folder/drive icon) in the Finder. If you'd like to move more than one file, you can hold down the **Shift** key while clicking to select more than one file. Then you can drag them as a group.

When you're done with the Items Found window, you can click its **close box**, choose **File, Close Window**, or choose ⌘**+W** to dismiss the results.

# Find by Content

Find by Content is a very cool addition in Sherlock, allowing you to search *inside* documents for a particular string of text (a word or series of words strung together). Best of all, it's really simple to use.

It's also pretty fast. But there's a reason for this. Find doesn't actually look through every file that's on your hard drive; instead, it consults an index that's created of all your files, where keywords are stored. That means documents can be found much more quickly, just as you can find terms and concepts in this book quickly by consulting the index in the back.

It also means that an index needs to be built before it can be referenced. And the index needs to keep rebuilding while you work so that you can search newer documents as well as older ones.

To begin a content search, select the Find By Content tab in the Sherlock window. Then, let's build an index.

## *Become an Indexin' Fool*

You'll need to create an index the first time you search a given drive, but it's fairly simple to do. Click the Index Volumes button toward the bottom of the Sherlock window. This brings up another window that allows you to create an index for any drives that haven't already had one created. To create the index, highlight the drive in question (click once on its name) and click the **Create Index...** button. This brings up an alert that lets you know that creating an index takes some time. Go grab a novel, and then click the **Create** button.

A dialog box appears showing you the indexing process and letting you know about how long things are going to take. You might want to get a little ice cream to go along with the novel, especially if you have a large hard drive. But once the index is created, it'll be worth it. (Just keep believing that.)

Finally, the index is created, and you're returned to the Index Volumes window. Now you can create an index for another drive, update the index for the selected drive, delete the index for a drive, or schedule regular index updates. Just select a drive and click the appropriate button if you want to do one of these things. If you don't want to do one of these things, I certainly can't blame you. Just click the close box on this window to get back to the Sherlock window.

## *Digging into Documents*

With your index created, you're ready to search the drive by content. To do that, get back to the Sherlock window (with the Find by Content tab selected) and enter some keywords in the **Words** text box. These can be any words you think might appear in the document; you can include as many or as few as you like.

In the Search window pane, put a check mark in the **On** column next to any volumes you want to search. You should also take notice of when the last index was created; if you think the file you're looking for may be newer, you'll need to update the index first.

To search, click **Find**. This results in an Items Found window that works just like the one that pops up when you search a Find File search.

# Find It on the Internet

The last little trick you can pull off with Sherlock is searching the Internet for a particular word, set of words, or a given phrase. The cool part is two-fold. First, you don't have to load a browser just to see if something out on the Internet can answer your questions. Second, you can search more than one search engine at a time—something that's tough to do from the typical browser.

**Index Scheduling**

This one is actually a good idea; if you'll be using Find by Content often, you should schedule regular updates to the index. Otherwise, every time you go to search by content, you'll be waiting a while for the index to update. In the Index Volumes window, click the **Schedule** button. A window appears that's fairly straightforward. Just select a time of day and the day(s) of the week that you want the indexing to take place. The indexes will then be updated for all your drives at the time specified. You might want to pick a time during which you don't plan to be too busy at the computer.

If you're used to using Internet search engines, you probably already know what to do: just jump into the Sherlock window and do it. If you haven't searched the Internet before, this is probably the simplest introduction you could get. It works pretty much like the rest of Sherlock!

The only difference: You'll need to be connected to the Internet to make this search happen. See Chapter 19, "Working the Web," for help if you don't yet have an active connection. And don't be alarmed if Sherlock fires up your modem for you; you'll need an *active* connection to the Internet while Sherlock is searching, too. Try not to forget this, especially if you share your data line with other phone extensions throughout the house.

### Executive Summary

Want to see a quick overview of what a particular file says? In the Items Found window, hold down the **Control** key and click the document in question. A contextual menu pops up. Choose the command **Summarize to Clipboard**. Now, switch to the Finder, and you can view the text in the Clipboard viewer. (You can also switch to any word processing application and select **Edit, Paste** to paste the summary into an open document.)

## Be the Net

Answers don't always just pop off the Internet. For some of us, there's a certain Zen to the art of searching, surfing, and seeking answers from Internet search engines. (For others, the term "Zen" has been utterly destroyed by being applied to more unrelated concepts than the suffix "-Gate" in popular American culture.) Whatever your take on the Zen of searching, realize that you're taking a step close to master with this helpful hand from the Mac OS's Sherlock-*san* utility. It's quite a boon.

Here's the drill. In the **Words** text box, enter the keywords you want to use for the search. In the Search window, put a **check mark** next to each of the search engines you want to use. Then click **Search**.

The Items Found window appears with a listing of Web pages it believes matches your criteria. To see a quick summary of the page, select its name in the top pane. The bottom pane will change to reflect that page's content. If you'd like to launch that page in your default browser, double-click the page's name. Your Web browser will launch (if necessary), and you'll be viewing the page.

*When searching for Web pages, you can check a quick summary of the page before committing to it and opening your Web browser.*

Select a Web page in top pane

Summary of page appears in bottom pane

| Name | Relevance | Site |
|------|-----------|------|
| Todd Stauffer on the Web | Unavailable | www.shutup101.com |
| Todd Stauffer on the Web | Unavailable | shutup101.com |
| Mac Chat | Unavailable | www.peak-computing.com |
| Mac Chat | Unavailable | www.peak-computing.com |
| Webintosh: Todd Stauffer's Happy Endi... | Unavailable | www.webintosh.com |
| Todd Stauffer on the Web | Unavailable | shutup101.com |
| Using Html 3.2 | Unavailable | research.firm.com |
| Shut Up Front Door | Unavailable | www.shutup101.com |
| Stauffer and Company's Individual Reso... | Unavailable | www.stauffers.com |
| Todd Stauffer on the Web | Unavailable | members.aol.com |
| HTML Web Publishing 6-in-1, by Stauffe... | Unavailable | www.discountcomputerbooks.com |
| No Title | Unavailable | elib.cs.sfu.ca |
| Mac Chat | Unavailable | www.peak-computing.com |

Items Found: terms contain "'Todd Stauffer'"
Items Found: 17
terms contain "'Todd Stauffer'"    **Stop**

Click here to begin a search on Goto.com!

**Todd Stauffer on the Web**
FAQs, Errata and Info Using HTML 3.2, 2nd Edition Creating Your Own AOL Web Pages HTML By Example Using the Internet With Your
http://shutup101.com/todd/

http://shutup101.com/todd/    Searching...

## *Update the Engines*

Occasionally, Sherlock will complain that it thinks the search engines are out of date. If you agree, you can choose to have them updated automatically. You can also update them yourself every once in a while by selecting the **Find** menu and selecting **Update Search Sites** from the menu. This will add new and interesting search engines you can use on your quest.

# The Least You Need to Know

Through some bizarre twist of time and space, the Finder got named "Finder" even though it's not really very good at finding—at least, not at searching for and finding things automatically. Fortunately, something is, and it's called Find (or Sherlock). In Mac OS 8.5, it's much better than it ever has been.

**Phrase Tip**

If you're searching for a particular phrase or string of words that appear next to one another and in order, try entering them between quotation marks (" "). Most Internet search engines know that this means to search for the specific phrase. An example would be a name. The keywords Todd Stauffer return entries that include Todd, Stauffer, and both in different parts of the document. Using "Todd Stauffer" in the text box results in much more pinpoint results.

You can start up Sherlock from the **File, Find** command in the Finder or from the **Apple** menu. Once started, you use tabs in the Sherlock window to switch between different types of searches. Sherlock can be used to search for particular files, for text within files, or for Web pages on the Internet.

To search for a particular file, you choose the drive to search, and then use different criteria, including names, dates, and so on. You can also choose the drive you'll search on or choose to search only the items that have been chosen in the Finder.

For text and Web searches, you use keywords to hone in on the subject. To speed things up, you need a current index of your drive to search for text; to search the Web, you need to update the search sites every once in a while.

# Chapter 5

# Getting Things Done

## In This Chapter

➤ Making applications go

➤ Multitasking: walk and chew gum

➤ The Apple menu: your personal launchpad

➤ The Mac's included tools

➤ Installing applications

Talk about a waste of time. This is the fifth chapter, and it's the first time we've talked about getting anything done with your computer! Up until now, it's all been about how to move the mouse, how to copy things, how to Trash things, how to find things, and so on.

Now we're ready to talk about getting something accomplished with your Mac—for that, you're going to need *applications*. Applications are the computer programs you use to create a document, explore information, or just to have a little fun. To get to that point, though, you'll need to know a little about how applications interact with other files, not to mention the Finder.

## Getting Applications to Work

Applications really are slightly different from the other sorts of files we've talked about thus far. An application is still a computer file—don't get me wrong—but it's the exact opposite of a data file (we also call them documents). While a data file is designed to store information you've organized, written, or otherwise created, an application program is designed to *create* and work with data files. That's the whole point.

An example of an application is SimpleText, the Mac's included text editing program. When you double-click SimpleText, you're presented with a blank document window and some menu commands that allow you to create and edit memos, notes, lists, or anything else you might want to type. You can then Save, Print, or perform other tasks on that document. (Chapter 7, "Mac OS Walkthrough," offers a walk-through of using SimpleText to create documents.)

So let's talk about applications a little bit. Applications work a little differently than some other files in the Finder—in fact, there are a couple of different ways you can go about starting up an application. We'll cover those, and then we'll stretch that into another topic: closing an application.

# Open Method #1: Keep It Simple

The easiest way to start up an application is to go to the Finder, find the application's icon, and double-click the icon. After a moment or two, you should see the application's name appear in the main menu bar at the top of the Mac's screen. Then you'll likely see a *splash screen* (some sort of graphics image that tells you about the program), followed by the application itself. Some applications will just show you a blank screen (you need to go to the File menu to create a new document or session) while others will present you with a default window or document.

# Open Method #2: Double-Click a Document

Another way to start an application involves the document. In the Finder, double-clicking a document will start up its associated application so you can edit that document. For instance, if you have a WordPerfect document, double-clicking that document's icon should launch WordPerfect on your Mac.

At least, this works most of the time. In some cases, you need to specify the application that's supposed to be associated with the document you double-click. For instance, in the preceding example, you might have a WordPerfect document on your Mac sent to you by a colleague. If you don't actually have the WordPerfect application on your Mac, though, the Mac won't know how to open the document. When the Mac gets confused like that, it asks you which application it should use to open the document. Often times, some applications you have on your Mac can open documents created in other applications: AppleWorks or ClarisWorks can open many WordPerfect documents, for instance.

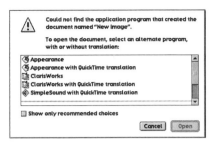

*A dialog box appears if the Mac OS isn't sure what application it should use to open your double-clicked document.*

This process is actually handled by a special control panel included with the Mac OS called File Exchange. In this control panel, you'll find preferences to govern the double-click-a-document behavior. To open this control panel, select the **Apple** menu by pointing to it and clicking the mouse, and then select the **Control Panels** menu item. Another menu appears, allowing you to select **File Exchange**.

To change the way a document is loaded when it's double-clicked, choose the **Translation** tab. Now you can click the **Add** button to create a new type of translation or click the **Remove** button to get rid of a translation (perhaps it isn't working correctly). Similarly, you can use the **check boxes** at the top of the control panel window to decide how many choices you want to see when the Mac gets confused about a document.

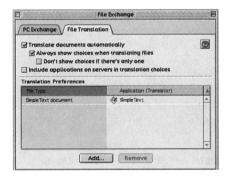

*The File Exchange control panel allows you to change the way documents behave when they're double-clicked.*

# Open Method #3: Drag-and-Drop Documents

The other way to get a document to load an associated application leaves little room for doubt: You simply drag the document onto the application's icon, and then drop the document. This will cause the application to fire up and load that document, if it possibly can.

Of course, not all documents are designed to work with all applications. So the Mac highlights an application when you drag a compatible document to it. (A darker shadow appears around the application icon.) This means that the application will attempt to launch the document when you drop it.

Even if the document does get launched, it may not necessarily work with that application. If the document isn't designed to be read by the application, you get an error message to that effect.

## Quitting the Application

When you're done working in an application, you can quit the application by choosing **File, Quit** from the menu bar or ⌘+**Q** on the keyboard. The application should resolve any unfinished business—like prompting you to save any changed documents—then shut the application down safely.

# Working with Documents

Once you've got your applications opening and closing on cue, you're ready for the next step: working with documents within those applications. You've already seen how to launch an application using a document, but what about creating new documents?

## Starting Anew

The only real problem with starting a new document is, well, there's nothing in it. You'll have to create things to go in that document, which can take lots of time, effort, and dedication. In fact, I would certainly suggest that you avoid creating documents whenever possible. The best plan would be to cash in your life insurance policy and get a little place by the ocean.

If you simply can't help yourself, it's certainly not tough to begin creating a new document. In almost every Mac application you'll encounter, you can simply choose **File, New** to create the document. One should pop up in the application, or maybe you'll see some options first in a dialog box. It depends on the application.

Any other ways? In applications that have a toolbar, you'll often see a small icon—it usually looks a bit like a blank document—that will create a new document for you. Click it once, and the new document should appear.

*The typical new document toolbar icon. Toolbars appear only in some applications, according to whether or not the application programmers think they're appropriate for the task at hand.*

## Closing Windows versus Quitting

Once you've got a document open, the logical thing to do is immediately close it; otherwise, you'll start to feel an inkling to do some work.

When you close a window (by clicking the window's **close box** or by choosing **File, Close** from the menu bar), you're not necessarily *quitting* the application. If you're working with folders in the Finder, you're simply closing that folder. If you're working in an application, you're closing that document (you might even get a dialog box that asks whether or not you actually planned to close that document). That doesn't necessarily mean you've quit the application, though. Some applications *do* quit when you close the window, but most don't.

If you're wondering if the application is still open, check the Application menu, which is the menu up in the top-right corner that has the current application's name and icon. If the application's name still appears in that menu, that means it's running. You'll need to switch to it, and then invoke the **File, Quit** command. How do you switch to a running program? Well, you'll have to buy the second edition of this book to find out!

Okay, okay. I'll tell you in the next section.

# Running More than One Application

Rules were made to be broken, so I'll break one now: I'll use parts of a word to define itself. *Multitasking* is the capability of an operating system to allow multiple tasks to run at once. The Mac OS, for instance, is capable of running two programs at pretty much the same time; it's okay to work in a word processor while your e-mail program checks for new messages. Of course, *you* can't really run more than one application at once, unless you're pretty darned special. Most people can only mouse and type in one application at a time. But that doesn't mean the Mac can't, especially if it's doing something more automated (like checking e-mail) while you do something that requires thought, like typing a report in your word processor.

For most people, the important thing about multitasking is that you don't have to close the application you're working in before switching to another application. That way you can move back and forth between applications if you need to—like between a CD-ROM encyclopedia program and a word processor in which you're typing a research paper. You can even switch back to the Finder and launch more applications, as long as you have enough RAM available.

## The Big Switcheroo

The key issue for the human being (that's you) involved in the Macintosh multitasking equation is figuring out how to switch between the open applications. After all, having another application open and ready for your input simply won't help much if you can't get to it so you can type.

### What's All This about Applications Running?

A guy calls me up the other day, says, "Todd, just thought I'd let you know that I've got five of my Mac applications running!"

I said, "Shouldn't you go and catch them?"

When we say an application is "running," what we really mean is simply that it's *active*. A computer application has two basic states: running and "closed" (or inactive). If an application is running, that simply means that it's been launched, the Mac OS has assigned it some memory to work with, and the processor realizes that it may receive computing requests from this application sometime soon.

Essentially, the Mac OS is put on alert that this application may do something. You're put on a similar alert, because the running application appears onscreen, complete with a menu bar and, often, a document window of some sort. And running applications appear in the Application menu, allowing you to switch between them almost instantly.

Closed applications aren't loaded into memory, and the Mac OS doesn't take notice of them until you launch one of them. Instead, these applications are simply stored on your hard drive. It's not until you double-click the application's icon in the Finder that it's told (by the Finder) to wake up, load its computer code into main memory (RAM), and alert the Mac's processor chip that it may have some tasks that need to be performed.

Up in the top-right corner of your Mac's screen is the Application menu; it should be displaying the icon and name of the application you're currently working in. Whenever a new application is launched, you'll find that its name is added to this menu. That way, you can easily switch to it if necessary.

To switch to a running application, just click once on the **Application** menu (the currently running application and icon), and then click on the **application name** you want to switch to. When you do, the application you chose will pop to the front, while other applications will be moved into the background.

## *Tear Off the Menu*

You might find something weird happens when you click on the Application menu and then move your mouse away from the drop-down portion of the menu...did the menu follow you? Ain't that spooky?

Actually, it's a *tear-off* menu. These menus not only drop down when clicked, but you can actually drag them away from the menu bar by moving the mouse pointer down and away from the top of the screen. Now the menu is just a tiny control window that you can position anywhere on the screen. And it's still an Application menu that will allow you to switch quickly between applications.

How do you switch between applications? Just click once on the icon of the application you want to switch to. It should pop right into the foreground.

You can also load new documents this way. Drag a document from the Finder to an application's icon in the tear-off menu, and the application will load that document.

### Ready for Close-Up

In computing lingo, the window that's on top (the one that has focus) is said to be in the *foreground*, while others, like the Desktop and the Finder, when you're running applications are said to be in the *background*. Something that's *running in the background*, then, is a task that is computed while you're looking at some other application. For instance, most Mac users choose to print their computer documents "in the background" so that they can continue to work in an application while the printer churns away.

*A tear-off Application menu.*

If you need to get rid of the tear-off application window, just click its close box, and it's gone. (You can retrieve it again the same way you tore if off in the first place. No need to glue it back together.)

## *Start Yet Another Application*

Don't have your fill of open applications yet? If not, the best way to start a new one is to switch to the Finder. Pull down that Application menu again, and you'll notice that the Finder is one of the listed applications.

To launch another application, **switch** to the Finder. Now find the application you want to launch and double-click its **icon** (or start it any of the other ways discussed earlier in this chapter). Now you're multitasking!

## Other Switches

There's actually another way to switch between running applications. If you can see one of the windows from the other application, you can point to the window and click once; this will bring that application to the foreground, just as if you'd selected it in the Application menu. To do this with the Finder, simply click on any part of the Desktop that you can see back there behind your applications. (You can also use the keystroke ⌘**+Tab** to switch between active applications.)

## Tricky Switch

Here's one quick Application menu trick: If you'd like to switch to another application while *simultaneously* hiding the application you're currently working with, it can be done, but only with some sleight of hand. Hold down the **Option** key while you select the application you want to switch to. Once you've switched, release the Option key. The original application *is* now hidden.

# Hide and Seek for Grown-Ups

Because multitasked applications can get in the way of each other—or just clutter the screen—the Mac OS includes a way to hide applications. They're still running, and their names won't disappear from the Application menu. You can still switch to them while they're hidden, and they'll pop up in the foreground. All hiding does is make the application's window and menu disappear from the screen so they can give you an unobstructed view of something in the background, like the Desktop.

The Hide menu item is a pretty smart one; it constantly changes to include the name of the application that's currently in the foreground. That way it's very clear which application you're about to hide. For instance, if you had Microsoft Word up on the screen in the foreground, you would pull down the Application menu and see **Hide Microsoft Word** as one of the options. If you wanted to hide it, you could select that option, and your Microsoft Word document window and menu bar would disappear from view.

You might also notice that, once hidden, the icon for Microsoft Word (or whatever application you ultimately choose to hide) will be *grayed out* a bit in the Application menu. This indicates that it's currently hidden but that you can still select it again to unhide it and bring it to the foreground.

The other option, Hide All, allows you to hide every application *but* the one that's currently got focus and is in the foreground. This includes the Finder (which can have focus even when the Desktop is obscured). In fact, this is best used with the Finder. If you can't see what you want to see on the Desktop, make sure the **Finder** has been selected in the Application menu, and then choose **Hide All** from that same menu. Now all applications but the Finder will disappear.

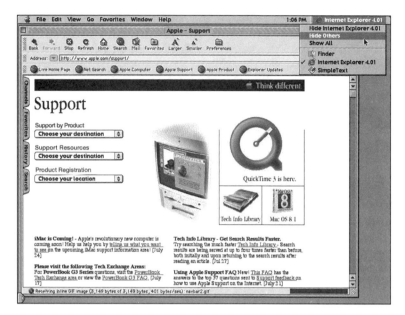

*The multitalented Application menu allows you to switch applications, hide applications, and shows you all your applications that are currently running.*

# The Apple Menu

Do you have a junk drawer in your house where you keep batteries, rubber bands, flashlights, birth certificates, and money in various international currencies? Me, too. It's in my kitchen, just in case you're hanging around at my place and suddenly need some fingernail clippers.

The Apple menu is sort of your Mac's equivalent of a junk drawer. The crazy Mac engineers have put quite a bit of stuff in the Apple menu, including some fairly important things like the Control Panels, Automated Tasks, and the Chooser. If your Mac is connected to a local area network, you'll probably find the Network Browser pretty useful, too.

The items in this menu work like regular menu commands, except for one difference: Most of the time, you use the Apple menu to launch applications. This is a little different from regular menus, where you're usually invoking commands like Print or Copy. In the Apple menu, you're actually starting up programs like the Calculator.

## Why the Apple Menu Is Cool

The Apple menu is handy because it's always there, no matter what application you're working in. So if you suddenly need to launch a calculator, the Chooser, the Find File command, or even enter a Web site address, you can do all of that without switching to another application or the Finder.

The Apple menu is also very customizable. You can put an application's alias on the menu, for instance, so you could launch Microsoft Word, Netscape Navigator, or even

**69**

a favorite game from the Apple menu—no problem. You can even add hierarchical menus, discussed in the next section.

So exactly *how cool* is the Apple menu? It's so cool that many old Mac hands don't use much else in the Finder. Their Apple menu is tricked out so that when they go to work with applications and documents, 9 times out of 10 they can use just the Apple menu. The only time you really need the Finder interface is for organizing and managing files. When it comes to actually doing something with your Mac, the Apple menu is the bomb. It's phat. It's bad.

## The Hierarchy of Menus

Actually, there's another thing that's a little unique about the Apple menu: its *hierarchical* menus. What does that mean? In the Apple menu, there are sub-menus that branch off to the right sort of like a family tree. To open one of these sub-menus, pull down the Apple menu by clicking the **Apple** icon once with your mouse. Then drag the mouse down the menu until it's pointed at one of the menu options with a **little arrow** next to it. A sub-menu pops up, showing you more choices.

*The Apple menu squeezes a bunch of stuff under that fruity menu icon because it allows for hierarchical menus.*

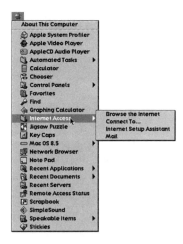

## Recent Stuff

The more interesting uses of those hierarchical menus are the Recent menus (Recent Servers, Recent Applications, and Recent Documents) that reside on the Apple menu. These menus are designed to watch what you're doing with your Mac and sort of take notes. The Mac OS remembers what applications, documents, and network servers you've recently visited and puts them on these menus.

The result? You can pull down the Apple menu, access one of the Recent sub-menus, and instantly launch an application or document you were recently working with. An example might be a chapter of this book: It takes me a few days to write each chapter, and when I'm doing it, I'm not doing too much else. To start again with an in-progress chapter document, I just head to the Recent Documents menu. The document will be hanging out right there (if it was one of the last 10 or so documents I worked with), so I can select it in the sub-menu to launch it. Ten seconds later, I'm writing again.

# Apple Menu Miscellany

The Apple menu includes some interesting built-in features and accessories to some included Apple applications. You'll find conveniences on the Apple menu, like the **Internet Access** menu. Open that menu and choose the **Connect To...** command and up pops a dialog box that asks you to enter an Internet address (an URL). Once you've entered an address and clicked Connect, the address is handed off to your Mac's default Web browser, and you're connected to the Internet site.

The Apple Menu gives you direct access to a few other interesting tools, including some small applications (sometimes called *desk accessories*) that add to the usefulness of your Mac. In fact, many of them even add to the Mac's Desktop metaphor, by representing things—like a calculator, notepad, or stickies—that you might have on a real desktop.

Here's a quick look at a few of them:

➤ *Apple System Profiler.* This handy little tool tells you a lot about your Mac, including the system software it's running, the peripherals installed, and other specifications. It's most useful when you're calling technical support lines or otherwise configuring and troubleshooting your Mac. This one will be discussed in Part Six, "Keep Mac Happy."

➤ *Apple CD Audio Player.* This little program allows you to play audio CDs that you've placed in your CD-ROM drive. The

**Add Your Own Menus**

One of the coolest things about hierarchical menus is that, because the Apple menu is completely customizable, you can actually add your own hierarchical menus. For instance, one of my favorite customizations is to make an alias of my main hard drive's icon, and then add that alias to the Apple menu. (I'll talk specifically about doing this in Chapter 10, "Let's Get This Mac Organized.") Because of hierarchical menus, it's then possible for me to get at *any file* on the hard drive through the Apple menu. I rarely switch to the Finder

**Duke of URL**

URL stands for *Uniform Resource Locator* and is often pronounced, "Earl." It's simply the standard way that Internet sites are given names, like **http://www.apple.com/**. The HTTP, name names, periods, and slashes all work together as part of the URL standard scheme. You'll learn more about how the URL works in Chapter 19, "Working the Web."

controls mimic those of a home stereo system. See Chapter 24, "Get Mac to Talk and Sing."

➤ *Apple Video Player.* If your Mac has TV-signal video capabilities built in, the Apple Video Player can be used to view that input onscreen. See Chapter 23, "QuickTime and Multimedia."

➤ *Calculator.* Select this option in the Apple menu, and a basic, functional calculator pops up onscreen. If you have a numeric keypad on your Mac's keyboard, those keys are tied directly into the calculator, so you can use them as you would a 10-key calculator (with some slight differences).

➤ *Chooser.* Select the Chooser to change your printer and network settings, among other things. The Chooser is discussed in various chapters in Part Three, "Print and Network."

➤ *Find File.* This is just a short-cut for running the Find File application discussed in Chapter 4, "Actually, Uh, Finding Things."

➤ *Graphing Calculator, Jigsaw Puzzle.* Have a little fun, do a little math, and perhaps build mouse skills with these applications. (Actually, the Graphing Calculator is a rather advanced graphing tool that also shows off the power of the PowerPC processor. If you're a mathematician type, you should check it out.)

➤ *Key Caps.* This program can be used to show you what keystrokes create special characters in certain font families. See Chapter 16, "All About Fonts."

➤ *NotePad, Scrapbook,* and *Stickies.* These applications are useful for dealing with text and multimedia "clips" that you want to hold on to, swap between applications, or just keep in a handy place. (Stickies are especially fun, working a lot like the physical sticky notes you probably have attached to your monitor right now.) We'll look at these in more depth in Chapter 25, "Other Mac Applications and Technologies."

➤ *SimpleSound.* This small program allows you to record sounds and change the alert sound. See Chapter 13, "Messing with Your Monitor and Other Peripherals," for more on alert sounds.

# Installing Applications

Before we take our leave of this chapter, it's important to touch on the art of installing new applications. Studies show that Mac owners are more likely to buy new applications and experiment with shareware than their counterparts using other operating systems like Windows. I don't know who did the studies, but let's at least feel comfortable saying the Mac owners are at least as likely to customize their Macs with new applications.

What's an installation? Before you can use an application, you have to install it. Generally you do this by popping the application's CD-ROM into your CD-ROM drive, locating the "Installer" application, and starting it up. (With some programs, like Microsoft Office 98, you can simply drag a folder from the CD-ROM to your hard drive's icon.) From there, you follow the onscreen directions. Your primary goal is to tell the installer anything it needs to know about your Mac (that it uses a PowerPC processor, for instance) as well as choosing the folder in which you want the application installer.

Fortunately, the process is rather painless. There are some very standard ways in which applications are installed; nearly all applications use a standard "installer" application that walks you through the process. (There are actually about three typical installers, and two of those are very commonly used. The only real exceptions to this rule are Microsoft installers, which are almost always weird.) Let's take a look at a typical installation.

## Installer VISE Installers

This is the installer you'll probably come across most often, even if by a slim majority. This installer is very full-featured, giving you some impressive flexibility when it comes to customizing the installation process.

### Desk Accessory Defined

In the old days of Mac System 6, there was no multitasking. The exceptions to this rule were the Desk Accessories—programs like the Calculator that could be selected in the Apple menu and popped up on top of your application. (They were also installed in very particular ways in the System Folder to get this trick to work.) Today, most desk accessories have been turned into actual applications. The only "true" remaining desk accessories are the Calculator and the Chooser. And the only difference is you can't change the amount of memory allocated to those two desk accessories; otherwise, they work like any other application on the Apple menu.

1. With these installers, you'll find the installer application (for example, AppleWorks Installer) and double-click it to launch it. Usually a splash window will appear to tell you which application will be installed. This is followed, most of the time, by a licensing agreement notice, which requires you to click the **Agree** button before moving on.

2. Then you're greeted by the main screen. On this screen, you can choose a number of options. In the top-left corner, you can choose an **Easy** or **Custom** install. If you choose Custom, you'll be given a checklist of options you can **check** or **uncheck** for installation. If you choose Easy, the installer will install the parts of the applications that it thinks are appropriate. (Some applications aren't complicated enough to include a Custom install option.)

3. Next, you'll have the option of choosing the disk you want the application installed onto; this one is in the lower-left corner. You can click **the Switch Disk** button to switch among the available disks, or pull down the menu to choose a new disk or the **Choose Folder** option. This brings up a dialog box that allows you to choose the exact folder where the application's new folder will be stored.

4. With that choice made, you click the **Install** button. Don't worry if the installer wants to automatically quit your background applications; you'll still be given the chance to save any data in those applications if necessary.

Choose the type of installation, Easy or Custom. You can also, in some installers, choose to Uninstall the application from this menu.

This is the message area, where the installer will tell you if you have enough disk space, among other things.

*The VISE installer is a pretty popular one. When you install an application, there's a good chance it'll look just like this.*

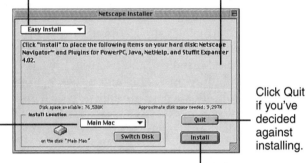

Click Quit if you've decided against installing.

Decide where you're going to put the application's folder. Clicking the Switch Disk button will rotate among the available disks. Choosing the menu will show you both the disks and an option for choosing a folder on the selected disk.

Click Install when you have all the options set up to your liking.

After the installation is complete, you'll either be given the option of restarting your Mac or quitting the installer. (If there's no restart option, you probably don't have to restart your Mac for the application to work.) Choose whichever seems correct, and you're done with the installation.

## Uninstall Easily

Notice that many of these installers also have an Uninstall option, as noted in the figure. This is a great boon if you decide you no longer need the application on your Mac. I have only one pretty serious uninstall rule: Don't forget to check to make sure you don't have any documents that require the application you plan to uninstall. If you do, try translating them to a document format that can be read by one of your other applications, and then uninstall.

## *Aladdin Installer*

The other popular installer is a little less complicated, but about as powerful. You're more likely to see it with shareware applications. This installer usually has a similar splash screen and license agreement screen that you need to click to get past, but then the interface is slightly different. In the bottom-left corner, there's an option for a **Custom** installation: Choose that button, and the window changes to reflect your options. When you have the options you want selected (or if you just want the easy install), click the **Install** button.

If you're doing a Custom installation, you'll make your choices here.

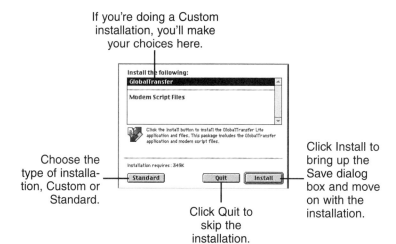

The Aladdin Installer is also a popular choice. It's similar but uses the standard Save dialog box for determining the folder into which you'll installer the application.

Choose the type of installation, Custom or Standard.

Click Quit to skip the installation.

Click Install to bring up the Save dialog box and move on with the installation.

Now you'll see a standard Save dialog box. Choose the drive and folder into which you want the application to install its own folder, and then click the **Install** button. The application will be installed, followed by a dialog box giving you options for leaving the installer. Sometimes you'll restart, but with most of these applications, you should be able to quit installing and return to the Finder.

# The Least You Need to Know

Up until this chapter, you've focused on finding things on your Mac; now you're doing things. This chapter focuses on using applications and documents to get your work done. You'll open applications, quit them, open documents, close documents—the fun never ends.

The Mac OS is capable of something interesting: It can run more than one application at once. Using the Application menu in the upper-right corner of the Mac's interface, you can switch between running applications or switching back to the Finder to start a new application. If you need to, you can also hide applications from this menu, and you can tear the menu off and place it elsewhere on the screen.

The Apple menu (upper-left corner) is a similar boon, only this one allows you to quickly and simply launch applications without switching to the Finder. The Apple menu is highly customizable and includes a number of applications, or desk accessories, for fun and productivity.

Finally, after you've used some applications, you might enjoy it so much that you want to install others. Fortunately, there are some standard installation programs that you'll encounter, so installing—and even uninstalling—should be fun.

# Chapter 6

# STUFF. Saving Stuff
STUFF

## In This Chapter

➤ The difference between storage and memory

➤ Open and Save dialog boxes

➤ File formats explained

➤ Back up your Mac

A messy desk is the sign of a, uh, *something* mind, right? Forgetful mind? I don't remember. The point is, if you're like me, you've got to appreciate the order that a Macintosh foists upon the chaos of your own existence. It's the only thing on my desk that forces me to file, organize, and, yes, save my documents. If only Rosie the Robot was around to help me with my physical papers.

Once you've gotten around to creating things on your Mac, you'll need to save them. For one thing, saving a file gives you a chance to give it a name, choose a folder for it, and keep it around for later use. Plus, if you don't save your files, they won't be there if you close the application or power down the Mac. That's the nature of the beast.

In this chapter, let's talk a little bit about how files are saved, and then how actually to save files. We'll finish up with perhaps the most important discussion in computing: backing up your files.

# What's to Remember?

You may have heard the term *memory* bandied about in discussions about Macs. All computers have a certain amount of random access memory (RAM) that is used for processing information and performing computations. (RAM is actually made up of small circuit boards that are installed inside your computer. They're usually in megabyte (MB) increments. Most Macs have between 8 and 128 or so megabytes of RAM, with some whiz-bang Macs for professional artists sporting a full gigabyte of RAM!) This is different from *storage*, which refers to the hard drives, floppy drives, and other media that are used to store data over the long term.

In fact, it's useful to think of RAM as short-term memory and storage as long-term memory. RAM is where *current* things are stored—things you're seeing on the screen at the very moment they're happening. If you're editing a document, that document is currently in RAM. If you've launched your e-mail application, that application is in RAM. Both applications and documents are placed into RAM so that they can be used by the Mac's processor chip.

## Short-Term versus Long-Term

If I see you tomorrow in the book store and we have a pleasant discussion, I'll likely remember your name throughout the conversation. I'll say, "You're quite right, Bob," and "I'd be more than happy to sign that, Bob," and "Could you lift your foot, Bob, you're crushing my toe." When I get out to the car, I'll immediately and completely forget your name. It's nothing personal, Bob, it's just that short-term memory is like that sometimes.

RAM is only short term. That means there's the potential for your computer to "forget" what's in RAM. For instance, electricity must be flowing to the RAM for it to maintain the data that's been placed in it; if you turn off your Mac, it'll forget everything that was in RAM. Similarly, if you close a document without saving (or if you close the application or it crashes), you can lose data that way, too.

Storage, on the other hand, can survive program crashes, Mac shut-downs, and other issues. In terms of human memory, storage is the equivalent of writing something down. The data is written to a storage device more permanently, as if it were long-term memory. Storage devices include internal hard drives (usually between 500 MB and 8 GB), removable drives like Zip and LS120 disks, and floppy disks. Storage is represented by the icons that appear on your Desktop; there aren't any icons for RAM.

## How Much RAM Do You Have?

Space must be available in RAM for you to run your applications. If you run more than one application at a time, this need for RAM can become a problem, depending on how much RAM you have in your Mac. Older Macs may have only 8 MB of RAM, which isn't even enough to run Mac OS 8.5, much less any applications. In fact, if your Mac has 16 MB of RAM or less, I wouldn't recommend running Mac OS 8.5.

If you have 32 MB or more, it's okay to run Mac OS 8.5. But then you're going to have to take notice of how many applications you're running—and how much RAM they require—if you're going to be running many applications at once. Fortunately, that's easy to do.

To see what applications are currently, running, how much RAM you have available, and how much RAM you have total, you can access the About This Computer window. Switch to the Finder (if you're not already in it) and choose **About This Computer** from the **Apple** menu. In the resulting window, you can learn quite a bit about what's currently going on in RAM.

## RAM Disks

Actually, there is one way to access RAM through an icon; it's called a *RAM disk*. This is simply a bit of RAM that's been set aside to allow you to save files to it as if it were a hard drive. Because RAM is much faster than a hard drive, a RAM disk is a clever way to save files more quickly. RAM disks are discussed in Chapter 11, "Change Settings for Better Performance."

The amount of RAM that's on chips installed in your Mac

Applications that are currently loaded into RAM

The amount of RAM available for launching new applications

The amount of RAM being taken up by applications

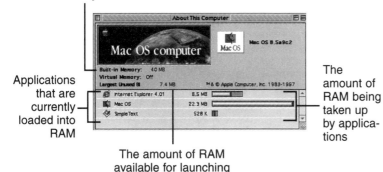

*The About This Computer window gives you a good deal of information you can use to work with RAM in your Mac.*

Looking at this, it becomes easier to judge if you have enough RAM to run the programs you want to run simultaneously. It can also explain things when you try to launch an application but are given an error message saying you don't have enough RAM available. In that case, you can try to recover some RAM by closing an application you're not using. Or you can adjust the amount of RAM required by your programs.

More than anything, though, the About This Computer window should give you some indication of whether or not you need to upgrade your Mac with more RAM. If you're constantly running out of available memory for your applications, you should

**Change RAM**

Chapter 11 discusses how to change the amount of RAM that's given to each application you run. Other RAM related enhancements are also discussed in that chapter.

probably upgrade. If you've always got plenty of RAM, you might consider a performance tweak like creating a RAM disk.

# How Much Storage Space Do You Have?

Although both memory and storage are measured in megabytes, it's important not to get them confused. Storage refers to your Mac's disk drives: the hard drive, floppy disks, and removable storage. Storage is *written to* whenever you choose the Save command in your applications or when you make a change in the Finder. In order to save, though, you need to have enough room available.

The easiest way to determine how much storage space you have available is to visit the Finder and take a look. When you open the main window (or any others, usually) of your hard drive or a removable drive, you can see how much space is remaining for storage.

The top of the window shows the number of items in the current window, along with the amount of space available on the entire drive for storage.

With the right options selected (in **Views, View Options**), you can see the calculated folder sizes in this column.

*Just double-click the icon of the drive in question, and you're presented with important storage-space information at the top of the window. You get more information when you choose **View, as List** in the Finder's menu bar.*

| | Name | Date Modified | Size | Kind |
|---|---|---|---|---|
| ▷ | App Launcher | Tue, Jul 21, 1998, 4:38 PM | | folder |
| ▷ | Apple Extras | Tue, Jul 21, 1998, 4:00 PM | 12.1 MB | folder |
| ▷ | Applications | Tue, Jul 21, 1998, 5:15 PM | 19.1 MB | folder |
| ▷ | Assistants | Tue, Jul 14, 1998, 12:27 PM | 438 K | folder |
| ▷ | Documents | Tue, Jul 21, 1998, 5:12 PM | 42.4 MB | folder |
| ▷ | Installer Logs | Tue, Jul 21, 1998, 5:11 PM | 131.8 MB | folder |
| ▷ | Internet | Tue, Jul 21, 1998, 4:38 PM | 15 MB | folder |
| ▷ | Mac OS Read Me Files | Tue, Jul 14, 1998, 12:31 PM | 716 K | folder |
| ▷ | System Folder | Tue, Jul 21, 1998, 4:33 PM | 116.8 MB | folder |
| ▷ | Utilities | Tue, Jul 14, 1998, 12:22 PM | 756 K | folder |
| ▷ | Web Pages | Tue, Jul 14, 1998, 12:28 PM | 324 K | folder |

11 items, 461.2 MB available — Mac OS 8.5

Notice that one of the things this number tells you is when it's important to start thinking about deleting things on the drive. If you're under, say, 100 MB on the drive, that's certainly time to start considering a way to dump your unneeded files. Of course, you'll want to back up and archive your files first, which is discussed later in this chapter.

You may also find that knowing how much space is available can explain error messages away. Sometimes you can encounter odd errors if you have too little space available on your hard drive. In that case, it's time for a bit of spring cleaning. Pop open your folders and find some things you can get rid of. (If they happen to be trade secrets or similar documents, perhaps you can hold a virtual garage sale.)

# Saving and Opening Things

In real life, I'm not much of a pack rat. Even as I get older, I've always tried to decorate whatever apartment I'm living in so that it reminds me of a nice but starkly modern hotel room. Maybe a suite with a kitchenette. It's important for me to be able to pick up and move at a moment's notice; the reasons why are shrouded in the past.

On my Mac I'm completely different. I have e-mail filed away in folders in my e-mail program that date from 1995. And it doesn't matter when you're reading this...I still have them. My Mac is where my sense of adventure and a need to always be correct collide violently.

**Slow Views**

Although having the **Calculate folder sizes** option enabled in the View Options window is certainly convenient, realize that it can also slow down your Mac quite a bit. That's actually why it's optional instead of required. If you notice a performance hit, you might want to leave the option turned off. You can still check an individual folder's size by selecting it with the mouse and choosing **File, Get Info** from the Finder's menu bar.

Don't call me and say you sent an e-mail about the Clinton re-election campaign if you didn't really do it. I can check up on you.

Saving documents on your Mac gives you this same opportunity, plus it allows you to work with documents again at a later date. Saving documents can also guard against crashes and other problems with your Mac; you bought a computer to be more efficient, so it's no fun when you have to do your work twice. Save vigorously and save often.

## The Save Dialog Box

Just because something is on your Mac's screen doesn't mean it's stored for later use. Things you create on the screen are in the Mac's memory, but that memory is good only as long as the computer is turned on. Turn off the computer (or lose power in your building), and that data will be erased from memory. So you have to tell your Mac to "write stuff down" by saving to the hard drive.

To save, you need to pull down the **File** menu. (Almost every single Mac application has a File menu, and almost as many have the Save command.) Then select **Save**. The Save dialog box appears, asking you what you'd like to name the file and where you want to put it. After you enter that information, click **Save** to store the document in that location, under its new name. If you're successful, your document window will change names, too, to reflect the name of the document.

If you're in a subfolder in
your hierarchy, you can
use this menu to move up
to a parent folder

Create a new folder
in which to save the
document

*Decide where you're going
to file your document, and
then save often.*

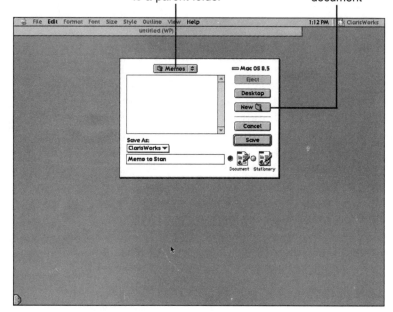

## Open/Save Metaphors

You know how we've been talking about the Mac's "desktop metaphor" and how
it's like using a real desk sometimes? That's often true in the Finder, except that
the Trash can is stored *on* the desk (most of us put our trash cans under the desk,
on the windowsill, or under one of those mini-basketball hoops). With the Open
and Close dialog boxes, things are a little more two-dimensional. It makes sense,
but you'll need to keep in mind the hierarchy of folders that you've created in
the Finder. If you're not happy with all these lists, though, here's a suggestion: just
save your file to the Desktop, and then switch to the Finder to store it using the
mouse to drag the file to your folders. Eventually, you'll see that the Open and
Save dialog boxes help you maneuver through the exact same folders as the Finder
does, just in a slightly less obvious way.

Notice that the figure shows you some of the different, powerful options that the Save dialog box offers you. You can use the dialog box to get anywhere in the hierarchy of folders that exists on your drives. In fact, you can even create a new folder if you want. When you do, you're automatically switched to that folder so you can save the document.

Now, if you make changes and again select **Save** from the **File** menu, the document automatically updates this file in the same location.

## Save As...

But what if you want to save this file with another name or to a different location? Because Save will now default to your original filename and folder (it won't ask you to enter those again), you'll need to use another command. Under the **File** menu, select the **Save As...** command. This lets you save another copy of the file, either by changing the name, the folder, or both. Remember that with the Save As command, you are saving a new copy of your document—not just changing the name or moving it to a new folder. Any changes you make in the new copy will no longer show up in the original.

## Closing Documents

You can see that saving documents and closing them goes hand in hand. If the document is at all important, you should save it before closing it and moving on to something else. In fact, most applications will prompt you to save a file that you try to close if it has any new changes or additions in it.

**New Wave Save**

In Mac OS 8.5, a new sort of Save dialog box, based on Apple's Navigation Services work, is beginning to appear (see preceding figure). In this sort of dialog box, you not only Save documents in traditional ways, you also get three new menus to work with in the top-right corner. In the Shortcuts menu (leftmost), you'll see links directly to the different drives on your Mac. In the Favorites, you can place your own shortcuts to particular folders. The Recent menu lets you instantly choose folders or drive locations you've recently been using.

To close most documents, you can either choose **File, Close** or click the **close box** on the document's window. If it hasn't been completely saved, you'll be prompted to save it. Make your choice in the dialog box. Once you do (and it's completed saving if that's what you've chosen to do), the document window will disappear from the screen. As mentioned in Chapter 5, "Getting Things Done," remember that the application is still open until you choose the **File, Quit** command.

## *Opening Documents*

You save documents so that you can close them and use them again later. To open and work with an existing document, you can do any of the things outlined in Chapter 5: You can drag a document to an application icon or double-click a document icon to open it and its associated application. (If the application is already open, the Mac OS will simply switch to it and load the document.) Or you can go one easier: Choose **File, Open** from the applications menu, and the Open dialog box appears.

This dialog box offers you some interesting choices. You can use it to navigate to the folder that holds your documents, and then find the document and pop it open. To open a document, click its name in the window and select the **Open** button, or simply double-click the name of the document.

If you're in a subfolder in your hierarchy, you can use this menu to move up to a parent folder

*The Open dialog box is very similar to the Save dialog box, only this one's mission is to help you find existing files, not create new ones.*

Choose which folder or file to open

Click over here to cycle through the different drives on your Mac

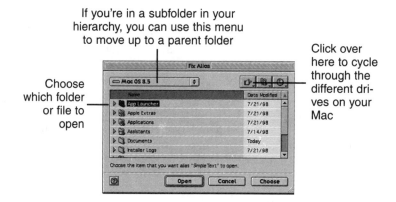

The result of a successful open command: The document pops up in your application, ready to be edited, augmented, or printed.

# File Formats: Exposed!

Every document on your hard drive has to have a particular file format. After all, different applications create different types of files, right? The Mac needs to know some basic things about a file if it is to work with that file, including things like the sort of file it is.

For instance, is the file a word processing document or a digital sound file? That's right: A particular document could easily be a bit of music that's been digitally recorded to the hard drive. Or it could be a spreadsheet document—a table of text and numbers used to calculate financial statements and other information in a program like Microsoft Excel.

The uniqueness of files means they need to have a particular format. At the most detailed level, this format includes the exact application and version of that application that created the file. For instance, a lot of this book was written and saved in documents that were Microsoft Word 98 format files, meaning they could be edited correctly only by Word 98 for Macintosh or Word 97 for Windows. The images, however, were saved in PCX, which is a particular type of graphics file format that can be created and used by many different PC and Macintosh applications.

## Working with Foreign Formats

So what does this mean for you? Basically it means you need to have some idea of what file format a document uses before you can load it into an application and edit it. Sometimes the icon will help you—for instance, an icon can make it easy to tell if a document is a ClarisWorks document. You could then drag and drop the document on the ClarisWorks icon or choose **File, Open** from the ClarisWorks menu to open the file, as described in Chapter 5. That should work most of the time.

Sometimes, though, knowing what sort of document it is also helps you determine if you'll need to *translate* it or not, a process also sometimes called *importing*. You need to import/translate the file from its original format into a format that your application can read. For instance, when you go to open a file that was created in another application (for example, if you want to open a Word file, but you only have Corel WordPerfect on your Mac), then you'll need to translate it as you open it.

## Launching Odd Documents

The Mac will often tell you when it believes you don't have the correct application for loading a particular document. All you have to do is double-click the document's icon. If the Mac can't figure out which application created that document, it presents you with a dialog box telling you as much. (This is discussed in more depth in Chapter 5.)

## Further Translation

If the double-click method isn't working well for you, your next best bet is to start up an application that you believe can translate the document. Try dragging a Word document onto the WordPerfect icon, for instance. This might work. Sometimes, though, the program is capable of translating a particular format, but it can't figure out on its own what format the document is in. So it needs a bit of help.

That's what you're there for: helping your computer. If you're willing, choose **File, Open** from the application that you believe is equipped to handle the foreign file. Now, in the Open dialog box, look for an **Open As...** menu or a similar translation menu. In this menu, select the file format you believe the document is in. Make sure you've selected the document in the file listing, and then open it as usual. (Click the **Open** button.) If you've chosen wisely, the file should begin to be translated by the application, and then be opened in an editing window.

*Use the Open dialog box to translate a file from its original format into a format that's acceptable to your application.*

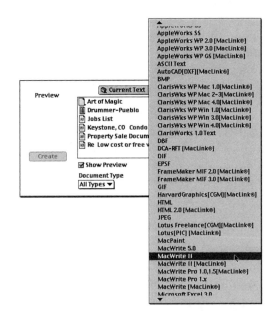

## Exporting Documents

I've already mentioned that the Open and Save dialog boxes are similar beasts; just as the Open dialog allows you to import certain file formats, the Save dialog box in many programs allows you to *export* a document into another file format. This is best done if you know you'll be sending the document to someone else, and they don't have the same application program you have.

Check in the Save dialog box for a menu that allows you to **Save File As...** or something similar. This should result in a menu that allows you to choose from a number of formats.

A few suggestions: If you want to be the most compatible with your fellow computer users, choose older file formats (like Word 2.0 instead of Word 6.0). Choose a file format that's designed for their computer platform; choose Word for Windows, for instance, if you're saving the file for a Windows-using friend. Also, if you're sending to Windows users, don't forget that Windows requires the little three letter ending, like ".doc" for Word files or ".txt" for plain text files. And, finally, use the least common denominator if you're not sure what your recipient uses: If it's a word processing document, nearly any computer can read Rich Text Format (RTF), for instance, which also maintains a lot of the document's formatting. In a pinch, all computers can deal with Plain Text or Text Only documents.

## Back Up Your Mac!

The only thing I can think of that's more important than backing up your Mac is not taking a fork and sticking it in the power supply fan. Aside from doing physical damage to your Mac or yourself, not backing up is the biggest mistake anyone can make. In fact, the loss of data could be *worse* than doing damage to your Mac; if you work with your Mac for a living, you could lose thousands of dollars worth of important files that can't be replaced as easily as the Mac can.

Unfortunately, there's nothing really built into the Mac OS that helps you back up things. Of course, there are great programs available to help you back up—check your store shelves for programs from Retrospect and Aladdin Systems, for starters. If you want to take a barebones approach, though, my recommendation is pretty simple. Create a Documents folder on the main level of your Mac's hard drive. Now you'll focus on backing up your documents. In most cases, this is good enough, because you should be able to reinstall the Mac OS and your applications easily (you likely have them on CD-ROM for easy installation). Documents you create, though, should be well safeguarded.

Next, you need some sort of storage media that allows you to back up all your documents. You probably will have quite a few files—at least tens of megabytes once you've been computing for a while. My recommendation is to get an Iomega Zip drive, an LS120 floppy drive, or something even bigger, like a SyQuest SyJet removable drive. That way you simply drag

**Determining Origin**

One of the most inexact sciences when dealing with your Mac is trying to figure out an unknown document's particular file format. The icon can give you some clue, but it still leaves you guessing, particularly about the version number of the application that created it. If the file was originally a Mac document, you can try selecting it in the Finder and choosing **File, Get Info** from the menu; that may tell you more about the document and the application that created it. If the file was originally a DOS/Windows document, turn to Chapter 22, "Deal with DOS and Windows," for more information. But if you're still at a loss, there's one more piece of advice: Ask the person that sent you the file. It's not as high-tech, but it can be most effective.

your Documents folder to the disk's icon on the Desktop and sit back while it copies all your files for safety. Then store the disk somewhere away from your Mac, maybe even off-site so it's safe in case of catastrophe.

You should also consider using a new disk every week or few weeks so you have a copy of your files that stays exactly the same, even if it's a few months old. This gives you a permanent archive of the files that you can revert to in case a subsequent backup disk becomes corrupted, lost, broken, or infected with a virus.

Of course, backup can get very sophisticated, with serious applications and services devoted to helping small and large businesses back up their important data. If you're using your Mac professionally, you might consider one of these backup applications or services (for Internet-based backup, for instance).

### Serious Backup

If you're into the idea of automating your Mac yourself, I have two suggestions. First, you can use the Find application described in Chapter 4, "Actually, Uh, Finding Things," to help you search in your Documents folder for files whose "date modified is after..." a particular date, allowing you to simply drag those changed files to your backup media. Even better, you can automate this using AppleScript and Folder Events, as described in Chapter 12, "Make It Automatic: AppleScript and Automated Tasks." Backup is discussed a bit more in Chapter 28, too.

# The Least You Need to Know

An important distinction to understand when you deal with your Mac is the difference between memory and storage. Memory is the short-term memory of your Mac, where currently used documents and applications reside; anything on your screen is in memory. Storage is longer-term memory: It's where files and documents are "written down" so the Mac doesn't forget them. Even after a particular application has been quit or the Mac has been turned off, a document placed in storage (or "saved") can be restored (or "opened") and edited again.

This saving and opening is done with the Save and Open dialog boxes, which offer quite a bit of power for managing documents on your hard drive. Notice that these dialog boxes give you access to the same folders and files you'll find in the Finder, just using a slightly different interface. This interface is designed to help you create files from within the application (in the Save dialog box), and then find those files again later (in the Open dialog box).

Another feature of these dialog boxes is the capability to import, or *translate*, foreign file formats. (A foreign file is one that wasn't created by the application.) From the Open dialog box, you may be able to choose that foreign file format and translate the document so that it can be opened in the current application. From the Save dialog box, you can often export a document into a format that can be read by other applications.

Lastly, a quick note on how important backup is when you're using your Mac. To make it simple, you can create a Documents folder you can use for keeping your documents organized in one special place. If you've done that, it's easy to back up that folder by dragging it to a removable media disk's icon, like a Zip disk or LS120 disk. Then you can store that disk safely away from the computer so you have access to your data even if disaster strikes.

# Chapter 7

# Mac OS
# Walkthrough

---

### In This Chapter

➤ Quick start: open an application

➤ Create a document

➤ Edit and invoke commands

➤ Save the document

➤ Print the document

---

Let's do a couple of different things at once here. First, I'd like to walk quickly through the process of opening an application, creating a document, and editing that document. At the same time, I'd like to introduce you to SimpleText, the Mac OS's included text editor.

SimpleText is an interesting program. While it's not quite a full-fledged word processing program, it's capable of many things, including some basic commands you'll see in this chapter. It's also capable of quite a bit more: Apple tends to use SimpleText as a test bed for some of its technologies. So SimpleText can support cut-and-paste graphics images, it can play QuickTime movies, and it can read text aloud using speech technologies. Throughout this book, you'll see SimpleText in action. Here, then, is where you can get a start with SimpleText.

By the way, aside from viewing in detail a few commands like Copy and Paste, there isn't much I'm going to cover in this chapter that we haven't already touched on. The point here is to recap many of the basics that you need to know to get started working with applications and the Mac OS. If you already feel comfortable launching and editing documents, you might want to just skim this chapter or skip it entirely.

# What Is SimpleText?

Aside from being such a showcase of Apple technologies, SimpleText is a great program to have hanging around. It's designed to work with Plain Text documents—the type you might get as e-mail messages, over the Internet or from computer users using different OSes like Windows or UNIX. Plain Text (or ASCII text) is the least common denominator among Internet-connected computers, so it's used for a lot of things. You can edit Web documents in SimpleText, for instance, or you can read email–based newsletters.

Documents that are often distributed in SimpleText format are the Read Me files that come with the Mac OS and many applications that you install. These files provide instructions and information regarding your new applications, including known problems, caveats to work around, and instructions for proper installation.

SimpleText will prove useful for you beyond these capabilities, too. For a plain text editor, it's pretty sophisticated, allowing you to change the way your document looks, with different fonts, sizes, and styles. You can also copy and paste parts of your document into other parts—procedures we'll discuss in this chapter.

You may notice that SimpleText is like a word processing program (like Nisus Writer or Microsoft Word) but less sophisticated. Where word processors are designed to create printed documents of considerable length and complexity, text editors are designed for dealing with onscreen computer text in smaller quantities. Not that SimpleText can't print—it can; but it's not designed to create reports, papers, and book chapters as you would in a word processor.

Of course, even word processors vary in their capabilities. Different word processors have different talents that set them apart from the others. But, just like cars, word processors all have a core set of functions in common. Nearly all cars "go," "stop," and "turn." All word processors allow you to enter text, arrange it on the page, and print it out.

## Where Is SimpleText?

If you're getting ready to launch SimpleText and begin working with a text document, you shouldn't have too much trouble locating the program. Head to the Finder and try looking in the root level (the main folder) or your main Macintosh HD. Double-click the **hard drive icon** in the top-right corner of the Desktop. You'll likely find SimpleText in the window that opens.

If not, check the **Apple Extras** folder (from the main folder of your hard drive) for a subfolder called **SimpleText**. The program may be hiding in there. (It could also be in the Applications folder, depending upon your particular installation of the Mac OS.)

If you don't have any luck there, either, try using the **Find** command in the Finder to locate a copy of SimpleText. If you've used your Mac for any length of time at all, you'll likely learn that you have quite a few copies of SimpleText lying around.

## How Do You Start It?

After you've found SimpleText, you can start it by pointing to it with the mouse pointer and double-clicking the mouse button. (If you already have a text document created, you can double-click that text document, or you can drag the text document over the SimpleText icon and drop the document onto SimpleText. This will launch the program and open the document at the same time.)

# Creating the Document

When you first launch SimpleText, it actually opens an Untitled Document for you to begin typing in immediately. So the document is already created. But if you want to create another, here's the procedure:

With the application open onscreen, you're ready to create a new document. In SimpleText, as in most applications, you create a new document by heading up to the **File** menu and choosing the **New** command. (Click once on the word **File** in the menu bar, and then click again on the word **New** in the menu that appears.)

A new document window appears, ready for you to begin creating your document.

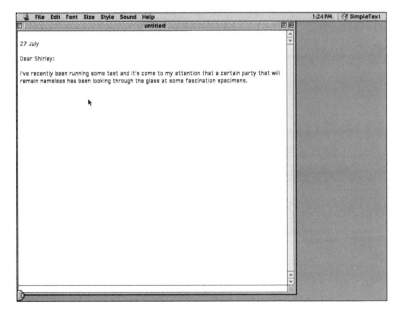

*Once you've invoked the New command, you're presented with a blank document. Just start typing.*

### What's a Font?

Technically, a font is a collection of letters and characters with the same typeface and size, such as Courier 12. Font families are sets of fonts in several sizes and weights. Some people get mad if you say typefaces and fonts are the same thing, but the term *font* is often used to refer to typefaces or font families.

### Who is Clarus?

It's Clarus, the world-famous dog-cow! That animal (whatever it is) is there to help you determine what orientation your paper will be in when it prints. The standard setting is portrait, which means the paper is normal; that is, longer than it is wide. Landscape means you're using the paper sideways: wider than it is long.

*You can easily change the style of text after it's been created as long as you highlight the text first.*

## Getting Text on the Page

The first and most important thing a text editor can help you do is get text on the page. Not just tossed out there, but in the right order, in an interesting font, and with all the *t*'s crossed and *i*'s dotted.

The place to start is the **Page Setup** command, found in the **File** menu, which is where you can choose the right size and orientation of paper you're using for what you plan to create.

In any text editor or word processor, you start out with a blank page, pick the first font you want to use, and start typing. You might want to **boldface** some things, *italicize* other things, or even underline a really good point or two. Remember keyboard shortcuts for changing text? That's ⌘+**B** for bold, ⌘+**I** for italics, and ⌘+**U** for underline. You can also choose these style commands from the **Style** menu on the menu bar. Then type, and the word is suddenly in the new style. If you want to turn the style off, just invoke the command again.

You'll also notice that you've got a little helper: the cursor, or *insertion point*. It's the line that goes along in front of whatever you're typing. Its sole job is to tell you where a letter will appear if you press a key.

If you'd like to change a word after it's been typed, drag to select the entire word with the mouse. Start by pointing the mouse at the beginning of the word, and then hold down the mouse button and drag the pointer to the end of the word. When you release the mouse button, that word should be highlighted. (In most Mac applications, you can also double-click a word to select the whole thing.) Then choose the Style command you want to use or use the keyboard shortcut to change the selected text.

## Advanced Typing

Remember that high school typing class you never really paid attention in?

There's an important rule while you're typing in most any word-related Mac application (a text editor, a word processor, or even a desktop publishing program). For the most part, the typing is just like a typewriter, with one small difference: When you get to the end of a line, don't press Return to get to the next line. SimpleText (and most other Macintosh text and word processing programs) automatically *wraps* the text from one line to the next. This makes it easier to reformat text later.

You do, however, still need to press the **Return** key whenever you want a new line or new paragraph. Notice in the figures that I've pressed Return whenever I wanted to represent a carriage return, like right after typing the "To" and "From" lines.

Another important rule: There's no reason to put two spaces after a period. That can actually confuse some word processors, resulting in bizarre spacing. One space should be enough to make it clear that a new sentence is starting.

If you make a mistake and mistype something, there are two ways to fix it. You can press the **Delete** key on your keyboard (usually two rows above the Return key) to back up and delete everything you've typed. Or you can use the **cursor keys** (the little arrows toward the bottom-right of your keyboard) to place your cursor next to the word you've mistyped, and then use the **Delete** key to back up over just the mistake. It's up to you.

You use this same concept for entering letters you've omitted. Just move the cursor to where you want to insert the letters and then type. (You can also place the cursor by pointing with the mouse to a spot in your document, and then clicking once.) You won't type over any other letters; your editor will automatically make space for your new letters.

## Cut, Copy, and Paste

So far, using the Mac to type a memo isn't much better than using a typewriter. But the Cut, Copy, and Paste functions are what make word processing really shine. What we can do, if we like, is pick up entire blocks of text and put them somewhere else in the document. Some people find this offers amazing freedom over writing things by hand or using a typewriter. It allows you to toss all your ideas down on the page and then arrange them in whatever way makes the most sense.

To move text in my document, I simply place the mouse pointer at the beginning of the text I want to move and hold down the mouse button. Next, I drag to the end of the selection and release the mouse button. That highlights the text. Then I pull down the **Edit** menu and choose **Cut**. The text will disappear.

*Cut, Copy, and Paste are ways to apply Mac's power to editing your documents.*

Notice that when you put the mouse pointer over text, the mouse pointer changes to a cursor that looks like the capital letter *I*. This is to let you know that it's acting as a text selection tool, which enables you to highlight text in a document.

The next step is to move the mouse pointer to the place you want to paste your text. Click once, and the cursor appears in the document. Head up to the **Edit** menu and select the **Paste** command. The cut text drops back into the document, just as if you'd typed it again.

The Copy command works the same as Cut, except that it leaves the text in the document and allows you to add a copy of that text somewhere else. Basically, it duplicates the selected text and allows you to paste as many copies of that text into the document as you desire.

### Drag-and-Paste

In many applications, you can simply drag text to a new destination instead of cutting and pasting. Try it: Highlight some text with the mouse, and then point to the highlighted text, hold down the mouse button, and drag the text to a new spot in the document. It won't work in all programs, but it works in a lot of them.

## Saving Your Creation

Have you typed even just a few lines? You should save the document. In fact, if you aren't already in the habit of using that Save command every few sentences (or every paragraph) or so, try to get into that habit right now. There's nothing more frustrating than losing your work because you encounter an error. And you will hit an error at some point. The more you save, the less actual work you'll lose when an error comes along.

My best advice is to get used to using ⌘+**S** to save your documents quickly and often, even if you don't use many other keyboard commands. That's one of the easier keystroke combinations to learn, and it's easy to toss it in while you're typing. I promise, one day, you'll get used to doing this.

Anyway, with all that said, saving is simple: Choose **File, Save** from the menu bar or use the ⌘+**S** keyboard sequence. After you've maneuvered to the desired folder and entered a name for your document in the Save dialog box, click the **Save** button to write the document to that location under its new name. If you're successful, your SimpleText window will change names, too.

*Decide where you're going to file your document, and then save often.*

## Save As...

As mentioned in Chapter 6, "Saving Stuff," you can use the **File, Save As...** command if you want to save this file with another name or to a different location. The reason you use Save As... is simple: Invoking the regular Save command, after the first time, no longer brings up the Save dialog box. Using Save As... will bring up that dialog box.

# Print When Ready

Done entering text for your document? If you've said everything you need to say and fixed it all with fonts and style the way you want it, then it's time to go ahead and print the document. This is pretty easy, too, assuming you have a printer connected to your Mac and selected for printing. (If you don't, see Chapter 15, "Getting Your Stuff Printed," for more on printing.)

To print the document, choose **File, Print** or ⌘**+P** on the keyboard. That brings up the Print dialog box. From there, you can choose the **number of copies** you want to print, **how many pages** of the document to print, and so forth. Some of the options may also be specific to your printer; check your printer's manual if you see something interesting in this dialog box.

When you've got everything set the way you like it, click the **Print** button. That will send the document to the printer, eventually returning control of the Mac to you. (If it doesn't return control quickly, and you instead watch the action in a dialog box as each page is slowly printed, then you may not be printing "in the background." Check Chapter 15 for more on this setting in the Chooser.)

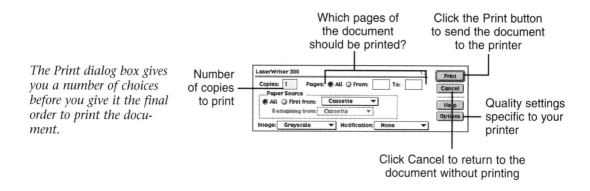

Which pages of
the document
should be printed?

Click the Print button
to send the document
to the printer

*The Print dialog box gives
you a number of choices
before you give it the final
order to print the docu-
ment.*

Number
of copies
to print

Quality settings
specific to your
printer

Click Cancel to return to the
document without printing

# Close and Quit

With the document is finished and printed, you're ready to close the document and
quit SimpleText. Actually, you can do both at the same time by simply selecting the
**File, Quit** command. But, for the sake of thoroughness, try quitting the document
first.

Choose **File, Quit** or click the document window's **close box** to close the document. If it hasn't been completely saved (perhaps you've changed something since
last changing the document), you'll be asked if you want to save changes to the document. Click **Save** to save the document, **Don't Save** if you don't want to save the
document, and **Cancel** if you want to return to the document without closing it.

*If you try to close a docu-
ment that hasn't been
completely saved, you'll
get a dialog box prompt-
ing you to save any
changes.*

With the document closed, you're ready to quit SimpleText completely. Choose **File,
Quit** or ⌘+Q. The application should close, and you'll end up in the Finder or another application if you have one open.

# Congrats!

Now, if you like, head to the Finder and locate the document you created just to make
sure it's where you expected it to be. You might try double-clicking it, too, just to
prove that that will open SimpleText and let you edit again.

Let me point out that, while this all focused on SimpleText, you've learned the most
basic commands that appear in nearly all Mac productivity applications. Open, Close,
Save, Page Setup, Print, Copy, Paste, Cut, and even text styles should work pretty

much the same in any application designed to allow you to edit text or edit a document of any sort. You're well on your way to using the majority of applications designed for the Macintosh.

# The Least You Need to Know

This chapter is a quick run-through designed to show you how to open an application, create a document, and save that document. It covers SimpleText, a text editor, so other commands, like fonts, styles, and text sizes, as well as Cut, Copy, and Paste, are also covered. After creating the document, you can print the document using the Print command in the application. Then close the document and quit the application. You end up back in the Finder, ready to give yourself a pat on the back.

# Chapter 8

# Get Help from Your Mac

---

## In This Chapter

➤ The Unbelievable Number of Different Types of Mac Help

➤ Using Apple Help

➤ Using an Assistant

➤ Using Apple Guide and Balloon Help

➤ Application-Specific Help

---

Mac people are supposed to be the sort of people who don't like to read manuals too much. Maybe you'll just read this one and no others, huh? Not a bad plan—after all, I could use the money. But it's also a good idea when you consider that the Mac OS, itself, can be pretty good at helping you along when you get stuck.

In every Mac application, including the Finder, you'll come across a Help menu. In this menu, you'll find the various ways that the application developer has made help available to you.

Usually, this help comes in the form of a searchable index of possible topics, along with clickable links that take you to definitions, walkthroughs, and step-by-step instructions. If you've got a question about how a feature works or why something doesn't seem to be acting the way it should, the first place to consult is the help command. The second place to consult? A second copy of this book. (I actually recommend purchasing one copy for each room in your house, if only for the sake of convenience.)

# The Unbelievable Number of Different Ways to Get Help from a Mac

Of course, the Mac is supposed to be easy to use. And many times, it manages to be just so. Usually that's because things get implemented efficiently, elegantly, and in an appealing way. Most of all, the best Mac OS interface touches come along because the engineers and designers who create those elements don't think *too much* about them.

That's exactly the problem with the Mac OS's help system. While every single change to Mac OS help has been an impressive innovation, the big issue is the fact that there have been way too many changes. From the clever balloon help system to the clever Apple Guide system to the clever HTML help system, Apple is loaded down with too many different *clever* ways to get help.

It's sort of like if your city's police department kept coming up with new and better services: They can automatically tell where you're calling from, they can locate you by satellite triangulation, they instantly send armed paratroopers at the first sign of trouble, but they also change the emergency phone number every three weeks from 911 to 10-911 to 10-10-911 to 10-10-911-2000.

Let's take a quick look at the different types of help and which problems they're most likely to solve. Then we'll move on to a more specific approach to each help system.

## How Many Types of Help Are There?

Uh...at least five. That's my quick count of how many different ways you can get help. Oh—six, if you count Read Me text files and that sort of thing. Actually, eight if you include the special DocMaker documents, tutorials, and sample files that a lot of software applications include as electronic manuals. Nine if you factor in printed texts and manuals. Ten if you've bought (one or more copies of) this book.

Actually, onscreen, from the Mac OS, there are about four different ways you'll encounter help, with the fifth being reserved as a catch-all "application help" category that covers any help for a particular application that doesn't use a Mac OS provided system. (Application help is something like the Microsoft Word help system, which doesn't use an Apple technology. The Apple technologies include things like Apple Help, Apple Guide, and Balloon Help.)

Just as the Mac OS provides standard methods for popping up an Open or Save dialog box, it also offers standard methods for offering help. An application doesn't have to follow those methods, though, if the programmers feel like creating their own help system. (Just as they can change the Open dialog box if they want to. Just ask Microsoft.)

## *The Different Types Revealed!*

So what are the different types of help? Here's the quick and skinny:

➤ *Apple Help.* Also called *HTML Help.* In Mac OS 8.5, for the first time, the main recommended help system is based on HTML (Hypertext Markup Language), which happens to be the language on which the World Wide Web is based. Essentially, Mac OS 8.5 help documents—as well as those written in new and upgraded Mac OS applications—use Web-style pages and links to offer you help.

➤ *Assistants.* Mac OS 8.5 includes more assistants than ever before. Assistants are small applications that walk you through the setup or configuration of certain parts of the Mac OS or other applications. The Mac OS Setup and Internet Setup assistants are examples of these.

➤ *Apple Guide.* Although no longer recommended by Apple for use in new applications, Apple Guide help was all the rage in the mid-1990s versions of the Mac OS. You'll still find it in many applications. It's actually sort of a hybrid of an assistant and HTML help, allowing you to be *actively* helped with certain problems. While it was telling you about a problem, it could also show you the solution onscreen. (The new HTML Help system is capable of some of this as well.) The drawback is that Apple Guide is time consuming for application authors to implement, and many of them didn't make the effort.

➤ *Balloon Help.* Once the only major help system available for the Mac OS, Apple doesn't really tout it much anymore. But you'll still find it popping up in Mac-centric and Mac-only applications. When you point the mouse at an item—a window or a menu item—Balloon Help tells you what it does by using a comic book-like talking balloon. (A lot of shareware vendors like to use it, and Microsoft Internet Explorer 4.0 includes a special version of Balloon Help.)

➤ *Application Help.* This is the catch-all category that includes all the sorts of help that different applications create for use within those applications. While Apple certainly recommends that software developers use the Apple recommended help systems, some of those developers have their own ideas and implement something slightly different.

Let's take a look at each type of help in turn.

# Oh the Help We Weave

I want to start by talking about the most recently conceived type of help first, because this is the type of help you'll encounter in the Finder and elsewhere in the Mac OS. It's called *Apple Help*, and it's based on the same technology that pages on the World Wide Web use to display text and move from one topic to another. This type of help system is new to Mac OS 8.5.

Basically, this help works by simply popping up articles written on a particular topic, like "Using menus." You'll also get definitions, diagrams, and the ability to search for different pages. The real differences, though, are the *hyperlinks*.

While the word "hyperlinks" sounds alittle like a fast-paced game of golf, it really refers to the clickable nature of an Apple Help page. Text that is underlined and blue is a hyperlink; it's linked to another page. When you click once on the hyperlink, the new page appears.

*The Apple Help systems is simply pages that include explanations, images, and links to new topics.*

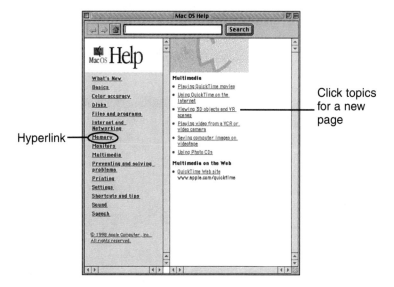

But before you can get too deep into how this help system helps you, you'll need to know how to start it up.

## Calling for Help

Most of the time, you'll access Apple Help like you will any other kind of help— through the Help menu in that application. (Just head up to the menu bar and choose **Help** to see where it leads.) In fact, it may not be up to you if you get Apple Help or not; it depends on if the applications developer has implemented Apple Help. In some cases, you might get a different type of help.

In the Finder and in other Apple applications, though, it'll be Apple Help. To start it from the Finder's menu bar, just choose **Help**, **Mac OS Help**. (You can also choose ⌘**+?**.)

Another way to get help is to click the ? icon you'll see hanging out in different places around the Mac OS. Usually, the ? shows up on control panels and small applications written by Apple, although you'll find them in programs written by other folks, too. Just click the icon, and up pops the Help viewer.

Want another cool way to get help? You can get help on a particular problem (a window, a folder, a document icon) by pointing the mouse at it and holding down the Ctrl key while clicking the mouse button. This brings up a pop-up menu. It's first option is Help. Choose Help and see where it leads you.

Help icon

*The ? icon shows up in different places around the Mac OS.*

## Getting Around with Help

The Apple Help system is a contextual help system; basically, it can sort of decipher what you're trying to do and will attempt to offer help articles that fit that problem. For instance, if you have the PPP control panel open when you click the help icon, the help will be focused on PPP issues.

Other times, you'll simply be given an index listing of various topics. To find an article that addresses your problem, click a related topic once in the Help Viewer. Now you can read that article or click on other topics that come closer to what you're trying to learn.

Although they call this hyperlink game "surfing" for information, you're really digging or tunneling through these links to find the information you need. It's like using the Table of Contents in an encyclopedia: You find the letter of the alphabet, and then the topic, and then the subheading. It's the same with Apple Help and hypertext links.

If you realize you've dug too deeply, you can click the left-facing arrow to move back up to the previous article. To move forward again, you can click the right-facing arrow. If the arrow is "grayed-out" (it shows less detail, and nothing happens when you click it), then there are no more pages to go forward to. Instead, you'll need to click a hyperlink on the page itself.

Go to the
Help Center

*The HTML Help controls.*

Go
back

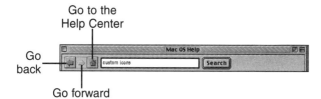

Go forward

See the little house icon? In World Wide Web parlance, that would mean "Go to the home page." In this context, it takes you to the Help Center, the home base for all Apple Help on your Mac. It's here that you'll find links to all the different types of Apple Help that have been installed on your Mac. If you think you have a question that isn't being answered by the current index of helpful articles, you can head to the home base. It's here that the help files for all of your applications reside. Click a link to open a particular application's help file.

### Unequal Links

You may notice that not all hyper-links are created equally. Throughout Apple Help, you'll find links that say "Open...for me." These links can actually jump out into the Mac OS and open an application or control panel for you. And there are others that perform tasks like running special AppleScripts automatically. It's great fun for all us "desk-chair" potatoes who don't want to mouse all the way to the Apple menu ourselves.

## Searching Apple Help

They say that the search is its own reward. Well, that couldn't be more wrong when you're on deadline, the cat is sitting on your research papers, you can't find your glasses, and the silly printer won't print! Then you want to get *immediately* to the help file.

Up at the top of the Help Viewer, you can enter words that tell the Help Viewer how you'd like to search for help. Once you've entered the words, click the search button. The results show up in the Help Viewer window, along with a relevance ranking. Based on how many times the words you enter show up, the Help Viewer tells you which help documents seem likely to answer your questions, and it puts those first.

You can ask us a full English question in the Help Viewer—such as, "How do I connect to a network server?"—or you can just enter keywords like "connect, network, server" in the Search text box. The results may vary some, but the approach is up to you. (I like full sentences, but then again, I would.)

*Searching for help may be the best way to get straight to the point in the Help Viewer.*

Search phrase            Click the button

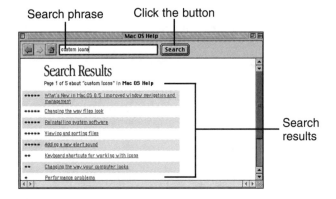

Search results

## Using an Assistant

Another popular way to get help in the Mac OS is to use an assistant. Assistants are small programs that walk you through the steps necessary to do something. Usually that "something" is configuring your Mac or an application to perform some new task, like getting on the Internet.

In fact, a couple of these assistants can pop up right when you first install Mac OS 8.5; they're the Mac OS Setup Assistant and the Internet Setup Assistant. Basically what they do is walk you through the steps of choosing some important settings, without forcing you to dig around in the System Folder to find the right files.

Enter configuration
information

*The Assistant's interface is fairly simple.*

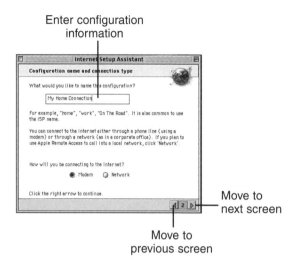

Move to
next screen

Move to
previous screen

There's really not much to learn about the assistants. You click the right-facing arrow to move to the next screen if you've finished configuring everything on the current scr en. (If you haven't, the next screen will tell you to go back and finish.) Otherwise, just follow the onscreen instructions. After you're done, you can simply use the close box to get rid of the assistant.

# Apple Guide and Balloon Help

These wicked stepchildren of the Mac OS help world used to be the shining glory and achievements of Apple engineers. And, in fact, they're cooler and more interesting than Apple Help and assistants. So what happened? Well, they're so cool that I imagine they're a bit tough for programmers to work with. And they can be a little slow, too, where Apple Help and assistants tend to pop right up on the screen.

### Can't Find Assistance?

Usually an assistant pops up "automagically" when you need it. But if you want to reconfigure something, you'll need to find that assistant again. Check the **Apple** menu, where they tend to hide. If it's not there, try the Assistants folder on your main hard drive. If you're looking for application assistants, look in the **Help** menu and the **File, Open** menu or dialog box for assistants; ClarisWorks and AppleWorks, for instance, let you access assistants through the Open dialog box.

You'll still encounter both types; in fact, if programmers want to, they can include them in their new programs. (An example is Microsoft Internet Explorer, which includes an implementation of Balloon Help.) You'll likely encounter them in some form or fashion, so it's best to be ready.

## *Follow Your Apple Guide*

Apple Guide is similar to Apple Help, at least in name. (Apple may be a creative company, but their naming schemes tend to follow certain patterns.) Still, the overall point of both help systems is to offer comprehensive, searchable help.

Apple Guide takes this further with a much more hands-on, tutorial approach. Hence the name "Guide." Apple Guide, in fact, has the technology to lead you through an entire process, opening windows, invoking commands, and even drawing on the screen to illustrate a point.

*Apple Guide is a combination assistant and Help Viewer, walking you through the help session. Notice the part of the screen that's been circled by the Apple Guide.*

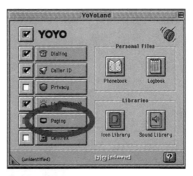

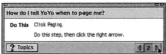

Apple Guides are accessed through the **Help** menu (usually called *something*-"Help" or *something*-"Guide") or by clicking the ? icon in some windows. Most Mac OS help has been transitioned to Apple Help, but you'll find Guides in other applications.

## *Balloon Help*

Balloon Help is really a different kind of help, essentially designed to help you figure out what different parts of a screen, window, or similar interface are designed for. That also makes Balloon Help good, for instance, for information about toolbar buttons and parts of a window.

When you point the mouse pointer at something for a few seconds (and Balloon Help has been turned on), a small cartoon-like thought balloon appears onscreen, telling you what that option, icon, or element does.

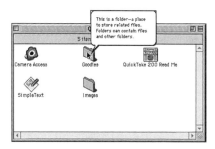

*After you leave the mouse still for a short while, Balloon Help tells you about whatever is under the mouse pointer.*

You turn on Balloon Help in the Help menu of the Finder or of applications. Choose **Help**, **Show Balloons** to turn it on. In fact, you can turn it on in one application, and then off in another—once it's on, it's on system-wide.

Then you'll likely also *immediately* turn off Balloon Help in the same way (**Help, Hide Balloons**). It can be a bit annoying.

The only exception to turning it on or off seems to be Microsoft Internet Explorer, which uses Balloon Help to tell you about different parts of the interface after you leave the mouse pointing at a part for more than a second or so.

# Application Help

Our last type of help is application-specific help. Most applications implement some sort of Apple-sponsored help: Apple Help, Apple Guild, or Balloon Help. They're certainly encouraged to. But other application programs just feel it's important to build their own help system from scratch, so they do.

In most cases, these help systems are still accessed via the Help menu in that particular application. (The Help key on 104-key Extended Keyboards will usually launch the help, too.) And, again in most cases, these help systems are usually some sort of derivative of the whole hypertext concept; you see a possible answer to your question, so you click the highlighted text to see the help article, and so on. Obviously, some of them have variations on a theme.

By the way, not all applications put their help commands on the Help menu. If you can't seem to find any help, check the Apple menu. The program may add a special help command under the About This Program entry. If not, choose **About This Program** and see if the About window offers any help.

What else might you encounter? While you've seen all the different options that appear under the Help menu, you might be able to find answers to other questions about applications in their folders on the hard drive. What follow are some common help documents and documents types:

➤ *Read Me files*. These files are basic, regular text files that can easily be read by a program like SimpleText. (Usually, you just double-click one of these files to use it.) Read Me files are supposed to tell you about known problems with the

**107**

application and new features, and they might tell you how to use it in some small detail.

➤ *DocMaker files.* These are a special sort of document created using DocMaker by Green Mountain Software. These special files offer tables of contents and other features that make them great as onscreen manuals. You just double-click to view these files.

➤ *Tutorials and Samples.* These can range from text documents to HTML-style help or even QuickTime movies that walk you through parts of an application or procedure. You may also find that applications include sample files or documents that you can use for learning purposes.

➤ *HTML documents.* These will work just like Apple Guide files but will require you to load them yourself in Internet Explorer or Netscape Navigator using the **File**, **Open File** command.

➤ *PDFs.* This stands for *Portable Document Format*, although most of the time, these are Abode Acrobat files. They're like text files, only they offer more complete and attractive formatting. They're a popular choice for onscreen manuals. You'll need the Adobe Acrobat Reader to view them.

*Microsoft is at it again. Their help in Office 98 is inspired by hypertext but adds the element of a cute little helper.*

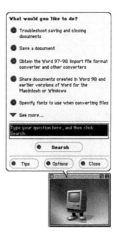

## The Least You Need to Know

The Mac OS offers tons of different ways to get help, although some of them are less popular than others. Currently, Mac OS 8.5 offers the Apple Help system as its help method of choice. Apple Help can be started from the Help menu in many applications (and the Finder) and uses a hypertext-based system to make getting help very much like digging around on the World Wide Web.

Assistants play a role in helping you configure things on your Macintosh—things like your Internet connection and your basic Macintosh setup. Other assistants can be found in applications, usually under the Help menu or via the File menu.

The older types of help include Apple Guide and Balloon Help, both of which you'll still encounter from time to time. Apple Guide is sort of a cross between Apple Help and assistants, allowing you to search for help, and then walking you through configuration issues. Balloon help is unlike any other; it's basically designed to tell you what different elements on the screen do, using comic strip-like balloons to tell you.

Finally, applications can have their own types of help, too. You'll probably find it under the Help menu, still, but other than that you'll just have to experiment.

# Part 2
# Tweak Your Mac

*Mac OS 8.5 offers the latest iteration of a computer operating system that's been lauded for years as easy to use, exciting, and attractive. The new additions in Mac OS 8.5 are no exception, allowing you unprecedented control and customization features to make using the Mac OS more enjoyable. (I think I've been reading a few too many Apple press releases.)*

*Many of these customizations, of course, are silly. You can change the background, the font, the color scheme, and the soundtrack for your Mac. But others are both enjoyable and useful—performance tweaks, automation, and settings for your peripherals. Most importantly, though, you can use a combination of all these tweaks to stop cluttering up your desktop and get your documents organized into folders and hierarchies.*

# Chapter 9

# Banish the Boring Mac!

---

### In This Chapter

➤ The Appearance Control Panel Explained

➤ Themes, Appearance, Desktop, and Sounds

➤ Set the Time; Change the Date

➤ Other Basic Settings

---

When you first install Mac OS 8.5, you're presented with the default, corporatized, logo-ified Mac look and feel that has been decreed from high atop a hill in Cupertino, California, home of Apple Computer. Frankly, it's a tad dull. Fortunately, you don't have to leave your Mac that way. There's a lot of stuff you can do to make your Mac a more comfortable, more personalized place to work.

Changing your Mac's appearance is more than just changing the way it looks. You can also change the appearance for practical reasons. Choose colors that aren't too garish to work with. Change fonts to make them easier to read. Make windows, menus, and folders work the way you want them to.

And there are some other settings you should know about, just to be thorough.

## Puttin' on a Little Mac Makeup

One of the most popular shareware downloads over the past few years (software that's distributed over the Internet on a try-before-you-buy basis) was a program called

Kaleidoscope. This program was designed to work with versions of the Mac OS before 8.5, giving them some of the characteristic options we now take for granted.

People downloaded this program by the truckloads! Hundreds of thousands of people visited the popular download sites to grab Kaleidoscope, especially when a new version came out. Why all the excitement? I guess people just love to change the way their Macs look.

Well, these days the flexibility is unprecedented. Once upon a time, you could change how gray a Mac's background was. That was about it. Today, you can make Mac look like something that isn't quite from this world.

*Hard to believe, but this is a Mac.*

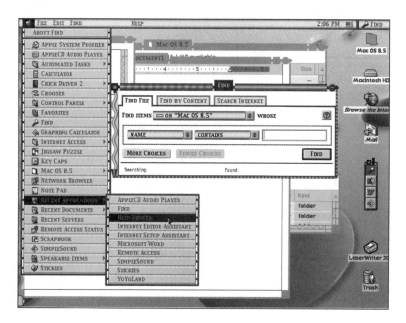

And even though changing your Mac's look is overwhelming but fun, that fun can have a purpose. In my experience, the more personal your Macintosh is, the more it's going to please you to work with it. That might help you be more productive because you'll be comfortable with your Mac—comfortable enough, in fact, to spend some quality time getting to know it better.

## Introducing the Appearance Control Panel

So how do you make these amazing sorts of changes? You'll make them through a single control panel, called the Appearance control panel. It's in this one command center that you'll find all the redecorating controls, from controls for the background picture or pattern (the unique settings for your Mac's Desktop) to settings for system-wide sounds. Somewhere in the middle there, you can even make universal changes to how windows, menus, and icons are going to look.

In fact, the Appearance control panel is another one of those things done right in Mac OS 8.5. If you've used previous Mac OS versions, you'll be glad to know that almost all appearance-related settings have been moved to this control panel, instead of being scattered through many different control panels and preference settings.

If you've never used a Mac OS version before, this is all new to you. (Sigh.) If only I could relive the experience of first sitting down with the Mac OS to change the colors around and mess with the sounds. I envy you.

Alter the overall appearance scheme

Change the Desktop's pattern or picture

Choose some miscellaneous settings

*The Appearance control panel features a tabbed interface so you can get at the myriad options available for changing a Mac's appearance.*

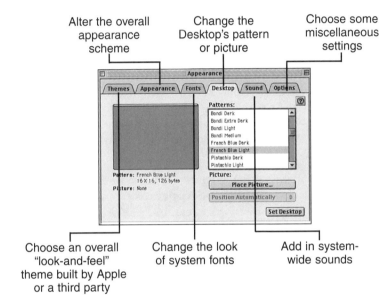

Choose an overall "look-and-feel" theme built by Apple or a third party

Change the look of system fonts

Add in system-wide sounds

The Appearance control panel uses a tabbed interface in its window to allow you to get to all the various settings. We'll touch on them all before we leave this chapter.

To open the Appearance control panel, pull down the **Apple** menu, choose **Control Panels**, and then choose **Appearance**. The control panel will then appear on your screen.

## Choose Your Theme

The Appearance control panel does one major thing, and a bunch of minor ones. Basically, the Appearance control panel allows you to choose a *theme* for how your Mac is going to look. A bunch of these themes are built in, and they're hiding right there under the Themes tab in the Appearance control panel.

What the themes do is set the overall tone of your Mac's interface. They'll change the background, the fonts, the way folders look—even sounds. Best of all, preset themes are usually designed by professional theme-decider types to look and sound pretty good. It's like your Mac has its own interior decorator.

But, once you've set the theme, the rest of the control panel is there, so you can customize it. If you don't like the background, change that. Don't like the sounds? Change those, too. Then, if you want to, you can even save the theme.

To choose a theme, click the **Themes tab** (if necessary), and then use the scroll bar under the themes to see the others. When you find one you like, just click it once to select it. After your Mac thinks for a moment, your Mac's appearance should change to reflect the new theme.

The rest of those tabs are hiding exciting ways you can customize that theme to make it more personal.

## Play with the Appearance

The Appearance setting is probably the coolest part of the whole control panel, because this is where you'll decide what the look and feel of windows and menus will be. This is brand new in Mac OS 8.5—the capability to make such wholesale changes in the way the entire Mac OS looks. And all you have to do is pull down a menu command.

### Put in an Appearance

Want to install a third-party appearance package? This should be a popular pastime for Mac owners: coming up with new and amazing ways to make your Mac look weird. If your software doesn't install the appearance itself, it should be easy enough to do it yourself. Just drag themes files onto the System Folder icon. The Mac will automatically file them away in a subfolder called the Appearance folder, in another folder called Themes folder. If you don't have the Gizmo and Tech appearance options, you'll need to install them, too. Just drag them off the Mac OS installation CD and onto the System Folder.

To change the appearance, choose one of the available options from the **Appearance** menu on the **Appearance** tab. You can use one of the Apple-provided appearances, or, if you've installed others, they'll show up here as well. Then choose the **Highlight color** (for when you select text with the mouse) and the **Variation color** (for when you select a menu item or something similar).

## A Font of Charm

The next changeable bits are the system fonts. Click the **Fonts** tab in the Appearance control panel, and you can choose what fonts will be used for the menus, window title bars, and secondary system text. It may not seem like it, but this can give a major change to the look and feel of your Mac.

To change a font, simple select the new font from the pull-down menus. You can choose a **Large System font** (for windows headings and such), a **Small System Font** for explanatory text (in a dialog box, for instance), and a **Views Font**, which is used in the Finder to show filenames and icon labels.

You'll also notice an option for smoothing fonts onscreen. This is quite a boon. In fact, I think this may be one of the biggest appearance issues yet on a Mac. If you've never seen a screen of smoothed-out fonts, you're in for a treat. Just wait until you see how much better Web sites look!

What smoothing does is it *anti-aliases* any fonts (over the chosen size) so that they appear smooth onscreen. This technology allows characters to look a little less jagged on the screen than they normally would. If you like this idea, turn on smoothing by putting a check mark next to the option: 12 points is about the right size to begin smoothing. Anything smaller is tough to read when smoothed.

### So What's a Font?

A *font* is a collection of letters and characters with the same typeface and size. For instance, Courier is the font that makes things look like they've been typed on a manual typewriter. Times is a popular published book-like font.

## Dabble with the Desktop

There are two basic things you can change about the desktop: the pattern and the desktop picture. If you choose a picture, it will overlay the pattern, making your choice of a pattern less important than, say, balancing your checkbook or getting the oil changed. If you don't use a desktop picture, your pattern is visible, making the choice suddenly as important as, say, changing the cat litter regularly.

The pattern takes up less memory, won't slow your machine down much (a picture can), and will often fit the theme you've chosen. A picture is *cool*, though, which makes all the difference. In the Appearance dialog box, click the **Desktop** tab to make your choice.

Choosing a pattern is simple: Just scroll through the list of patterns until you find a name that intrigues you, and then click the pattern once to see what it looks like. If you like it, click the **Set Desktop** button.

### Designers Beware

There's one place where smoothing can be a problem: when you're designing something, especially a Web site. Remember that older Macs and Intel-compatible PCs don't currently feature smoothing technologies, so screen fonts will often look better on your Mac than they will on other computers. If you're designing electronic pages for consumption by other types of computers, you might want to turn smoothing off, at least while you're

For a desktop picture, click the **Place Picture...** button. This brings up a special Open dialog box that includes a preview window (it also opens you to the Desktop Pictures folder). Find the picture you like; if you select it in the file listing, a preview appears on the right side of the dialog box. Once you're happy, click the **Open** button.

**117**

### Build Your Own

If you're creating your own Desktop Picture in an image editing, note, it should be the same size as your screen's resolution if you want it to fill the screen. You'll get best results if the image conforms to one of the following sets of dimensions (in pixels): 640×480, 800×600, 832×768, 1024×768, and so on, depending on how you have the resolution set in your Monitors and Sound control panel.

Back in the Desktop settings, the picture shows up as the preview. If you'd like to change how the picture will be positioned on the desktop, you can use the positioning menu. Pull it down and make a choice: It can be positioned automatically, centered on the screen, tiled (a bunch of the same images will be used if it's a reasonably small image), scaled to fit, or forced to fit.

Obviously, this is where you can get an image and a pattern to show up together. If you've got a photo of your favorite folks (or your dog), you can center it or scale it to fit the screen. Any desktop that doesn't get filled by the image shows the pattern.

Once you've made your choices, click **Set Desktop**. The Desktop changes to reflect your desires, determination, and state of mind. (Or, at least, all that could fit into that tiny dialog box.)

*If you'd like, you can place an image in the center of your desktop, surrounding it with the pattern of your choice.*

## Mom! Mac's Making Funny Noises!

Sounds aren't just for panicking anymore. It used to be the Mac made funny little sounds only when it had a problem or concern it needed to discuss with you through an alert box. These days, not only will Mac alert you to problems, but he'll just whistle, prattle, toil, and sing constantly if you let him.

To make the sounds stop (or start), click the **Sound** tab in the Appearance control panel. There you'll see four different check boxes; click the box to check it or uncheck it, turning the feature on or off, respectively.

At the top of the panel, there's also a pull-down menu that allows you to choose the sound track you want to use; certain sounds have been created and assigned to work with certain Appearances (like Apple Platinum and Gizmo). Of course, you don't have to live your life according to Cupertino's strictures. If you want to associate a different sound track with your custom theme, just select it from the menu. It's really that simple.

### More Pictures

Want your desktop picture to change every time you restart your Mac? Just drag a folder full of pictures onto the preview window in the Desktop panel. That's right—drag-and-drop works—for individual picture files or a whole folder. The pictures need to be copied onto the startup disk first, though, and they should be in PICT, JPEG, or

## Gene Splicing for Windows

The Options tab gives you a few more choices for the road. These apply to windows, allowing you to set preferences for the scroll bars or to see how collapsing a window will work.

You can place a check mark next to **Smart Scrolling**, which changes the scroll bars so the scrolling arrows are clustered together and so the scroll box (the floating box on the scroll bar) is proportional to the amount of content in the window.

Your other option? You can choose whether or not double-clicking a window's title bar works the same way the collapse box does. Finally, an answer to your wildest dreams.

### Adding Sounds

Want to add your own sound sets? Well, I don't know how to make them, but if you find a reputable source, installing them is cake. Just open the System Folder, open the Appearance folder, and you'll see the Sounds Sets folder; that's where they're stored. Of course, you can simply drag a sound set onto the System Folder, and it'll be put in the right place. If only my dresser drawers worked that way.

*These options, new in Mac OS 8.5, make mousing around in large documents a bit easier to do.*

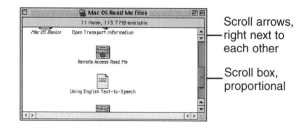

Scroll arrows, right next to each other

Scroll box, proportional

## Saving Your Monster

If you're like me, you've now thoroughly messed up the attractive theme that Apple's team of designers created, turning it into a frightening hodgepodge of color swatches and harsh lines. Not to mention the fact that you have a few nuts and bolts left over, and you swore you were following the directions.

If you actually like what you've done, though, you can give it a name and save it for posterity. (Who knows? Maybe Apple will have a contest one day.) To do that, switch back to the **Themes** tab and click the **Save Theme** button. This brings up a quickie dialog box, allowing you to enter a name for the theme. Click the **OK** button, and your theme joins the ranks of the others in the scrolling list. You've arrived as a digital artist: Adjust your beret and smile. You deserve it.

# Setting the Clock and Calendar

One day, we'll get past the "I can't even set my VCR" joke. Frankly, I can't wait. I don't want to just swap it for the "I can't set the clock on my DVD Player" joke, either. I want a whole new joke about the choking effect that technology has on society. That's my demand.

In the meantime, I will say that programming your Mac's clock and calendar should prove much easier than setting your VCR. (That's not a joke, just a point of fact.) First, the Mac has an assistant that pops up when you first install the Mac OS, so you should have already set these things. If you need to change them, though, they're just a control panel away.

From the **Apple** menu, choose **Control Panels**, and then **Date & Time**. This opens the Date & Time control panel (funny how that works), giving you a fighting chance at saving the planet and solving the world's ills.

## Time and Date

These are easy enough. At the top of the Date & Time control panel, you can click once on any part of the date or time (click the months or the minutes, for instance) to change them. Highlight portions to change them with the keyboard, or use the arrow keys next to the entry boxes to count up or down.

Each entry also has a button under it that allows you to pick the format for the date or time. If you have some special preference as to how dates are shown to you, make that change by clicking one of these buttons.

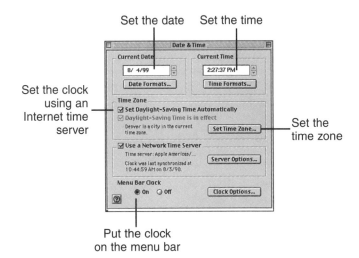

Set the date   Set the time

Set the clock
using an
Internet time
server

Set the
time zone

Put the clock
on the menu bar

*There are enough options in the Date & Time control panel that we can fairly say this is approaching overkill.*

## Getting in the Zone

It's important that your Mac know what time zone you're in so it can reason out its own approximate location on the earth and order pizza when you're away and unsuspecting. It also helps things like getting the dates right on incoming e-mail messages and knowing when to switch off the computer if you've told it to do that sort of thing.

Click the **Set Time Zone...** button if you have reason to suspect that the time zone setting is incorrect. This brings up a dialog box that helps you find the city that's closest to you. (Actually, it's not much help. You'll need to have some idea what larger cities are near your current location. Always good info, anyway, just in case you need to find an airport or a Starbucks regional headquarters building.)

Once you've located the city, select it and click **OK**. Now, back in the Date & Time control panel, choose whether or not you want the Mac to figure out if daylight saving time is in effect. (You can also set daylight saving time manually if you're in one of those locales that only celebrates daylight saving time on alternative Tuesdays. Just turn off **Set Daylight-Saving Time Automatically**, and then check **Daylight-Saving Time is in Effect** whenever you get the urge.)

## Net Time

Feel like logging into Central Command to check with the Total Chronographic Vortex to see what time it is in Universal Clicks? Well, it's easy enough to do. If you've got an Internet connection, you can log into an Internet Time Server that tells you the exact atomic time down to the sub-molecular level. You will never miss another arena football game.

Check the box next to **Use a Network Time Server**, and then click the **Server Options** button to choose how things will be updated. From the pull-down menu, choose the time server that's closest to you. Then, if you don't mind Mac checking whenever it feels like it, choose **Automatically**. (This could be a problem if you have a modem-based Internet account instead of constant Internet access.) Otherwise, you can choose to check every so many hours or to check only manually. To do a quick manual check yourself, click the **Set Time Now** button. You'll see the clock change after a moment.

## Watching the Clock

Lastly, let's get that clock up on the menu bar. If you want to see the time, no matter what you're doing, select **On** in the **Menu Bar Clock** section of the Date & Time control panel. If you don't think the standard clock is up to snuff, you can change things by clicking the **Clock Options** button. Here you've got plenty of choices, including the opportunity to turn on an hourly, half-hourly, or quarter-hourly chime. Plus, using the typical font controls, you can change the clock's typeface to something a little more palatable.

**Other Sound Stuff**

So what's this other stuff? Sound Monitoring Source is where you pick the source of sounds that the Mac listens to when it's recording sounds. Sound Output Quality tells how well certain sounds should be played when sent out through the speakers. More on both those topics in Chapter 24, "Get Mac to Talk and Sing."

# A Little More on Sound

It seems like we've talked about enough sound to last a lifetime, at least until the next Mac OS update, by talking about the Appearance control panel. But there's actually somewhere else you'll need to worry about sound, too. Well, two places, but they're both in the same place. Sorta.

Got a volume problem? Head over to the **Control Panels** on the **Apple** menu and select **Monitors and Sound**. Choose the **Sound** button up top there. Now you're in sound control central. You control the volume; you control the balance. To change either of these, click and drag the little slide (just as you would an icon in the Finder). Release the mouse button when you've got a good volume.

If you need to change the alert sound (the sound Mac makes when it's not happy about something and shows you an alert dialog box), click the button in Monitors and Sound marked **Alerts**. To change the sound, click to select a new sound's name in the listing at left. Use the slider to change sound volume.

If you've got a microphone handy and attached, you can create your own alert sound. Just click the **Add** button, and some tape recorder-like controls appear. Click the **Record** button, make some noise, and then click the **Stop** button when you're done. Click **Play** to listen to it. If you like it, click **Save** and give it a name. Now you can select it in the Alerts box.

Unfortunately, you get points deducted if your self-produced masterpiece alert sound is just you saying, "Red Alert!," "I am not a crook!," or "You can't handle the truth!" If any of these cause increased crashing on your Mac, don't come crying to me. I warned you.

# The Least You Need to Know

This chapter is all about making things pretty and getting them to sound good. That's accomplished in a few different control panels, all of which are accessible from the Control Panels menu in the Apple menu.

First is the Appearance menu, which allows you to choose themes for the way your Mac is going to look—then offers you countless ways to mess up the theme and get it looking pretty bad. These options include the Appearance, Sound Track, Fonts, Desktop background, and Color choices.

You can set the date and time through another control panel—the Date & Time control panel. Here you'll set the time, the date...is this getting a bit redundant?

Finally, there are the sounds. Change volumes and pick alert sounds in the Monitors and Sound control panel. In fact, you can even create your own alert sounds if you've got the time on your hands.

You have another choice, too. You could skip all this window treatment and finish that novel you started.

TEN-HUT!!

# Chapter 10

# Let's Get This Mac Organized!

---

**In This Chapter**

➤ Create Your Filing System

➤ All About Folders and Subfolders

➤ Adding Labels and Colors

➤ A Closer Look at Aliases

➤ Getting Serious About the Apple Menu

---

So you've got all these great capabilities built into the Mac OS: You've got little folders, aliases, duplicate commands, Apple menus, and Ctrl+Click contextual menus. But how can you use all this stuff to your advantage?

One of the keys is to forget about these things as technologies and think of them more as office tools. Not that I mean you need to create an office analog for each tool. I certainly don't want you running around your office for days trying to find a Chooser in your office. What I'm getting at, though, is the idea that you just use all this stuff—folders, labels, icons—to create whatever sort of filing system and organization is most convenient for you.

# How Should I Organize My Folders?

I used to know every program and every document on my hard drive. Then, one day, I finally got work and had to start using my Mac for something other than games and surfing the Net. That day, the realization hit me that I actually had to start organizing things, or I'd never find them again. How did I do this? It's not tough; all the tools are built right into the Finder.

There are about as many organization schemes for Macs as there are Macs. How you organize things is up to you, for the most part. If you don't mind, I'll make some suggestions, but feel free to get up and have a bite to eat if this part bores you at all. It won't take too long for me to get through it.

## *Arrange by Major File Types*

I've found it's best to arrange my hard drive into main folders that separate the different sorts of files I save: Applications, Utilities, Documents, and so on. In fact, the Mac OS sort of starts you down that path to begin with, creating many of those first-level folders (Utilities, Internet, Applications) for you.

### How to Lock?

This locking thing got you intrigued? It's easy enough to do. Select the folder icon (or an application or document icon) and choose **File**, **Get Info**. In the Get Info window, look for the **Locked** option at the bottom-left. Click it to place a check mark and activate it. Now it's locked and can't be emptied from the Trash until it's unlocked (or if the **Option** key is held down while the Trash is emptied). You can lock the Applications and System Folder folder separately using the General Controls control panel (welcome to the Department of Redundancies). That's discussed in Chapter 14, "Stuff That's Buried in the System Folder."

Doing this also makes some housecleaning ("disk-cleaning") tasks easier. For instance, backing up your documents becomes very easy—just copy the Documents folder to a removable media drive. (After all, you can likely re-install your applications and the Mac OS in case of catastrophe.)

And you can do things like lock your Applications and System Folder folders, so that those folders can't accidentally be deleted.

Once I've created these major folders for organizing by file type, though, I always try to organize my subfolders by project. (For projects that require only a file or two, I'll save multiple projects in one folder by client name.) As a book writer, most of my files get put in folders like "Mac OS 8.5 Book" with subfolders for things like "Images," "Chapters," and "Copy Edits."

I see a lot of people who file their documents in subfolders according to type, like spreadsheets, Word documents, and graphics files. But I recommend against doing this. Why? Because it isn't the way most people work. You wouldn't file things by letter, chart, and picture in a physical file; you'd file them by the relevant project or subject. It makes the whole project difficult to retrieve if you've stored a graphical image in one place, a memo in another, and a page layout document in a third. How will you tell what files you created for that project?

Instead, I'd say organize by the different reasons you create documents (Articles, Books, Newsletters, Annual Report), and then by projects. If you create a lot of sales presentations, put all the letters, memos, figures, and graphics that went to make up those presentations in the same folder (or better yet, use aliases).

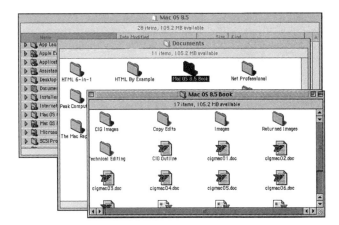

*Here's how I like to organize my hard drive.*

## Manage Your Projects with Aliases

I'll actually talk about this one more in depth a little later in the section in which I talk about aliases a lot, "Choosing Your Aliases Wisely."

Tons of alias stuff coming up after a short break. Be there.

Consider this: I was telling you about my project-by-project folders. But I've also got some document-centric folders I like to keep intact, like my Invoices folder. Because I don't want to store one invoice in the CIG Mac OS 8.5 folder and another in the MacinSplash Magazine folder, I'll keep them all in the Invoices folder.

But I can also very easily put an alias to a particular invoice in the project folder, just so I can see everything I've done for a project in one quick glance. (If I've sent an invoice to MacinSplash, I can store the invoice in the Invoices folder, and then create an alias in the MacinSplash folder, just for recordkeeping.) In this way, I can use the folder not just for storing documents, but also as a sort of To Do (or "have done") list that helps me track my progress. Make sense?

Okay, that's all I'm saying for now.

# How Do You Make Things Stand Out?

Are your files becoming lost in a sea of icons, names, and gray (or sort of bluish-gray) file folders? If you're having trouble finding what you want at any given time, you'll need to take matters into your own hands and set out a firm grip and a bold stroke. This, my friends, is the crossroads where organization meets art.

## Use Descriptive Filenames

You heard me. Already I feel giddy from the right-brained rush of creativity we've unleashed on such a left-brained pursuit as organization. Foldersand documents can have up to 31 characters in their names, *so why not use them?!*

Every name you give a folder or document can—and should—be meaningful. Not just for you, but for those who come after you. (If you haven't already looked into that whole life insurance thing, at least you can leave your family a well-labeled electronic version of your will. They'll know exactly what folder to find it in.) This one step will go a long way toward making your files easier to manage.

## Choose the Right View in the Finder

The View menu allows you to see things in basically four different ways. You can view things by regular icon, by small icon, and in a list. Oh...and you can view "as buttons" if you get your kicks that way. Some might say the room's lighting is the most important consideration when you choose a view in the Finder. But I disagree. The truth is that which view you use should depend almost completely on what it is you're looking at.

When should you use each? Here's my system. I use "as Icons" often, because I like to see the regular icons almost any time I can. They're prettier, they look better on the screen, and they're easier to recognize. So I use those for many of my application and utility folders.

I almost never use the "as Buttons" view, but they can be fun if you want to turn a folder into a one-click launcher—maybe even a tabbed folder at the bottom of the screen that's sort of a pop-up launcher.

The "as List" view is really convenient, especially when you want to get a ton of stuff on the screen at once. What's more, the List view also gives you access to other information about each file—things like file size, document type, date created, and so on. It's a very convenient way to look at files. And it's highly customizable.

## Arrange Your Files in Their Folders

I like being very regimented with my folder views, which, again betrays my split personality. (I clean out my refrigerator, on average, once every time I get ready to move. But my Mac's desktop is spotless.) Fortunately, there are options that make arranging and keeping your folders arranged a piece of cake. Even if it is moldy cake wrapped in tin foil.

In the Finder, open a folder you'd like to arrange and make sure the folder is selected. Now choose **View**, **Arrange**, and one of the options that follows (**By Name**, **By Date Modified**, and so on). You've got all sorts of opportunities to make things right again with the world.

Click headings to reorganize window

Drag the line between columns to change column size

Click direction box to change order

*Mac OS list views are great for folks with a flair for organizing things.*

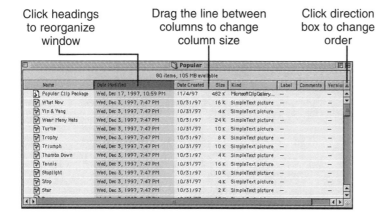

If you already have the window in a list view, you don't need to use the **View**, **Arrange** command. Once you've got a folder in list view, there are a few different things you ways you can use the mouse to do all your arranging for you:

➤ Click a column label, like **Name**, and you'll organize the folder by name. Click a different heading, like **Date Modified**, to organize the folder by that information.

➤ To change the direction in which the folder is arranged (from oldest to newest versus from newest to oldest, for instance), click the direction box—the staggered lines at the top-right corner of the window.

➤ You can also resize the columns themselves. Place the mouse pointer on one of the lines that divides columns. The cursor will change to two arrows. Hold down the **mouse button** and drag to change the size of a column.

➤ Hate it? Choose **View**, **Reset Column Positions** to put ëem back where they were when you started.

## Change Your View Options

You've seen how to arrange folders—but would you like them to *stay* that way all the time? Want folders to always place icons precisely in line when the icon is dropped? Want to change the size of icons? You can do all these things and more.

The answer to your needs is the **View Options** command. It's there that you'll find control for all sorts of window controls. With a folder window selected, choose **View**, **View Options** from the Finder's menu bar. Now you can make a few interesting changes.

129

*View Options actually vary depending on the type of "View As" you've set for the window. Shown are the "As Icons"*

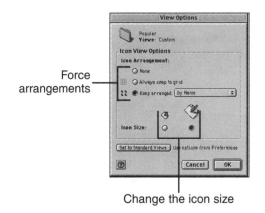

Force arrangements

Change the icon size

**List Options**

If you've got a window arranged by list, then View Options gives you a few other options. You can choose the columns that appear in the list window, as well as whether or not folder sizes are calculated and how dates are displayed.

Using the radio buttons, you can choose to force the icons to snap to a grid (align perfectly compared to one another) after you've moved them around. You can also force them to always snap into alphabetical order, for instance, or according to some other **Arrange by** criteria.

Notice that you can also choose to have a folder "Set to Standard Views." All you have to do is click that button in the View Options window, right? But what's standard?" Choose **Edit**, **Preferences** in the Finder, and then click the **View** tab. Now you get the same View Options window(s); use the pull-down menu to switch between the different view types. The difference is, this sets the standard; all windows will now conform to these settings unless you individually alter them.

## Go Nuts with Labels and Colors

Do you use colored file tabs on your physical file folders at work or in your home office? If you do, check out the Label menu in the Finder. Here's where you can decide how to define your colors for filing excellence.

To change the label for a folder, just select that folder in the Finder, pull down the **File** menu, choose **Label**, and then choose your color. That's it.

But those colors and labels can't possibly suit everyone. If you'd like to make them more descriptive and personal, that's easy, too. Just open the Finder Preferences (**Edit**, **Preferences**) and choose the **Labels** tab.

To change a color, click that color. The Color Picker opens. You can choose one of the different ways to pick colors (my favorite is the Crayons). Choose your color and click **OK** to have it selected and to close the Color Picker.

If you want to change a label description, click to place your insertion point next to one of the existing labels (such as "Essential") and edit it to create your new label name. It's that easy. Now, when you pull down the **File**, **Label** menu, you'll have your own custom color scheme!

# Choosing Your Aliases Wisely

Let's start by talking a little more in depth about aliases. I already mentioned how to create them in Chapter 3, "Finder Basics." Remember, an alias is just another way to access the same program or document; it's not a copy of the entire file, just a copy of the icon that you can put somewhere else.

One easy way to create an alias is to **Ctrl+Click** on the icon and choose the **Make Alias** command from the pop-up menu. (You can also use the keyboard command ⌘+**M**, or you can hold down the ⌘ and **option** keys while dragging and dropping files around in the Finder.) An alias appears. The alias can be renamed to anything you think is meaningful. You can move the alias to just about anywhere in your Mac's organization of files, and it will still open that original document or application when you click on it.

## How Can an Alias Help?

If you've worked with your Mac for a while, you probably already noticed that it can be a pain to go searching through folder after folder to find the applications you use the most. Sure, it won't kill you to double-click three times before you finally get to Microsoft Word, but it would be nice to have it a little more conveniently placed. And the same goes for all the rest of the documents you use over and over again.

Aliases allow you to have icons for the same file in different places. Right off the top of my head, I can think of two places that can make life a little easier: the Desktop and project folders.

**Trashin' Aliases**

Throwing away an alias will not trash, delete, or otherwise harm the original file. But you need to be careful about putting aliases on floppy and other removable disks. Because the alias just *points* to a file on your hard drive, it won't be useful with anyone's Mac but yours. Make sure you copy the actual file to your floppy if you're going to use it with another computer.

## Pile Up that Desktop!

For applications you use every day, just make an alias of the application icon and drop it on the Desktop. Now all you have to do to start the application is double-click the alias on the Desktop!

*Just like your desk at work, you can put stuff you deal with every day right on the Desktop.*

### Rename Your Alias

If you don't like having the "alias" appendage all over your desktop, edit the name back to the original. (You'll have to move the alias to a new folder first, though, because you can't have two files of the same name in the same folder.) You can rename an alias just like any other icon. You can still distinguish the alias from the original because the name on the alias's name appears in italic. (You can also use the **File**, **Get Info** command to learn whether or not you're dealing with an alias. The FBI could use this sort of power.)

## Create Your Own Tabbed Application Launching Interface

Get ready, cadets. It's time to build ourselves a *TALI*, or a *Tabbed Application Launching Interface*. (If you're doing this specifically for your Home Office Mac, you're cleared to call this mechanism a TALI-HO.)

In recent versions of the Mac OS, another interesting use for aliases has popped up: You can easily access aliases through pop-up windows. It makes it easy to create your own folder specifically for launching files. I like to have all my applications easily available, especially for drag-and-drop access. (I want to be able to drag and drop a file to the application's icon and to open the document.) My method for doing that is to create an Application Launcher.

First you create a folder called "App Launcher" or something similar. Put it on the first level of your hard drive. Now copy a bunch of aliases of your applications into that folder. Open up the window, drag it to the bottom of the screen, and it becomes a tabbed window. Now to access any application, you just drag to the tab, the window opens up, and you've got access to your applications.

*Tabbed windows make it convenient to create your own quick launcher.*

# Create Project Folders

If you find yourself working on projects that use the same files over and over again, create a project folder and drop aliases of the documents you need into that folder. Make aliases and drop them all in a single folder you can file in any way that pleases you. When you're ready to work on that particular project, just open the folder.

In fact, because aliases can be anything, you could even put aliases of the relevant *applications* in the folder. It depends on how you like to work. If you do it this way, you can drag and drop your documents onto the application quickly to get everything started when you begin to work on the project again.

### The Real Launcher

There's actually something else provided by the Mac OS called the "Launcher," and it seemed like a really good idea in the early 1990s when it first came out. These days, it's a little passè, because you can create a folder that pops up from the bottom of the screen and does other cool stuff. Still, it's a part of the Mac OS, so I need to tell you about it. Check out the discussion in Chapter 14.

*This project folder is for a Web site I'm working on. I can keep the document, image, and application icons all in the same place using aliases, even though these actual files are scattered all over my Mac.*

If you have a place on your Mac where you'd like to permanently store your projects, create your project folder there. Then you can drag it from its permanent place to the Desktop when you're ready to work. When you're done, you can use one of my favorite commands—the **File**, **Put Away** command—to send it back. You don't even have to remember where the file came from! (Which is good if you're like me. I have trouble remembering which one is Labor day and which one is Memorial day.)

# Aliases that Break

The Mac OS is pretty good about tracking down aliases, although sometimes they can break and no longer point at the original file. This happens most often when the original file gets moved from its original hard drive to another drive or is deleted. Then the alias has nothing to point to.

Fortunately, the Mac OS addresses this. If you double-click an alias that's broken, you'll be shown a dialog box. You select **Delete Alias...** to automatically move the alias to the Trash, or you can choose **Fix Alias...** if you'd like to find the original. This brings up an Open dialog box you can use to find the original icon. Or click **OK** if this is all just too much to worry about.

# What's Special About the Apple Menu?

In Chapter 5, "Getting Things Done," we talked about how the Apple menu is a little like the junk drawer in your kitchen; it can hold a lot of tidbits and utilities you can use with your Mac. But it can also hold just about anything else. If you want, you can add so many things to your Apple menu that you'll never have to double-click on the Macintosh HD icon again. Sound good?

The Apple menu is a drop-down menu just like the typical File or Edit menus on any menu bar. But, unlike most of the other menus we've encountered, the entries on the Apple menu can be easily changed.

Open the System Folder, and you'll find a folder called Apple Menu Items. Here's where you can add or delete things from your Apple menu. What the Apple menu does is read all the items in this folder and turn them into menu items. If you drop an icon—like an alias—in here, it shows up as a standard menu item. If you drop a folder in here, it turns into a hierarchical menu item. Put a folder within a folder, and it adds a second level to the hierarchy. Get it?

*The Apple Menu folder in the System Folder is a mirror image of everything that shows up on the Apple menu. Adding icons and folders here is how you change the menu.*

# What Can I Add to the Apple Menu?

The first Apple menu enhancement you might want to try is adding an alias to one of your applications. This way you can quickly launch an application without having to switch back to the Finder. Those saved seconds add up to months of quality time spent on cruise-ship jaunts to the Antarctic later in life.

Select the icon of the program you want to add. Choose **File**, **Make Alias**. (Or do the old **Ctrl+Click** thing, and then choose **Make Alias**.) Open the System Folder to open it and find the Apple Menu Items folder. Drag and drop the alias on the Apple Menu Items folder. Remember that you can also drag a file to a folder, and it will spring open after a few seconds, giving you access to its contents.

That's all you have to do. You should see that application's name as one of the options on your Apple menu.

The Apple menu organizes its items alphabetically. If you want your alias to show up at the beginning of the list, rename the alias with a space at the beginning. If you want it to show up at the end, start the name with a bullet point (**Option+8**). Then type the rest of the name.

**Beware the System Folder**

Remember that the System Folder contains important files that your Mac requires to operate. Throw away the wrong file, and, at the very least, you're in for some major headaches. My advice: Think at least three times before moving or trashing any files in here.

## Add Your Own Menu to the Apple Menu

If you don't like the idea of adding all your applications directly to the Apple menu, there's a less messy way to get this accomplished. Create your own menu.

All you have to do is a put a new folder in the Apple Menu Items folder, and you've created a second-level menu within the Apple menu. (A second level menu works just like the Control Panels menu does; it pops out a second menu with additional items.

1. Open the System Folder and then the Apple Menu Items folder.
2. Choose **File**, **New Folder**. A new folder called "untitled folder" appears.
3. Type the new name for the folder (for example, "App Launcher").
4. Select the program icon of the application you want to add to the Apple menu.
5. Choose **File**, **Make Alias**.
6. Drag and drop the alias in your new Applications folder.
7. Repeat steps 4 through 6 to add more applications.

And that's it. Close your windows and check out the Apple menu. You should have a new Apple Launch menu item. Select the App Launcher item, and a secondary menu appears with any application aliases you've added to the folder. Select one of the application names, and that application is launched.

*Add a new App Launcher folder to the Apple Menu Items, and you've got a new way to access your favorite applications.*

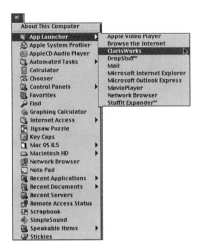

This doesn't just work for applications, by the way. You can make a second-level menu for anything you can alias. Or create aliases for commonly used folders, like your Documents folder, and you'll be able to access the whole thing from the Apple menu.

### The Easy Way

Okay, want to know the *real* way to add items to the Apple menu? Doing it the way I just showed you is like using a protractor, compass, and a look-up chart to figure out your trigonometry homework. Here's the calculator method: Select a file or folder (to create a menu) in the Finder. Now pull down the **Apple** menu, choose **Automated Tasks**, and choose **Add Alias to Apple Menu**. AppleScript will do it for ya!

## Add Your Hard Drive to the Apple Menu

So far we've talked about creating aliases for applications and documents. You can create aliases for hard drives, too. Why would you want to do this? With the hard drive in the Apple menu, you can access anything on that drive without switching to the Finder. It's like having a universal remote control for your entire hard drive.

Start by making an alias of the hard drive icon. Just select it and choose **File**, **Make Alias**. Next, open the **System Folder** and drag the alias to the **Apple Menu Items** folder. Now close everything up and check out your Apple menu. You've got a menu that represents your whole hard drive.

# The Least You Need to Know

Getting organized on your Mac is really about two things. First, you need to take a good, hard, honest look at your files and make a point of coming up with the best combination of file-type versus project-oriented folders that you can. It's best to store like files together, but then break them up into logical project subfolders.

Second, you need to take advantage of all the different wild and crazy ways that the Mac OS will allow you to add aliases and put away documents automatically. Then, to make things easier to find, you can rename files, use label colors, and change the way you view windows in the Finder.

Next, it's time to make full use of the Apple menu. You can add aliases to that, too, allowing you to quickly launch applications or access entire menus of applications and documents. The trick is that the Apple menu allows you to do this not only quickly, but also from *any* application—not just the Finder. It's quite a coup.

# Change Settings for Better Performance

Eventually, I think we all sit down at our Macs one day and decide we'd like things to go a little faster. Sometimes it's a particular task that puts us over the edge; sometimes it's just a general feeling of Mac sluggishness that might send us scrambling for that book we bought about Mac OS 8.5 that we read a few pages of, and then accidentally dropped into a pile of magazines destined for the recycle bin. After months of going it alone, finally we dig that book back up and start looking for some hints about speeding things up.

Well, you've found that chapter. Unfortunately, you probably won't see huge speed improvements from the tips in this chapter—at least, not the sort of improvements you'll see compared to buying one of those hot new Macs with the amazing amounts of RAM, storage space, and incredible new processors.

But there are some things you can do to make life a tad easier in the interim. Most of what you'll see in this chapter focuses on some important control panel settings that can slow your Mac down if they're not set optimally. At the same time, there are some other things you can do to improve performance of individual applications or in certain situations. Take a look!

# What Affects Performance?

There are a few different things that can affect performance, most of which you can change with settings inside the Mac OS. Without going too deep into it, let me say that, for the most part, your Mac's processor is going as quickly as it can. That's not the problem right now (although a new Mac might show marked improvements in speed). What you're worried about when it comes to optimizing the Mac OS is avoiding bottlenecks.

I like to compare Mac bottlenecks to traffic bottlenecks for two reasons. First, nearly all computer book authors have a very strong affinity for automotive metaphors because they're very trite and annoying. The only other writers who have even approached this level of cheesiness in the past two decades were the lyricists in mid-80s MTV hard rock bands.

The second reason is that, in both cases, the concept has the same name: bottleneck. It would have been much harder to use a metaphor like "butterflies."

A bottleneck simple means what its name suggests: You've got to fit a lot of something through a small opening (like the neck of a bottle). If you tried to pour a liquid directly through a straight tube, the liquid would have no impediment and would flow freely. Send it through a bottle's neck, though, and you'll see it backing up and slowing down while it all tries to squeeze through.

That's what can happen in your Mac. The difference is, instead of moving liquid around, your Mac is trying to move data around. When it encounters a bottleneck, the data gets backed up and has to wait its turn. Even if your processor is fast enough, for instance, you may be experiencing slow-downs with another part of your Mac, meaning data isn't getting to the processor quickly enough.

Here are the major bottlenecks:

➤ *Not enough RAM.* If you don't have enough Random Access Memory (RAM)—the main memory in your Mac—then you'll experience a slow-down. Each currently running program requires RAM to store its data while it's working. If it has to leave data on the hard drive, that'll slow things down.

➤ *Not enough cache.* (This is the problem I always seem to have in taxicabs.) If you don't have a high cache setting, you may be slowing down your Mac. Again, because RAM is faster than your hard drive, a cache of RAM can help speed up access to that drive.

➤ *Too much RAM.* This might not really be a bottleneck, but there are ways to manage things so that you get a speed boost if you have a lot of RAM. The major one, creating a RAM disk, is covered later in this section.

➤ *Energy saving.* There's another important trade-off with Macs, especially newer Macs and PowerBooks (Mac portables). That's the trade-off between energy and performance. The more energy you try to save, the slower your Mac is likely to be. Still, it's important to do your part to conserve energy.

➤ *Too much thinkin'.* At the end of this chapter, you'll go into the lightning round, where I'll tell you what settings you've learned about in other chapters can actually slow down your Mac. They're little things, usually, but they can add up quickly.

In the rest of this chapter, then, you'll look at these trade-offs and see how to set things up so you get great performance from your Mac. Ready?

# What to Do About RAM

There are a couple of indicators that you don't have enough RAM. If your Mac won't allow you to open more than a few applications (you go to launch another one in the Finder, and it says it can't do it), that's a sure sign that you're running out of RAM. Or if your applications (or the Finder) complain that they can't get something done because there's not enough RAM, that's another sign. Other things can happen, too, like more random errors or failures on the part of an application or the Finder.

In this case, there are really two things you can do. The first is to check up on some things in the Memory control panel. The second thing you can do is to help individual applications get more RAM.

You'll begin by pulling down the **Apple** menu, choosing **Control Panels**, and opening the **Memory** control panel.

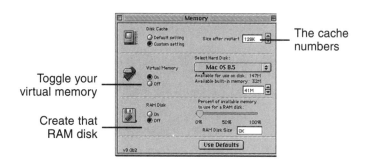

Toggle your virtual memory

Create that RAM disk

The cache numbers

*The Memory control panel is a great place to get your Mac a boost—if you know the right things to change.*

## Sounds Good, but What's the Cache?

One of the ways that your Mac makes things move more quickly is by *caching* (pronounced "cashing") information from the hard disk into memory. It's the same basic concept squirrels use when they gather nuts for the winter. Once November comes around, they could still go out into the forest every single day and get some nuts. But it's cold, they've got better things to do, and winter nut-gathering is a slow process.

Instead, they cache away some nuts in the fall so they can get at them more easily later on.

Same thing with caching hard drive data. Your Mac just stores the most recently used data in RAM, which is faster (warmer? drier?) than the hard drive. If it needs to use that data again, it can quickly grab it out of RAM instead of venturing out onto the dark, cold, ugly hard drive.

In most cases, you won't have to worry about the cache settings; the Mac automatically sets the cache if you have **Default Setting** selected in the Memory control panel. You should be pretty optimal if you leave the setting this way.

When should you change it? If you're running very low on RAM, you may find it's useful to choose **Custom Setting** in the window, and then enter your own value. The same may be true if you use a program (Adobe Photoshop comes to mind) that has its own caching scheme. You may occasionally come across an application that suggests you turn down the cache setting to its lowest level.

If you do have to enter a value, what should it be? The general rule is 32 kilobytes (KB) of cache for every megabyte of RAM you have in your system. The minimum cache is 128 KB, and each click on the up arrow will increase the amount of RAM set aside for cache.

So if you have 32 MB of RAM, the recommended cache value would be 1,024 KB (which would also be what you get with the Default Setting). If you're running low on RAM, though, you might have better use for that RAM. It's a trade-off between speed and the ability to run more applications, but you may find that 256 KB or so is enough to get the best of both worlds.

Remember, too, that you have to restart the Mac for changes to take effect.

## I'm Always Running Out of RAM!

Here's the other side of the spectrum. What happens when the squirrels fill their tree with nuts? They have to start storing them outside of the tree, out in the forest. Sound counterproductive? Well, when you don't have much tree space, you've got to keep shuffling things around.

If you don't have much physical (actual, installed on computer chips) RAM, you can use virtual memory as a RAM substitute. What the Mac does is send data that should be in RAM—but is currently not in use—to the hard drive. The trade-off is that the hard drive is slow. As a result, virtual memory slows down your Macintosh a bit. But it lets you run more programs (or programs that require more RAM) than you otherwise can.

You can also turn virtual memory on and off in the Memory control panel; just click your choice. You'll have to restart your Mac every time you make a change. You can also choose which hard drive to use (if you have more than one) and how much hard drive space to dedicate to virtual memory by clicking the up and down arrows next to the amount.

In Mac OS 8.5, virtual memory has become rather sophisticated, to the point that having it on can actually speed up some operations—and most PowerPC native applications benefit from having it on. In most cases, unless a specific application recommends against it, you should leave virtual memory turned on.

## How Much Is Enough Virtual Memory?

There's no hard and fast rule here, because virtual memory depends on how much hard drive space you have free. You probably don't want to set virtual memory any higher than double your actual RAM. Recommendations tend to be a bit more conservative than that; if you can, just set it for a few MB over the RAM you have installed in the Mac. It may seem odd, but just turning Virtual Memory on gives the Mac certain freedoms, meaning you actually gain more than it may seem from your setting.

**Lots of Cache**

This disk cache isn't the only one in your Mac, by the way. You may have heard of other caches: like L2 cache or "backside" cache. These are both physical RAM modules, unlike the disk cache setting, which is just a variable amount of system RAM used for caching purposes. Those other cache's can't be adjusted unless you open up your Mac and pull out the RAM modules themselves.

If you have 32 MB of RAM, anywhere from 33 to 40 or so MB should be good. Got 64 MB? Try 65 to 70 MB. Any more than that, and you may slow your system quite a bit. The faster the Mac, the more virtual memory it can handle. But remember that a faster Mac will really *sing* if you put in more physical memory—and memory is pretty cheap.

## The Macintosh Paradox—RAM Disks

Okay, so we've got these squirrels, right? Let's say they've moved to a slightly more upscale tree, and now they've got some room to play with (RAM). Instead of storing their nuts in the forest (hard drive), they store all the nuts they want in their tree (RAM again). Then they figure out they can put some other things in their tree: like rocks for sitting on and a nutcracker (bear with me) for opening nuts. Now they're in business.

Somehow this relates to a *RAM disk*. A RAM disk allows you to set aside a certain amount of memory for holding data or application files. It looks like a disk and acts (for the most part) like a disk, except it's really, really fast.

### Exceeding the Limit

Will virtual memory help if you've got a program that requires more RAM than is installed in your Mac? No. If a program requires more RAM than your system has installed (it requires 16 MB, and you have only 12 MB of physical RAM installed), virtual memory won't help, even though your About the Macintosh box suggests you've got enough RAM free.

That said, virtual memory does decrease the memory requirements of applications slightly. So if you have a program that requires only slightly more than the physical RAM *available* (when you look in the About This Computer window), it will likely run once virtual memory is enabled.

But the real reason for virtual memory is to allow you to run more programs, not those that require tons of RAM. Now, if you have two 8 MB applications and only 12 MB of RAM, virtual memory can help there because each program, on its own, will fit.

## What's the Difference between a RAM Disk and Other Disks?

The difference is that the RAM disk is still RAM, and it's still volatile. Turn off your Mac's power or get hit by a blackout or power surge, and the stuff on that RAM disk is gone. Forever. (PowerBook users have an additional tool in their arsenal: a check box in the Memory control panel that allows you to Save at Shut Down. That way you can use a RAM disk regularly, because spinning down the hard drive saves battery power.)

Otherwise, a RAM disk acts like nearly any other disk. You can drag things to it, copy things from it, and start applications that are on it. You can even save data files to it, although it's very risky. Make sure you copy those files to disk often. Any power interruption, and you will lose your hard work.

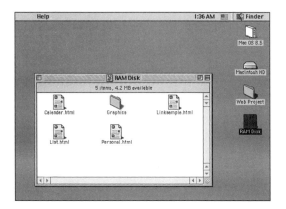

*Looks like a disk, acts like a disk, but it's volatile and needs power to maintain data, like RAM.*

## When Should You Use a RAM Disk?

The best time to use a RAM disk is whenever you want a particular application to run very quickly—and losing the files on that disk wouldn't be a huge problem. For instance, I often put games on a RAM disk, because there's nothing about the game files that I'm likely to change. When the game needs me to save a file, I just specify a folder on the hard drive instead of a folder on the RAM disk. (If I lose the RAM disk, I can always reload the game from disk or CD-ROM.)

Another option? Put a Web browser's cache files on a RAM disk. (You can usually choose where the cache is stored from the browser's Preferences window. Some programs, like versions of America Online, are less accommodating.) These cache files are downloaded from the Web and stored on your Mac to make the browser faster. It's even faster still if those files are stored on a RAM disk. Plus, if those files are lost, you'll automatically download them again the next time you're browsing the Web.

## I Want One!

Remember, you need to have more than enough RAM available before a RAM disk will do you good. If you create a RAM disk, but then you don't have enough RAM for your applications, it's a waste of time. The rule? If you have less than 64 MB of RAM, you probably shouldn't worry about a RAM disk. If you have more than 64 MB and you use regular office/productivity applications, you can consider a RAM disk. (PowerBook owners who spend a lot of time on battery power might might want a RAM disk even if you have less system RAM than I've suggested. Keeping your current documents—and maybe even smaller applications—on a RAM disk can significantly improve battery life.)

You can create a RAM disk using the Memory control panel. Just open the control panel and turn on the RAM disk option, and then select the size for your RAM disk. Keep in mind that you still need RAM left over to actually *run* your applications. It's probably not a good idea to use more than half of your available RAM for the disk. When you're done, you'll have to restart your Mac to get the RAM disk to show up.

**145**

With your RAM disk created, you can drag-and-drop copy files to and from your hard drive just like any other disk. You can open files there, too, by double-clicking them. You can even create folders.

### How Do I Get Rid of This RAM Disk?

You can't just toss a RAM disk in the Trash. First, start by saving any files you need to keep to a folder on your hard drive. Then drag and drop everything on your RAM drive to the Trash. (If the files are important remember to copy them to the hard disk first!) Empty the Trash. Now you can go back into the Memory control panel and turn off the RAM disk. It should disappear from the Desktop.

## Energy Savings versus Performance

There's another control panel on your Mac where some interesting trade-offs occur. It's the Energy Saver control panel—accessible in the usual ways (**Apple** menu, **Control Panels**, **Energy Saver**). And while you might think energy savings is something that only PowerBook owners need to worry about (after all, they're the ones with computers that run on batteries), the truth is that some parts of the Energy Saver control panel affect everyone.

### Sleep, Monitor, and Hard Drive Power Savings

The place where all computers—desktop models and portables—can get some power savings is with the monitor and the hard drive. Using the Energy Saver control panel, you can actually have your Mac go into "sleep mode," power down the monitor after a certain amount of time. Similarly, you can have the hard drive inside your Mac spin down, which saves energy. (Only certain Power Macintosh models have these features. If you can select the options, yours is one of them.)

*The Energy Saver control panel offers interesting options, even to desktop users.*

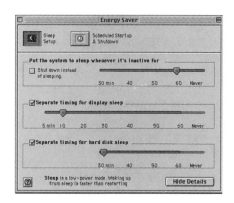

When you first open the control panel, you may see only a sleep controller, allowing you to decide how long the Mac should be idle before it's put to sleep. (This is a low power mode. When you press the Power key, the Mac will wake right up again where it left off.)

The slider bars are designed to work like those sliders you'll find, uh, on a DJ's mixing board. (Like we all deal with one of those daily.) Anyway, all you have to do is drag the little handle doo-hickie to the left or the right to pick how long your Mac should be idle (without pressing a key or moving the mouse) before the Mac will shut down the monitor or spin down the hard drive.

Looking for the other options? Click the Show Details button. This will reveal the display and hard drive sleep controls. You can time them separately if you like, although you'll notice that the Mac OS cleverly won't allow you to cause the display to sleep *after* the entire Mac sleeps. That would cause a space-time paradox, forcing open a portal to other universes behind your desk. Portals like that are exactly the sort of thing you don't want the maid service stumbling on. Am I right?

You've got to put a check next to the **Display sleep** and **Hard disk sleep** options to activate them separately from the system sleep. And if you'd prefer to have your Mac just **shut down** instead of go to sleep, check that option.

## PowerBook Dimming and Processor Cycling

If you've got a PowerBook, you've got some other options. These work like the regular Energy Saver stuff (at least, they've got slider bars), but they do some different stuff, including the capability to set two different types of criteria—how the PowerBook acts when it's running on batteries versus when it's plugged in.

PowerBooks can save a little energy by having their screens dim without shutting all the way off; just creating that backlighting can take a lot of battery power. Set this up by choosing the Dimming slider bar and choosing an amount of time before the screen dims.

Processor cycling is a bit different: This can actually power down *part* of the processor so that things go a bit slower but take up less energy. You can use the slider, in this case, to

### Sleep Timer

Want to turn your Mac on and off automatically? You can do it pretty easily. Just click the **Scheduled Startup and Shutdown** button in the Energy Saver control panel. Now you can set the times for each occurrence—it's just like setting the click in the Date & Time control panel. Oh, and don't worry. It'll warn you if you're still working when it's supposed to shut down. It won't just blink out on ya.

choose a balance between speed and power conservation. If things seem too slow, bump up the speed a little bit, but remember that you'll be using more power. It's like walking a mile and running a mile for exercise. You burn the same amount of calories doing either; you just get done with it more quickly if you run.

# Other Fascinating Performance Enhancements

I know what you're thinking: It's infomercial time. I can feel him gearing up to start pitching me on some silly program he wrote that's probably the whole reason he's doing this book in the first place. Well, that's not true. I wrote the book for the love of writing and the desire I have to help people. If you'd like more help, though, I do have a 12-cassette system you can use 45 minutes a day in your car...

You can squeeze some performance out of your Mac by avoiding some things that I tell you how to do in other parts of the book. Sure, I could have simply not told you, but I want you to make that choice freely. I'm not going to force anything on you.

So here are some places where you can pick up some extra speed and performance:

➤ *Extensions and Control Panels*. The fewer of these you add, the fewer you'll have to load when the Mac starts up, saving time. You'll also be making more memory available for applications, because many extensions and control panels require memory. (See Chapter 13, "Messing with Your Monitor and Other Peripherals.")

➤ *Fonts*. The more fonts you have, the more slowly most of your *applications* will start up when you launch them in the Finder. You may experience other slow downs, too, like a slow Font menu in the application itself. (See Chapter 16, "All About Fonts.")

➤ *Desktop Pictures*. A large desktop picture file takes up memory and can slow down the way your Mac redraws the desktop. (See Chapter 9, "Banish the Boring Mac!")

➤ *Colors and Resolution*. The lower your screen resolution and the fewer colors you use, the faster your Mac's windows, icons, and screen will redraw (in most cases). (See Chapter 13.)

➤ *Finder Calculations*. In List views in the Finder, you can set View Preferences so that folder sizes are calculated in the lists. This takes time and slows down the Finder. (See Chapter 10, "Let's Get This Mac Organized.")

➤ *Subfolders*. Using multiple subfolders within folders that have many files in them can speed up things. The more files a folder has to keep up with, the longer it will take to open up. (See Chapter 4, "Actually, Uh, Finding Things," and Chapter 10.)

➤ *Optimize the Drive*. The more fragmented a hard drive gets, the slower it is. (See Chapter 28, "The Macintosh Maintenance Routine.")

# The Least You Need to Know

If speed is important to you, but you're sure your current Mac still has some life in it, then it's time to tweak the Mac OS. You can change some basic settings to make it possible for you to run more applications, larger applications, or to get a little more speed out of your day-to-day operations.

The place to start is the Memory control panel, where you can change the size of the disk cache (assuming you have sufficient funds), turn on virtual memory to use your hard drive for pretend RAM, or use your extra RAM (if you've got it) as a high-speed hard drive. These may not all speed up things, but there's a balance between capabilities and speed, and all you've got to do it strike it. ("C'mon 10 pin!")

Another place where a balance between performance and something else is the Energy Saver control panel. (In this case, it's a balance between performance and political correctness.) Use the slider bars—apparently meant to act as digital metaphors for another typical American household item, the steel guitar—to change the amount of time before the Mac goes to sleep, puts its monitor to sleep, or spins down the hard drive. If you've got a PowerBook, you've got other sleep options, including but not limited to dropping the thing from your backpack and giving it a concussion.

Finally, there are a ton of other things that can affect the way your Mac runs, and none of these requires a special upgrade card from your local Mac retailer. Not that one of those wouldn't help, too.

# Chapter 12

# Make It Automatic: AppleScript and Automated Tasks

---

## In This Chapter

➤ What is AppleScript?

➤ Playing with the automated tasks

➤ Creating your own scripts

➤ Creating folder actions

➤ Building the better script

---

Not enough Mac owners take advantage of AppleScript the way they could. The fact is, AppleScript is all about automating everyday computing tasks: things you do repeatedly that can be done another way. Even I'm not very good at remembering to create an AppleScript when I realize that it'd be a better way to accomplish some redundant task.

But, after all, computers are supposed to easily automate things, right? And many, many Macintosh programs are designed to work with AppleScript. Even if you're creating only very basic scripts (which you can record automatically using the AppleScript tools), you'll find that AppleScript is a great way to get things done faster. And it's another reason to love your Macintosh; some of the most popular operating systems for PCs don't even have scripting.

You'll really love AppleScript in Mac OS 8.5, though, because now it's faster than ever (it's all "native" PowerPC code, meaning it computes very quickly on modern Macs). Apple has also added some new AppleScript-aware features in the rest of the Mac OS, including a new feature called Folder Actions. Want something automatic to happen when you open, close, or copy to a particular folder? We'll discuss how later in this chapter.

# What Is AppleScript?

*AppleScript* is a scripting language and technology that allows you to write small computer programs, called scripts, that can be used to automate tasks on your Mac. A scripting language generally isn't as complex as a full-fledged programming language like C++ or Java, both of which are used to create complete productivity applications and other programs you'll find on your Mac.

Scripts tend to be a bit more focused on doing only one or a few things at most. You can think of a script like a script for a movie versus the novel upon which the movie is based. The novel is a complete, full-fledged account of the story; the script is usually just instructions and dialog for actors. Similarly, AppleScripts are usually just instructions and dialog for regular Mac applications, allowing them to work without human intervention.

Of course, like any programming-type endeavor, AppleScript can get pretty complicated rather quickly. But, unlike other programming languages, it's possible to use Apple's built-in tools to get your tootsies wet with AppleScript without first needing a master's degree in computer science.

There are three basic ways we can get at AppleScripting without needing a book-length primer in its usage. (There are certainly book-length primers, by the way.) The first is simply by installing and invoking AppleScripts. Apple has already built some into the Apple menu that you can use to your heart's delight.

Secondly, we'll take a quick look at the Script Recorder. This allows you to create your own scripts by simply doing what it is you want the Mac to do—something tedious, like switching printers or choosing a different file server that's on the network.

Finally, we'll take a quick look at Folder Actions, a new addition in Mac OS 8.5 that allows you to respond with a script when something happens to a particular folder. Want all the files you copy to a particular folder translated into Mac text or uploaded to your Web server? It can be done.

# Playing Around with Automated Tasks

If you've started reading this chapter and said to yourself, "Ugh. I certainly don't want to learn programming of any kind," then rest assured that I've said something very similar myself. When I looked at this chapter on the outline, I said, "Ugh. I certainly don't want to write about programming of any kind." I say we just skip this chapter and go grab a bite to eat.

Before we head out, though, I should mention that just working with scripts and the Automated Tasks folder really isn't tough—and know that Apple's prewritten scripts might help speed up your sessions with the Mac a little bit. So let's take a look at those, and, while we're doing it, you think about whether you want Mexican or Italian food.

Pull down the Apple menu and select the Automated Tasks menu, and you'll see some of the AppleScripts that Apple has included with the Mac OS to show what AppleScript can do and to help you get some work done.

## Apple's Automated Tasks

These tasks are pretty easy to use. In some cases, you just select them as you would any menu item. In others, you'll need to select an icon in the Finder first, and then choose the task.

For example, one of the automated tasks is the Add Alias to Apple Menu task. This one is a great boon for people who like to customize their Apple menus (as discussed in Chapter 10, "Let's Get This Mac Organized").

All you have to do to use this task is select an icon that you want added to the Apple menu: It can be a folder, an individual application, or whatever else you'd like put on the menu. Next, with the icon selected, pull down the **Apple** menu, choose **Automated Tasks**, and then choose **Add Alias to Apple Menu**. This actually creates an alias of the item, and then adds it to the Apple Menu Items folder in the System Folder. Now, the item's alias appears on the Apple menu.

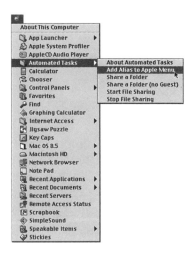

*With the item selected, pull down the **Apple** menu and choose **Automated Tasks**, and then the task you want to perform.*

See what I mean by "automated tasks?" This is something you could easily do for yourself, but it involves two more steps (creating an alias and copying it to the System Folder). Whenever you have a basic task that involves two or more steps—and it's something you're likely to repeat—that's a great time to create an AppleScript.

That includes things like turning AppleTalk on and off, which would otherwise require you to open the Chooser, choose the correct button, and then close the Chooser. That's not tough, but it can be automated to run a little more smoothly.

**Speakable Items**

You may have noticed the Speakable Items menu in your Apple menu. Did you know that those are simply AppleScripts? That's right; they're more automated tasks. If you want to, you can simply select them in the Apple menu, and they'll be run just like regular automated tasks. Of course, their primary purpose is to respond to spoken commands, but it's cool to know that they're just scripts. See Chapter 24, "Get Mac to Talk and Sing," for more on Apple's Speech technology.

## *Adding Scripts to Applications*

Have you chosen a type of food yet? If so, you might want to concern yourself with the wine selection while I quickly discuss one other aspect of task automation: adding scripts to applications. This is probably one of my favorite ways to get something done with AppleScript; I like to surf the Internet, find scripts written by *other people* that do amazing things, and then add them to my own Mac. Cool, huh?

This is one reason that Mac folks like to know what sort of AppleScript support an application has. I, for instance, am partial to Claris Emailer for my day-to-day e-mail tasks for two reasons. First, it's the only Mac e-mail application I know of that can access both Internet and AOL e-mail, so I'm able to download from all my accounts. Even more interesting, though, is the support that Claris Emailer offers for AppleScript.

I haven't written a single one of the AppleScripts that I've added to Claris Emailer; they've all been written by folks who know more about AppleScripting than I do. But these AppleScripts have added tons of different capabilities, including allowing me to forward a group of messages, extract the e-mail addresses from a folder full of e-mails, or even change the status of a read message back to "unread" so that it shows up, boldfaced as if new, in my Inbox.

Applications that support AppleScript often have a script menu like the one shown in Claris Emailer—that's sort of a universal sign for scriptability. It's not necessarily the case that you'll have one of these menus; many applications don't offer this level of AppleScripting but still respond externally to AppleScript. That means you can write scripts that are invoked from the Finder (to launch that application or cause it to quit, for instance), but you can't add scripts in a menu within that application.

For those applications that do support an AppleScript menu, generally you'll find that there's a corresponding AppleScripts folder that's a subfolder of the application folder. That's how you'll add scripts to this application.

*AppleScripts can be added within many programs to automate repetitive tasks within the application itself.*

First, make sure the application has been quit, and then find the AppleScripts folder within the application folder. When you find that folder, all you need to do is move the scripts into that folder, and then launch the application. The scripts should be available from the menu once the application has started up again.

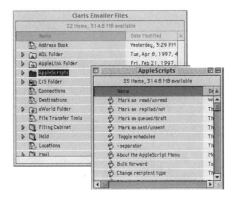

*Some Mac applications have an AppleScripts folder that allows you to add automated tasks that can be accessed from within the application itself.*

So where do you find good scripts? You can start with some of the typical download Web sites for Macs (see Chapter 19, "Working the Web"). I'd also recommend that you stop by the software developer's Web site to see if they've posted any scripts. Often, they'll appreciate that users have added features to their program and post those AppleScripts for downloading.

### More (Hidden) AppleScripts

You'll find some other AppleScripts that Apple has hidden away in the More Automated Tasks folder, that's in the AppleScripts folder that, itself, is in the Apple Extras folder.

Here's my favorite: It's a script included by Apple called Synchronize Folders. You tell this script about two different folders that you want to look exactly the same (with the same files, folders, and so on). Then you attach the script to the folders. Now, when a new file is added to one of the folders, it's automatically added to the other.

What's this good for? Backup! If one of those folders is on your hard drive and the other is on a removable disk, then you're backing up your documents in the background without even worrying about it. Is that cool or what?

# Creating Your Own Scripts

You've probably gotten so into AppleScript by now that you're not even hungry anymore, right? Well, even if you are, let me quickly show you something else that's interesting about AppleScript: the Script Editor and its recording ability.

As I've said, learning the breadth of AppleScript will cost you another book; it's sophisticated enough to require some training. For simple tasks, though, and to just get started with the whole concept, there's an important shortcut you can take. It's called script recording.

Within the Script Editor, you can actually set it to record your actions—either within the Finder or within some other application. Then you've got a script that you might be able to use over again to automate a task. It's sometimes just that simple.

## The Script Editor

To start creating AppleScripts, you'll want to familiarize yourself with the Script Editor. You'll find it hiding in the Apple Extras folder, in a subfolder called AppleScript. Find the Script Editor icon and double-click it to start up the editor.

The Script Editor can be used for some basic script building tasks: recording a script, editing the script to make it work better, testing the script, and saving it. In fact, you can even use the Script Editor to save the script as a mini-application, complete with its own icon, ready to be added to the Apple menu, your Desktop, or wherever you decide to put it.

## Recording Your Script

To create an AppleScript that affects an application, that application needs to be *scriptable*. That just means the application developers have implemented AppleScript internally, allowing you to script the program's menus and commands.

To find out if an application is scriptable, you can drag its icon over the Script Editor: You don't have to drop the icon, just hover over the Script Editor icon. If the Script Editor icon becomes highlighted, you know that the application is scriptable. (If you do drop the application icon on the Script Editor, it'll open that application's AppleScript Dictionary, which shows you all the application's internal AppleScript commands.)

**AppleScript Help**

The Apple Help system for AppleScript is pretty good. For instance, it'll tell you some of the basics of AppleScript and how to use it with the Finder. If all this is proving pretty interesting, choose **Help, AppleScript Help** from the **Script Editor**'s menu.

If the application is scriptable, you can record a script using the Script Editor. Here's an example. I'm often editing my Web site, which means I open the same documents in my Web editor, PageSpinner, which is scriptable. Instead of going through those motions every time, what if I create a script that opens the program, loads the files I always use, and then allows me to just start editing?

That's one of the real strengths of the Script Editor. I can just record myself doing that once, and then I can access the script as much as I want to. Here's how:

1. Start in the Script Editor and click the **Record** button.
2. Switch to the Finder. Double-click the application to start it up.
3. When the application is open, choose the **File, Open** command to load a document.
4. Adjust the window if you want to (the Script Editor will even notice window position in many applications). Then open more applications.
5. When you're done, switch back to the Script Editor and click the **Stop** button.

That's it. You've created a script that will launch an application and some standard documents. To test it, click the **Run** button and watch the script unfold.

*After having watched me perform tasks in the Finder and in an application, the Script Editor has generated a script that can duplicate my efforts.*

Consider the implications of just this sample script. Do you open the same applications and documents every time you sit down to your Mac? Could you automate it? You've got to think a little like a computer to get this automation thing down, but once you realize the power, you may never go back. By using the Script Editor, you could record much of your "startup routine" if you go through one every morning when you turn on your Mac. Create a script, save it, and drop it in the Startup Items folder in your System Folder, and it'll be done automatically.

## Saving Your Script

Once you've got a script created in the Script Editor, you'll want to save it. There are actually a few different ways to save a script.

The first one is as a script-in-progress—that is, a document that you want to continue working on in the Script Editor. In this case, you don't want the script to run when you double-click it in the Finder; instead, you want the script to open as a document in the Script Editor that you can edit.

To do this, choose **File, Save As...** from the menu. Choose the folder you want to save in and give it a name as you would any document. Now, in the **Kind** pull-down menu, choose **Compiled Script**. This makes it an AppleScript but requires that the Script Editor be loaded before the script can be run.

If you want to be able to double-click the script to start it (or if you want to put it in a menu on the Apple menu for quick access), you'll want to turn it into an application. Choose **File, Save As...**, give it a name, and choose a folder. Then pull down the **Kind** menu and choose **Application**.

This pops up a few more options. If you choose **Never Show Startup Screen**, the AppleScript will run immediately after it's launched. (Otherwise, after the script is launched, a screen appears asking if you really want to run the script. I'm not sure why, exactly.) You can also choose **Stay Open**, which leaves the script open after it's performed its required tasks. This might be useful if you want the script to hang around to perform the same task again, but only with more advanced scripts (those that accept drag-and-dropped files, for instance).

## Making Your Script Go

With the script saved as an application, you've pretty much created a mini-program that can be launched like any other application. You can change the icon (see Chapter 11, "Change Settings for Better Performance"), put it anywhere you want on your Desktop or in folders, and double-click it to start it up.

Script applications can go anywhere else that application icons and aliases can go, like on the Apple menu, in a subfolder on the Apple menu (like in the Automated Tasks folder in the System Folder), or even in the Startup Items or Shutdown Items folders in the System Folder.

**Other Saves**

You can also save the script as **Text** using the **Kind** menu. This allows you to open the script in some other editor, like SimpleText, if you want to. From the **File** menu you can choose **File, Save As Run-Only...**, which works the same as a Save As... except that the script can't be re-opened for editing. Only a good idea if you know the script works well and you want to distribute it to others, but you don't want them to see all your hard work (or you don't want them messing it up).

# AppleScripts Based on Folders

One of the interesting new additions to AppleScript in Mac OS 8.5 is its capability to react directly to things that you do in Finder folders. In fact, you can create AppleScripts that are attached to folders, forcing them to run every time something happens in that folder. Sound pretty useless?

Here's one good folder action that's included with Mac OS 8.5: have your Mac alert you when a new file appears in a particular folder. If you work on a network of Macs, you'll know when someone passes a document on to you, for instance, because a Folder Action results in a dialog box that alerts you to the new file.

What makes these different from regular AppleScripts is a very basic change: Instead of being double-clicked or otherwise started in a normal fashion, they react to an *action*. There are five different actions they respond to when attached to folders: the folder is opened, closed, the folder's window is resized, items are added to the folder, or items are removed from the folder. So scripts can be written specifically to react to any of these circumstances.

## Getting Folders to Run Scripts

Apple actually provides some folder actions along with the Mac OS installation that you can use to get started; for instance, the two described earlier are included. You'll find them in the System Folder in the Scripts folder. You'll also find them by **Control+clicking** on the folder in question and adding a folder action through the contextual menu.

Point to a folder that deserves a folder action, and then hold down the **Control** key while clicking that folder. In the pop-up menu, choose **Attach a Folder Action...**, which results in a dialog box. In the dialog box, choose the action you want to attach to this folder, and then click the **Open** button. The action is now attached.

You can tell an action is attached to a folder because its icon changes slightly: A small script icon will appear in the bottom-left corner of the folder icon.

*The folder icon changes when you attach a folder action.*

You can attach more than one folder action, if desired, or **Remove** or **Edit** the current one by returning to the contextual menu.

## Where Folder Actions Are Stored

Folder actions are somewhat sophisticated scripts. You may not find yourself immediately writing them on your own. You may, however, find them distributed on the Internet or elsewhere and want to add someone else's to your collection. (Assuming they don't mind.) In that case, all you really need to do is drag the actions to your System Folder and into the Scripts folder.

# The Least You Need to Know

AppleScript is a special language built into the Finder and many Mac applications that's designed to help you automate repetitive tasks. It's not nearly as daunting as a programming language like Java, although there's certainly some learning involved.

Of course, if you know anything about the Internet, you know that it's a great place to download programs that have been written by other people. You can find AppleScripts out there, too. So knowing how to install and use them are half the battle. Hopefully, someone has already written the one you need.

If not, you can use the AppleScript Script Editor to quickly automate tasks by allowing it to watch you and record your movements. This is script recording, and it allows you to create scripts without programming. Then you can save the scripts as double-clickable applications that you can put in the Finder or on the Apple menu and access quickly.

Now, in Mac OS 8.5, you can attach special scripts to folders that notice when something happens to that folder and react by running the script. Because it's a new capability, the reasons to use this are only starting to appear, but it should be a very popular way to automate some parts of Finder and folder management in the near future.

# Chapter 13

# Messing with Your Monitor and Other Peripherals

---

### In This Chapter

➤ How do I change monitor settings?

➤ Setting up your sound equipment

➤ Working with the modem

---

So far you've looked at quite a few different ways to configure the Mac OS itself—assuming you're still awake. You can change the appearance, the performance, and the behavior. But what about all the stuff that's attached to your Mac? What can you do about that?

Well, you can poke, prod, and adjust it. In this chapter, you'll take a look at the Monitors and Sound control panel, where you're free to tweak a number of things about your Mac's video output: what it's showing you and how. Then you'll work with the sound portions of the Monitors & Sound control panel. Lastly, we'll take a look at installing and working with a modem and the Modem control panel.

## The Monitors and Sound Control Panel

If you've got a monitor for your Mac—and I know you do—you'll want to pay attention to the Monitors and Sound control panel. It's here that you can do a whole lot of interesting things to make your experience with the monitor a tad more enjoyable. Seriously, I think that's pretty important. You're going to spend quite a bit of time in front of that monitor. In my opinion, it should be quality time.

### Opening Monitors and Sound

How do you open the Monitors and Sound control panel? Pull down the **Apple** menu, and then select the **Control Panels** menu item. Now select **Monitors and Sound**.

Now, if you got your monitor at a garage sale in the late 1980s, even if it has a tilt-swivel base, it still may not be the best thing for your eyes. But, hey, that's your call, right? I'm just here to do the best I can for you.

The Monitors part of the Monitors and Sound control panel basically gives you control over three different major issues when it comes to computer screens: the color depth, the resolution, and the color matching characteristics of the monitor. Sound like Greek so far? (Unless you speak Greek, in which case maybe it'd be safer to say, "Sound like silly technobabble so far?") It'll make sense. Take a look.

*The Monitors and Sound control panel is fairly easy to get around in, even if it offers quite a number of different settings to alter.*

Click to alter different types of settings

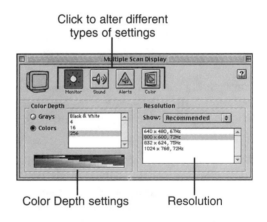

Color Depth settings          Resolution

## *Changing Your Monitor's Color Depth*

Color depth is a pretty straightforward concept: It's simply the number of different colors that a Mac is capable of showing on the screen at one time. The more colors available, the more distinct your color choices are. It's not that you necessarily have to have a million colors on the screen at once. It just gives you more choices. With 256 colors, you'll probably be able to pick a pretty shade of light blue. With millions of colors, you could pick a light blue that was exactly 68 percent blue, 36 percent green and 24 percent red.

Exactly how many colors your monitor can show depends on the amount of video RAM that's installed in your Mac and the resolution of the screen, discussed in the next section. The typical color depth possibilities you'll see include 16, 256, thousands, and millions of colors. Which is best? Depends.

For high-end graphics work, you'll probably want to work with at least thousands and probably millions of colors. After all, the printed output you're creating (for instance, for a magazine spread) is also capable of showing that many colors. For other sorts of design work—even for the World Wide Web—having only 256 or thousands of colors is probably okay. If you have only 16 or 256 colors available, though, that might be a time to consider either changing resolutions or adding more video RAM. (The lower the screen resolution, the higher the color depth you can have.)

The only other caveats are that having more colors on the screen may slow down your Mac slightly, although it isn't likely to be noticeable. And you may need certain color settings for your Mac to be completely compatible with some games, multimedia entertainment programs, or similar graphics-oriented applications.

So how do you change color depth? In the Monitors and Sound control panel, make sure the Monitor button has been selected. Then in the Color Depth box, select the number of colors you want to use on your Mac's display. The display should switch to the new color level instantly.

## Viva la Resolution

Resolution, resolution—I keep talking about it, so what is it? The resolution your screen displays represents the number of pixels, or picture elements, that make up the screen. If you have a higher resolution, you'll be looking at a screen that offers more information but smaller icons and text. At a lower resolution, you'll see less information (you'll have to scroll to see more of your document, for instance), but the onscreen elements will be larger.

Which will you choose? Actually, there are some standard resolutions recommended for various screen sizes. The reason? Because, at a given screen size, a particular resolution will give you a *WYSIWYG* (What You See Is What You Get) effect. (That's a real acronym, by the

**Strip Control**

Do you have the Control Strip active? If so, you should be able to use it to quickly change the color depth—and resolution—of your Mac's screen. Look for the Control Strip panels that have little monitors as icons. The one with color bars is for color depth; the checkerboard pattern is for resolution.

way, pronounced "wizzy-wig.") That means that the dimensions of the page on your screen will be very close to the dimensions of an actual page when it comes out of your printer.

## Recommended Resolutions

| Monitor Size | Resolution |
| --- | --- |
| 12" | 512×384 |
| 13-14" | 640×480 |
| 15-16" | 800×600 (or 832×624) |
| 17-19" | 1024×768 |
| 20-up | 1280×1024 |

Many monitors can be driven at resolutions other than the recommendation: The typical 15" monitor on many Mac models like the iMac can actually be viewed at 1024×768, although it's not recommended because it makes the icons and menu items on the screen appear very tiny. But that same 15" monitor might be good-looking at 800×600 (and that's the closest to WYSIWYG). If things are still too small, try 640×480 instead.

How do you change resolution? In the Monitors and Sound control panel, make sure that the Monitors button is selected. Now click once on the resolution you'd like to switch to in the Resolution box. The resolution should change instantly.

If you like the results, click OK in the alert box that appears; this keeps the screen from reverting back to its previous resolution. If you can't see anything on the screen, wait a while. The resolution should switch back automatically after a few seconds.

## Calibrating Your Monitor

One of the big deals with Mac OS 8.5 is the addition of new color-matching technologies, especially one called ColorSync. The idea is simple: A computer has pretty much no idea what color you're seeing on your monitor compared to the color you expect to see. It's a simple question of the number of different monitors, monitor manufacturers, and colors out there that have to all get along. If you create an image on your screen, and then print it, you may be surprised at the resulting printed colors—especially if you don't have a color printer.

Even if you do have a color printer, you'll likely see quite a difference. Why? Because monitors aren't all alike, and, even if they were alike, we'd all still be up under them playing with their dials and making the picture look bad.

So Apple has come up with a way to help correct this, and it's built into the Monitors and Sound control panel. It's an assistant that helps you calibrate your monitor correctly and choose a ColorSync profile.

To start up the assistant, choose the Color button in the Monitors and Sound control panel. The control panel will change to offer a list of monitor names. These are ColorSync profiles that are built into the Mac OS for various popular monitors. Choose the one that corresponds to your Mac's monitor model.

You can also calibrate your monitor at this point. To do so, click the Calibrate button. The Monitor Calibration Assistant appears. This assistant will help you set up your Mac's monitor so that you can be reasonably assured that the color on your screen will match the output of your color printer (or it'll match the output at a professional printing house if you take your Mac files to such a shop).

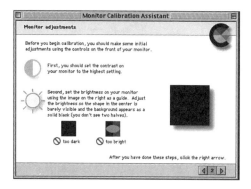

*The Monitor Calibration Assistant walks you through various monitor settings to make your ColorSync profile more meaningful.*

The Assistant is pretty friendly, so there isn't too much I can add. You'll be setting the brightness, contrast, and some other levels on the exterior of your monitor as well as in software, so you'll need to know how to change your brightness and contrast settings. Other than that, just do what the assistant tells you and don't talk back. It will be giving me a full behavior report later on.

## Impress Your Date: Two Monitors at Once

Got an extra monitor hanging around? Sure you do. We all do! If you really do have an extra monitor—and you've got a second video card in your Mac or a Mac that supports two monitors—then you can add that monitor and use them both at the same time.

First, shut down your Mac and attach the monitors. Now start up the Mac and open the Monitors and Sound control panel. You'll see a new button called Arrange. Click it, and you're in another world—a world with two monitors! (Wow.)

### Geometry Lessons

If you have an AppleVision monitor, iMac, or a Mac model that supports similar technology, you may find a **Geometry** button in your Monitors and Sound control panel. If you do, you might want to experiment with it; it's hiding software controls for the height, width, angle, and other issues dealing with your screen's visible shape and size.

*If you've got two monitors hooked up to your Mac, you can decide how they'll behave by clicking the **Arrange** button.*

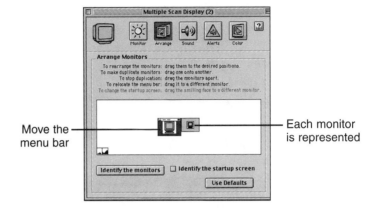

Move the menu bar

Each monitor is represented

Basically, this screen allows you to set up your monitors in reference to one another. That means you can decide if you're going to mouse off the right side of one and onto the left side of the other or the other way around. You can also choose which monitor will get the menu bar: just drag it across to the other screen if you feel like it. When you're happy with your settings, just close the control panel and enjoy your new-found freedoms!

Oh, I almost forgot. Adding a second monitor also changes some other settings in your Monitors and Sound control panel, because you now have two resolutions and two color depths to set. But don't despair. As long as you know which monitor is monitor number one and which is number two, you're fine.

Give up? On the **Arrange** screen, click the **Identify** button. That'll show you which is which.

# The Sound Part

So we've talked about the monitor settings—what about sound? Monitors and Sound is where you'll pick just about all the sound-related settings for listening to, recording, and improving the sound coming out of your Mac. You can also change the "alert" sound that your Mac uses when it pops up an alert box or encounters some other difficulty. In fact, you can even record a new alert sound if that's what floats your boat.

## System Sound Settings

You can set the volume, balance, and other options by selecting the Sound button in the Monitors and Sound control panel. That results in a number of different slider-bar settings, nicely accessorized by a couple of pull-down menus. And, unfortunately, some of you have the garish surround sound entry as well—not that it isn't a nice feature, but the logo adversely affects the balance of the dialog box.

What should the sound be played on? (Assuming you have more than one choice)

Volume and balance

*The Sound portion of the Monitors and Sound control panel gives you enough options for the audiophile, while keeping them friendly enough for the rest of us.*

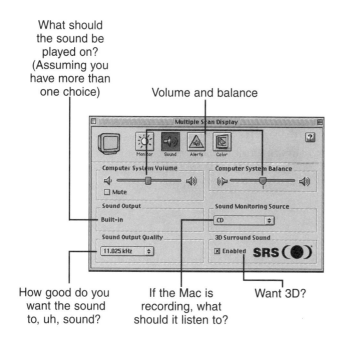

How good do you want the sound to, uh, sound?

If the Mac is recording, what should it listen to?

Want 3D?

Anyway, you can change quite a bit. Here's a look at the settings:

➤ **Computer System Volume.** Move the slider bar to change the main *software* volume for your Mac; note that this doesn't affect the external volume if you happen to have speakers with a volume switch. Every once in a while, something will accidentally bypass the main volume. If you've got your speakers way up and the Mac's volume way down, you may still get the occasional very loud sound. There's also a mute button that allows you to change it so that no sound is uttered by your Mac. Alerts, in this case, will flash the menu bar instead of making any sounds.

➤ **Computer System Balance.** The balance slider does what it says: It balances the sound between left and right speaker channels. If you like a lot of left, go for it, dude.

➤ **Sound Output.** If you have more than one type of output—you have both internal and a line-out to an external amplifier, for instance—then you'll be able to choose which to use in this pull-down menu. If there are no options, don't pick one. (Isn't that a famous flower-power song?)

➤ **Sound Monitoring Source.** If you plan to do some recording (even if it'll be extemporaneous recording), you'll need to choose what the Mac will listen to in this menu. If you end up belting your best version ever of *Give My Regards to Broadway* into the Mac's mic, only to find that the Sound Monitoring Source has been set to your CD-ROM drive the whole time, you'll be more than disappointed. You'll be heartbroken. Learn from my experience.

**167**

➤ **Sound Output Quality.** If, for some reason, you'd prefer to switch from CD-quality sound output (44.1 kHz) to, say, AM-radio quality sound output (11.025 kHz), then be my guest, weird-o. I'm kidding. Actually, there's good reason to do this. If you're playing a digital sound file that's been recorded at a lower quality level, playing it back at a higher level makes it sound worse than it already is. More on that in Chapter 24, "Get Mac to Talk and Sing." This setting doesn't affect sounds played from audio CDs, by the way—just sounds that are stored on your Mac in a digital sound file format.

➤ **3D Surround Sound.** Want your surround sound enabled (assuming you have a Mac that supports this option)? Click the check box, and it's on. Don't forget to turn it off when you're wearing headphones, though, or things will probably sound pretty strange.

## Putting Yourself on Alert

Click the Alerts button in the Monitors and Sound control panel, and you're ready for some real fun. Instead of going "beep," you're ready to make your Mac go "quack" or make a sound like a waterdrop. Whoopie! To choose a new Alert sound, just select its name in the Alert Sound box.

You can also use the slider bar in System Alert Volume to change the volume level for alerts. Notice that this is only for alerts, not your entire system volume. Other sounds will play at the regular level. If you want alerts off entirely, slide the bar all the way to the left. This will cause alerts to blink the menu bar instead of making a sound.

Want to record your own alert? If you've got a microphone, some duct tape, and the leaderless edge to a 45 minute high-bias L230 audio tape, you're in business! (Actually, you just need the microphone.)

With your mic properly hooked up and chosen as a Sound-in source back in the Sound pane of Monitors and Sound, you're ready to rock. Click the Add... button in the Alert Sound box.

*You can record your own alerts using this small recording control left over, by the look of it, from the original Macintosh prototype back in '36.*

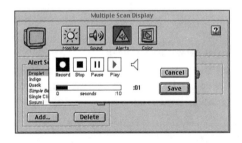

Up pops a little control that looks like a cassette recorder's controls. To begin recording your sound, just click the **Record** button and start making noise, preferably near the microphone. When you're done, click the **Stop** button. Hit **Play** to test it out. If you like the sound, click the **Save** button and give the sound a name. Now it appears in the Alerts box, where it can be chosen like any other alert sound.

# Getting Along with a Modem

Modems are devices designed to allow your Mac to communicate with other computers. The word *modem* stands for *modulate/demodulate*, which describes the process by which computer data gets turned into sounds that are then transmitted over phone lines. On the other end, the sounds are translated back into computer data. This is how you can get access to an online service like America Online or the Internet at large through a special Internet service provider.

Mac modems attach to the modem port on the back of your Mac (or come as an internal part of your Mac in some cases). They also attach to the phone line coming from the wall in your house or office, and a telephone set can often be attached to the modem as well.

On top of all that, your modem may need software to work correctly. Some modems work just fine using the settings in your Modem control panel or in the communications application itself. With some modems, special software should be installed along with your modem (assuming you bought it after you bought your Mac). If the software is included with your Mac, you'll find a control panel governing its actions in the Control Panels menu. Apple menus are commonly given a control panel called Express Modem or Apple Modem.

To get all that working will probably take a trip or two to the modem's documentation; modems are different enough that I can't cover all the different ways they get connected here in this text. What I do want to talk about are some very common modem-related settings in Mac OS 8.5.

### The Modem Standard

Modems are actually all designed to adhere to certain standards, including a set of modem commands (called the Hayes AT command set) and certain speed standards, like the V.90 standard that allows modems to communicate at 56 kilobits per second. These standards mean that, ideally, you don't need a special control panel for your modem at all, because it should be able to communicate with the Mac using standard commands. This is sometimes the case, especially with third-party modems. Apple modems and some made by companies like Global Village and Boca Research, however, use special control panels because part of the modem is implemented in software; it actually requires the computer's processor to help it be a modem. In other cases, though, you might be able to survive a special control panel if you're trying to get on the Internet; you can use the Mac OS Modem control panel if it's properly configured.

## Setting the Modem Control Panel

Unfortunately, this control panel isn't as far-reaching as its name might indicate. It'd be great if Apple could write one control panel that could control all modems, but it doesn't do that. Instead, this control panel is specifically for Internet or AppleTalk Remote Access connections. (Programs such as America Online manage the modem connection on their own.)

Open the Modem control panel, and you'll see a drop-down menu that allows you to choose the port that your modem is connected to. If it's an external modem, you likely connected it to the Modem port, so choose that in the menu. An internal modem should cause an "Internal modem" option to appear in this menu.

Next, head down to the Modem pull-down menu. Here you'll choose the exact model of modem you're using. This allows the Mac's Internet connection software to properly configure and dial the modem. You should see pretty much the exact name for your modem. If you don't, consult your modem's documentation to see if it recommends any alternate modem names you can use. (A company might tell you that their B324 Roadsurger model is compatible with their B334 Roadsurfer, for instance.) If that doesn't give you a hint, you may need to head over to your modem manufacturer's Web site to see if they've posted an updated modem script.

**Script Storage**

Modem scripts are stored in the System Folder, as you might have guessed, in the Extensions folder in a subfolder called Modem Scripts. If you have a new one, just drag it to this folder, and it should appear in the Modem menu.

With the correct modem selected, you can make some other choices, like if the modem should let you listen to it dial and connect (Sound on or off) and how it should dial: most of the time, choose Tone. If you have a rotary phone line, choose Pulse. And if you're having trouble getting your Mac's modem to dial out even though there's nobody on the line, click the Ignore Dial Tone option, and you'll have better luck.

Congrats. Your modem's configured. Now what do you do with it? You either turn to Chapter 17, "Networking Macs," to learn about AppleTalk Remote Access or turn to Chapter 18, "Getting on the Internet," to figure out how to get that modem on the Internet.

## One More Modem Thing: Faxing

This isn't strictly a Mac OS 8.5 thing; in fact, faxing from your modem is usually controlled by special software, provided with the modem, that you need to install. After installing that software, though, you'll find that a lot of it works alike.

In general, there are two ways to fax from an application. (And you can fax from just about any application that allows you to print.) The first is with a keystroke combination; the second is through the Chooser.

If you've got a modem hooked up and fax software loaded, you'll likely be able to perform a little trick to get a fax sent. With a faxable document open, start acting like you're going to print. (Look around at your neighbors and friends with that telling "I'm about to print something" look.) Next, you'll be heading up to the File menu.

But wait! First, hold down the Option key before selecting that menu. Now, with the Option key duly held, click the File menu. Did it replace your Print command with a Fax command? Ain't that something? (If it didn't try ⌘+Option and then the menu. If it still doesn't work, consult your Fax software's manual.)

Now you can set up a fax like you would a print job: most likely choosing the number of copies, a recipient, and entering a fax number to call. You might even need to fill out a quick cover sheet if you plan to send one.

*With my fax software, I get a print-like dialog that allows me to send a fax of the document instead.*

Now, your faxing might not be as seamless and pleasurable as all this. If you're having trouble dialing out or setting something up, you'll probably have to configure the fax software first before you can get this "Option+Click" dialing to work.

So what's the other way? Every fax package for the Mac that I've come across puts a fax driver in the Chooser. This is just like a printer, except it represents your fax/modem. Select it in the Chooser as you would a printer, and then print from your application as normal. For all this trouble, you should get a dialog box that lets you fax instead of print. Just don't forget to switch back to a printer when you're done.

# The Least You Need to Know

The Monitors and Sound control panel offers a unique opportunity to do quite a bit of Mac tweaking; specifically, you can get under the hood of your computer screen and computer speakers to create the best possible sensory experience.

**More on Choosing**

The Chooser is covered in more detail in Chapter 15, "Getting Your Stuff Printed."

The Monitors part of that control panel allows you to do a number of things, including configure the color depth and resolution of the screen. You can also calibrate the monitor for ColorSync—an important step if you plan to print any color documents. Oh, and if you happen to have an extra monitor lying around, you might be able to hook it up to your Mac, too, and configure it through the Monitors and Sound control panel.

Not to mention the Sound part: This control panel allows you to configure your Mac in pretty much the same ways you would adjust your home stereo system. You can change the main volume, change the balance, choose which audio-out device you want to have playing, and, on some Macs, you can turn surround sound on and off. Also part of sounds is alert sounds, which you can change the volume of or change completely. In fact, if you ever find yourself home alone on a romantic evening—just you and a Mac-compatible microphone—you can wile away the time by recording your own alert sounds.

After that, move on to the Modem control panel, where you'll find glorious days and nights on the beaches of the Internet. In this chapter, you learned how to use your modem for good, instead of evil. (In Chapters 17 and 18, the evils of using your modem on the Internet or for a remote networking connection are discussed.)

# Chapter 14

# Stuff That's Buried in the System Folder

**In This Chapter**

➤ What's in the System Folder?

➤ Why care about extensions and control panels?

➤ Managing your extensions

➤ Meet your control panels

➤ The Launcher, Location Manager, and other goodies

The System Folder is sort of like the fuse box in your house. It's the backbone of everything on your Mac, you'll need to get to it occasionally in emergencies, and you'll likely need a flashlight if you plan to poke around in it. You're less likely to store an old, rusting bicycle in front of the System Folder that you can trip over in the dark, but I've seen it done once or twice.

The System Folder is where you'll find quite a bit of the stuff that makes itself known through the Finder and other interface elements. Control panels, for instance, are stored here, as are Fonts, Control Strip modules, Contextual Menu items, Apple Menu items, and other things. In a sense, it's a convenient repository of some important things you'll want to access when you go to tweak the Mac OS.

At the same time, though, there are some things you definitely won't want to mess with in the System Folder. After all, the System Folder needs to be present and in fighting shape if your Mac is going to start up successfully; if there's something wrong with the System Folder, you will encounter grave errors and complaints from your nonworking Mac. So this isn't a place to suddenly get an unshakable urge to have a garage sale and get rid of all your System Folder stuff. You need the stuff that's already there.

# What's in the System Folder?

The System Folder is where you'll find most of the Mac OS proper; these are the files that are actually responsible for getting your Mac up and running. These files range from the Finder application icon and the System file (a single file with a bunch of programming gobbledygook in it that's responsible for keeping the Mac running), to a bunch of folders designed to hold different sorts of add-ons and enhancements. In fact, the System Folder is sort of customization central for people who want to get under the hood of their Mac a bit.

Some of the more important things that are stored in the System Folder include:

➤ *System File.* This file is necessary for your Mac to start up and run successfully. Even with very little else in the System Folder, the Mac could run, barely, with an active and present System File.

➤ *Finder.* The Finder's icon is located in the System Folder. Even though the Finder doesn't have a Quit command, it's still an application.

➤ *Extensions.* The Mac OS allows for files that can extend the Mac's capabilities, called extensions. These have their own folder.

➤ *Control Panels.* You've already seen some of the control panels, which can be accessed through the Apple menu. There's a folder in the System Folder where these control panel files are stored.

➤ *Apple Menu Items.* This folder allows you to add items to the Apple menu simply by placing an application or alias icon in the folder.

➤ *Fonts.* If you want to add fonts so that all your Mac applications can access them, they're added (or otherwise moved around and managed) here in the System Folder.

➤ *Preferences.* The files that hold the preferences settings for most of your applications can be found in this one folder.

➤ *Favorites.* Drag items (usually aliases) that you'd like to have appear in the Favorites menu found in the Apple menu and in the Mac OS 8.5 standard Open/Save dialog boxes.

➤ *Launcher Items.* Drop aliases in here if you'd like them to appear in the Launcher, an optional method of starting up programs discussed later in the "Ordering General Controls Around" section of this chapter. Folders created in the Launcher Items folder become new tabbed menus in the Launcher itself.

➤ *Startup Items, Shutdown Items.* These folders allow you to add application or alias icons that are launched as the Mac starts up or as it shuts down, respectively.

➤ *Configuration folders.* There are a number of different folders designed to store files, aliases, or other icons that help to configure that particular interface element. For instance, you can add special Contextual Menu items to a special folder to give the contextual menu new capabilities.

Actually, there's quite a bit of stuff in that folder. But once you get the hang of where everything is and what everything does, having all this stuff centrally located actually makes it pretty easy to customize your Mac and tweak it with some nice add-ons.

## What Are Extensions?

Extensions and control panels are arguably the most important of the files you'll be dealing with in the System Folder (with the exceptions of the System file and the Finder). These files are designed to augment the Mac OS, add features and capabilities, and even more.

An *extension*, also called an *init* (meaning, computer code that is loaded at the time of Mac initialization), is a small program that gets added to the Mac OS as the Mac starts up. It's designed to patch the Mac OS in a way that wasn't originally thought of, either to add a new capability or to change an older feature.

For instance, there's a Printer Share extension that gives your Mac the capability to share a serial printer with other computers on a network. If you didn't have that extension, you wouldn't be able to share that printer, because the capability to share printers (in that fashion) isn't built into the core of Mac OS instructions.

Extensions can come from Apple (and many of them do) or from third parties for more specific reasons. For instance, a company that makes Ethernet cards might have you load a special extension. AOL and Microsoft throw some in the Extensions folder when you install their programs.

## Okay, So What's a Control Panel?

*Control panels* are similar to extensions; in fact, many control panels also happen to be inits. The difference is that a control panel is a bit of startup code that needs to have an interface with you, the human.

That's why they're "control panels": They give you control over something. All control panels (if they're loaded correctly) appear in the Control Panels menu in the Apple menu. Select one of them, and you'll get a little window, complete with an interface that allows you to change some setting or make some important choices.

**Whence Loaded, Init?**

Inits are pretty easy to spot as your Mac starts up. They're the little icons on the Welcome to Mac OS screen that pop up. If they don't have a big "X" over them, they've successfully patched the Mac OS, adding their own functionality to the Mac OS's more basic capabilities.

So control panels are put in their special folder for that reason: so you can access them more easily. Some of them also happen to have an init part to themselves; they're extensions that need an interface for a human. So they're stored in the Control Panels folder, too. Make sense?

# Managing Extensions and Control Panels

Now that you've learned all about extensions and control panels, you're probably asking yourself, who cares? You're probably right. Hopefully you won't have to care too much about this stuff, because it's really not too much fun to worry about.

Obviously, you'll need to open a control panel every once in a while, and you know how to do that from the Apple menu. But no matter what you do, after a while you'll come up with a reason to deal with your extensions and control panels. You might want to just check to see how many are loading. You might want to get rid of one or two that are designed to work with an application or add-on you've decided not to use. Inits can take up extra RAM, so you might want to cut down on how many you load if possible.

And if disaster strikes, you'll likely have to do more than that. You'll need to dig into these extensions and control panels to see if you can find the problem.

Fortunately, Apple offers a tool to help you do that. It's called the Extensions Manager, and it's designed to help you deal with all your extensions and control panels. Oddly enough, it's a control panel itself. To open the Extensions Manager, choose **Control Panels** from the **Apple** menu, and then choose **Extensions Manager**.

## How the Extensions Manager Works

The Extensions Manager is sort of a hybrid between the Finder's interface and the Sherlock application. It allows you to browse through all the extensions, control panels, and a few other important files that are all part of your Mac's startup process. At the bottom of the screen, the Extensions Manager will also give you a little information about most of these files, perhaps to help you decide whether or not you want to keep it.

The basics of the Extensions Manager are pretty straightforward: You use the check boxes to decide which extensions will be loaded and which won't. Click once on an extension's name, and information about that extension will appear in the window below. Click a column name to organize the files by that criterion.

The best part is that the Extensions Manager isn't throwing anything away. Back in the System Folder (if you go looking), you'll find folders called Extensions (disabled), Control Panels (disabled), and so on. These folders are where unchecked extensions and control panels get stored. So if they disappear from the Extensions Manager and you need them back for some reason, they'll always be there. Before the Extensions Manager, a lot of extensions and control panels were getting thrown away accidentally.

If you're adept at moving around in the Finder, you'll probably be fairly comfortable in the Extensions Manager. There are a few options you should be aware of, though.

Choose a set of extensions
from the Selected Set menu

Get Help

*The Extensions Manager offers fairly complete control over your extensions and control panels.*

Click to
check, and
the file is
loaded;
uncheck,
and it won't
load

Click arrow
to reveal
information
about an
extension

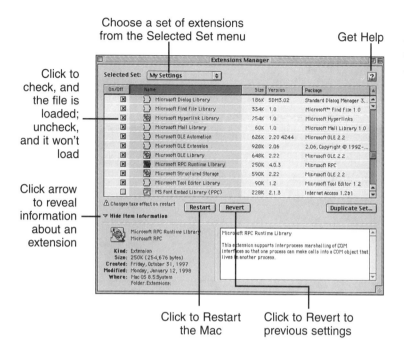

Click to Restart
the Mac

Click to Revert to
previous settings

# Get the Extensions Manager the Way You Want It

How, exactly, you view the files shown in the Extensions Manager can make a good deal of difference. For instance, if you know that you've just uninstalled your modem (you've unhooked it from the back of the Mac), you might want to know which extensions *and* control panels had something to do with that modem. It'll be tough to sift through them all in the default view. Head up to the **View** menu and choose **As Packages**, and you'll be looking at the files organized by who created them (and, often, for what reason). Now scroll down and find the grouping that was installed for your modem and uncheck the entire package if you'd like.

This is actually a really useful way to look, because it allows you to uncheck groupings of extensions and control panels that are likely not to affect any other applications or groupings. Not that they won't; sometimes a file in one package is actually being used by a different application, too, but you'll have a better fighting chance if you view by package.

If you know exactly what you're looking for, you can choose **View, As Items**, which just gives you one long list of files. What's convenient about this is you can put the files in alphabetical order, which might help you find extensions and control panels that work together, that are in the wrong place, or that are duplicates with similar names.

You'll also find the window is as customizable as most Finder List windows. You can drag the size of the columns, you can change the "least-to-greatest" order using the order box (the small, stacked lines), and you can use the **Edit, Preferences** menu to add a few extra columns.

## Saving Profiles and Using More Than One

If you're a gamer, if you like to experiment, or if you sometimes need a lot of RAM to work with graphics software, for instance and other times you want full Internet access or full network access, you might want to create different sets of your extensions. This allows you to create different preset arrangementswhere some extensions are loaded and others aren't and then pick between them to restart under different circumstances. Basically, you're creating a few different "outfits" for your Mac, so it can dress appropriately depending on where you plan to take it.

For instance, every so often I like to mess around with Apple's Web Sharing technology, but I don't use my Mac every day as a Web server. By creating different extension sets, I can regain some of the RAM that the Web Server extension uses when I don't need that technology.

*The Selected Set menu can help you create a number of different sets that allow you to load different sets of extensions under different circumstances.*

Another reason to create a new set might be to play a very demanding (RAM and processor-wise) game or multimedia title. You could turn off all of your third-party extensions or shareware extensions, for instance, but then add in the gaming ones Sprockets, joystick controllers, and so on allowing you to have the most RAM possible but still the correct extensions for the game. When you're done playing, just change the Set back to your daily extensions and restart.

To create a new Set (which you should do *before* you make major changes in the Extensions Manager), pull down the **File** menu and choose **New Set**. You'll be asked to give the set a name, and then you can add and change the extensions that are part of that set by clicking the check boxes next to each. If you'd prefer to work from the last set you created, make sure it's chosen in the Selected Set menu, and then choose **File**, **Duplicate Set**. Name it and make your changes.

You don't have to explicitly save a set; once you've gotten it the way you want it, just restart (you can click the Restart button in the Extensions Manager). The set will be saved and used to start up the Mac.

### Disable the Familiar

Of course, you should disable an extension only if you know what that extension does. Some of the important extensions can have odd or obscure names that make it difficult to tell how important they really are. If you're not comfortable with the idea, you might decide against creating different extension sets. They're certainly not mandatory.

Likewise, now that you've got the different sets, you can switch to the Extensions Manager at any time, use the Selected Set menu to switch to a different set, and then Restart. You're in business.

# Using Control Panels

You've already seen how to work with control panels through the Extensions Manager but that's only half the battle. Once you have control panels properly loaded and installed, you're ready to actually use them.

Throughout this book, we've already talked about a number of control panels, like Appearance, Energy Saver, even Extensions Manager. In general, control panels work just like small applications, allowing you to set some quick preferences regarding whatever technology that control panel covers. They allow you to configure your Mac for different scenarios.

### Startup Switch

Want to change your Extensions Set as your Mac is getting started? Hold down the Spacebar as the Mac is starting or restarting (start holding it down right after the Mac makes its startup chime). On most Macs, this will cause the Extensions Manager to appear shortly after you see the Welcome to Mac OS screen pop up.

There's also no one way control panels can look; they vary widely. You've seen most of the elements you will encounter already: slider bars, text boxes, pull-down menus, and so on. With a little experience (especially if you've already worked through some of the earlier chapters), you already know pretty much how to work with a control panel.

So what else do we have to talk about? Let's talk about some specific Mac OS interface-related control panels that aren't covered elsewhere.

# Ordering General Controls Around

The General Controls control panel has been hanging out in Mac OS Apple menus for years, but I imagine a lot of folks overlook it. There are actually some interesting configuration issues that can be dealt with in this control panel. Among them are the Launcher: A special program that worked like a folder with View As Buttons enabled, and the capability to hide the Finder icons when you switch to a new program. You can select either of those by clicking the respective check boxes.

### Discussed Elsewhere

If you don't see a control panel in this chapter, it's probably covered in another chapter that relates to the technology that the control panel configures. For instance, the Modem control panel is discussed in Chapter 13, "Messing with Your Monitor and Other Peripherals," and Chapter 18, "Getting on the Internet."

*The General Controls panel offers a few basic settings that control different behaviors in the Mac OS.*

Shut Down warning  Finder settings  Speed of cursor

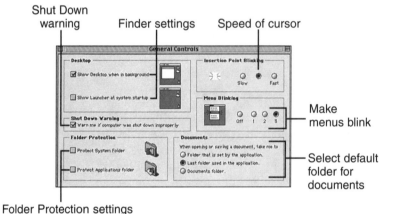

Make menus blink

Select default folder for documents

Folder Protection settings

### Launcher Settings

The Launcher can be configured by dropping aliases in the Launcher Items folder in the System Folder. As detailed earlier in this chapter, you can create new tabbed menus by creating a folder within the Launcher Items folder and copying program or document aliases to that new folder. Now when you use the Launcher, you'll click the new tab to show the added items. (By the way, you can also start up the Launcher at any time by choosing **Control Panels**, **Launcher** from the **Apple** menu.)

Here's what the other General Controls options do:

➤ **Shut Down Warning.** If your Mac crashes or isn't shut down using the Shut Down command, it will do a diagnostic check and a warning as it starts up again. If you don't want it to, uncheck this box.

➤ **Folder Protection.** Check these boxes if you'd like the System Folder or the Applications Folder to be permanently locked. This will keep users from being able to delete the files within those folders accidentally.

➤ **Insertion Point Blinking.** This choice allows you to choose the speed at which the insertion point (the cursor that shows you where you'll be typing text) blinks.

➤ **Menu Blinking.** When a menu acknowledges your command selection, it does so by blinking the selected item quickly. Click the number of times you want the item to blink before being executed.

➤ **Documents.** When the Open and Save dialog boxes open, they need someplace to open *to*. What folder should they show you every time? Make your decision here by clicking the choice.

**More Than Warn**

The diagnostic check performed after your Mac crashes is actually a pretty useful thing. It uses Disk First Aid (discussed in Chapter 26, "Dealing with an Unhappy Mac") to check your Mac's hard drive for any errors that may have resulted from the crash. In most cases, I'd recommend leaving it turned on.

## Controlling the Control Strip

Originally made just for PowerBooks, recent versions of the Mac OS have given us all a chance to play with the Control Strip, a little interface for activating a number of different options. The Control Strip control panel determines if this little wonder is turned on, how you show or hide it, and what font it'll use.

The Control Strip is really pretty handy; the Mac OS ships with Control Strip modules for doing things like turning AppleTalk on and off, enabling on File Sharing, changing the number of colors being displayed on the monitor, changing monitor resolutions, changing the volume, and many other settings. You can also add to the Control Strip using third-party panels you can download from the Internet. You install these additional Control Strip panels by dragging them to the Control Strip Modules folder in the System Folder.

*The Control Strip is a great way to get at some important settings without going through the Control Panel menu.*

Change Control
Strip settings

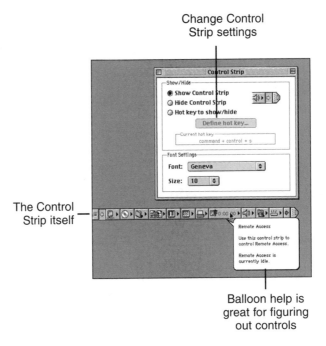

The Control
Strip itself

Balloon help is
great for figuring
out controls

### Raising the Bar

Wondering how to move the Control Strip around? Hold down the Option key while you drag the bar around the screen. This allows you to move it up and down or switch sides of the screen. Let go of the mouse button and the Option key when you've got the strip where you want it.

## *Living with the Location Manager*

Another control panel that was born to the PowerBook is the Location Manager, a really powerful piece of software for anyone who moves his computer around (PowerBook, iMac, or similar Mac owners take note). The basic gist of it is this: It allows you to set up your Mac the way you like it, and then tell it, "Okay, this is my home configuration" or "This is my office configuration." Then you can create a different configuration if you're somewhere else: on the road, taking your Mac home, and so on.

Why is this cool? Well, if you have an AppleTalk network at work or school that you hook up your PowerBook to every day, then you need AppleTalk settings active, and you'll access the Internet over the network while you're there. But when you get home, you may need to turn off AppleTalk and change other settings to use your home-based printer and modem.

Switching back and forth between the various settings you'd need for those two different setups will be new and exciting for about three days, after which it'll become an annoying chore. Instead of doing that, you could set up two locations home and work and just go to the Location Manager when you need to make a change.

Here's how you do it. In the Location Manager (**Control Panels, Location Manager**), select **File, New Location** to create a new location profile. Now give it a name (wherever you are right now: home, work, traveling). The Edit pane appears in the Location Manager window.

Here's what you do first: go configure your Mac (the Internet connections, the network connections, your Extensions, even the sound level) the way you like it for this location. With that done, you simply put a check next to every setting that you want the Location Manager to keep track of.

Choose an
existing
location

Edit a location

*The Location Manager, after some initial configuration torture, makes moving your Mac a breeze.*

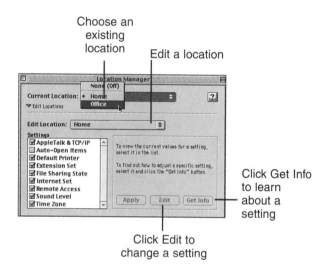

Click Get Info
to learn
about a
setting

Click Edit to
change a setting

Click **Apply**, and the Location Manager will begin tracking everything you've selected.

If you need to create another configuration, go through the process again: choose **File, New Configuration**, configure your Mac to taste, and then put check marks next to all the settings that need to be tracked. Click **Apply** again to put this new configuration into effect.

Now you can use the Current Location menu to choose between your configuration, based on your current location.

But here's why this is really special. The Location Manager doesn't just store the settings you've selected when you click the Apply button. It actually *tracks* those settings. Let's say you've chosen as the Current Location a configuration you called "Home in SF." If you change the printer in the Chooser because you bought a new Epson printer the Location Manager will recognize this and remember that you made the change. What I'm saying is: You don't have to specifically go change a setting in the Location Manager. It's watching you, and it remembers that if you select "Home in SF," you now have an Epson printer as the default, not the old one. Ain't that cool?

## Select Your Startup Disk Wisely

To be a startup disk, a disk (whether it's a CD-ROM, a hard drive, or a removable like an Iomega Zip disk) needs to have an active System Folder on it. If you choose a startup disk that doesn't have an active System Folder on it, it's possible (but unlikely) that your Mac won't start up correctly. In most cases, the only result will be a slight delay while your Mac tries to find the correct startup disk. But why put up with that delay?

In fact, this control panel is usually important only to people who have more than one hard drive and more than one System Folder. Because it's possible to have a System Folder on any of your drives, you might find it useful to start up from one or the other of them under certain circumstances. In that case, you'll want to change the startup drive using this control panel.

If you know a particular disk has a good System Folder on it, click it once in this control panel to choose it. Now when the Mac starts up, it'll use the System Folder on that new disk.

## The Lesser Control Panels

Although no less important, I've grouped these control panels together in this section because I couldn't really think of all that much to say about them. My usual recourse for a situation like that is to create a bulleted list, and, frankly, I'm not feeling creative enough to bypass the list this time. So, here goes:

**CD Startups**

If your Mac has an internal Apple CD-ROM drive, you don't need to change the Startup control panel to start up from a Mac OS CD that's been placed in that drive. Instead, just hold down the C key as your Mac starts up. It should find the System Folder on the CD and start up from there.

➤ *Apple Menu Options.* If you'd prefer not to have hierarchical menus in the Apple menu, you can click the option in this control panel to turn them off. You can tell the Apple menu if it should remember previously used documents, applications, and servers and, if it should, how many of each item to remember.

➤ *Auto Power On/Off.* On some Mac models, you can use this control panel to turn the Mac on and off at a certain time. (You can also do this with some models in the Energy Saver control panels.) You can also tell those same models to automatically restart themselves if they encounter a power failure a good idea if you're running a file server or an Internet server of some kind.

➤ *Numbers.* This control panel basically allows you to set your preferences for displaying numbers, especially currency. Use the text entry boxes to change around decimal points, commas, and currency symbols, or you can just choose a nationality from the pull-down menu.

➤ *Text.* This quickie control panel allows you to choose a different type of lettering, if appropriate, for your Mac. It also determines the behavior of the text, changing sort orders and other things that are specific to individual languages.

## The Least You Need to Know

The System Folder is like the fuse box in your house: It's where you'll find some of the little annoying bits that like to blow out when you've finally sat down to get some good entertainment in. Actually, it's where the basic configuration files and folders are stored for your Mac. For instance, if you need to add something to your Favorites, your Control Strip, your Apple Menu, or even as a Script, you'll find a folder waiting patiently in the System Folder.

You'll find some other folders in there, too: the folders that hold extensions and control panels. Extensions are bits of computer code that patch the Mac OS, allowing it to do something different or new. A control panel is a small program that offers a configuration interface to you, the humble user, allowing you to make choices about your Mac's behavior. Together, they're the, uh, extensions and control panels.

Oh, yeah...together they're also the main reason that the Extensions Manager exists. The Extensions Manager helps you manage these files by giving you Finder-like abilities to sort extensions and control panels. And, using the manager, you can set up different sets of control panels and extensions, allowing you to decide which to load and which to ignore.

Finally, it's on to the almost endless number of control panels you'll encounter. A number of them should prove very interesting, including the General Controls, Location Manager, and Startup control panel, all of which give you extra control over how your Mac acts. Plus, explore the Control Panels more, and you'll find some lesser panels that allow you to change some specific settings on your Mac.

# Part 3

# Print and Network

*There's really nothing like watching your Mac—after careful preparation, love, and understanding—ready to head out and start communicating with the world. In this part, your Mac leaves the nest to begin printing documents and communicating with other Macs and PCs over networking cable. Try to be strong for your baby.*

# Chapter 15

# Getting Your Stuff Printed

## In This Chapter

➤ The different types of printers

➤ The wiring and the software: getting connected

➤ Choosing the printer correctly

➤ How to print: testing things out

➤ Using your desktop printer

➤ Sharing the printer on a network

There's a good chance you'll be using a printer at some point in your Macintosh career. After all, a lot of what the Mac does well is help you create documents to be printed, and printed nicely. Unfortunately, it's often up to you to get the printer connected and configured correctly so that some Mac application has that golden opportunity to help you create an attractive page.

To get started printing, you'll need to set up your printer. First, you'll need to focus on getting the wiring and hardware correct. Then you'll need to make sure driver software for your printer is correctly installed. Then it's on to the Chooser, where you'll set up your printer and have a desktop printer created for you.

Finally, you'll get a chance to test the printer out and take a look at your other printing options, which might include sharing that printer over a network.

# The Different Types of Printers

In this section, I'm not really talking about the different sorts of printers you can buy—whether you should get a laser printer or an inkjet, for instance, is up to you. What I'm really after is *how* the printer creates its images and *how* it connects to your Mac. That's what's important for getting it set up.

There are really only two different types of Macintosh printers: QuickDraw and PostScript. This refers to the way the printer creates the printed page. Technically, a printer has to be able to take what's on the screen and translate that into its own internal language so it can figure out how to print it, right? In a way, it's like being a freehand artist. Even though a lot of art is having the innate talent to reproduce something you see in your mind, there's a whole lot of skill-building and technique that goes into drawing. For a printer, the technique it uses is a big part of how you'll set it up.

A QuickDraw printer uses the Mac's own internal graphics capabilities (QuickDraw is the technology that makes windows, icons, and other graphics appear on your screen.) QuickDraw printers are usually inkjet printers, they usually connect directly to the Mac's printer port, and they usually aren't particularly fast.

PostScript printers, on the other hand, use the standard PostScript language created by Adobe Corporation. This is a sophisticated language that works with many different types of computers, not just Macs, and is very popular with professional artists, desktop layout, and publishing types. The printers tend to be more expensive, bulkier, and more sophisticated. One of the requirements of a PostScript printer (in almost all cases) is that it's actually a computer in its own right; it has a processor and RAM that allows it to create printed pages. That means it's faster and less bothersome to your Mac than a QuickDraw printer, but it also means the printer is connected in an interesting way.

A PostScript printer, because it's a computer, is actually *networked* to your Mac. The connection can look the same; it may be a connection through your printer port. But, in this case, the printer is actually connected using LocalTalk network cabling and an AppleTalk (networking) connection. Other PostScript printers are connected using Ethernet—the most prevalent networking hardware.

So, after wading through all of this lingo, you've got to ask yourself a question. "Do you feel lucky, punk?"

Whoops—wrong question. What you need to ask yourself is whether you have a QuickDraw printer or a PostScript printer. Most inkjet printers are QuickDraw; most lasers are PostScript, although that isn't a hard-and-fast rule. If you have a cross-platform printer (one that touts PC and Mac compatibility), it's a PostScript. Once you've got that figured out, you're ready to connect it. So do you know which you have?

Well do you...punk?

**Networking Jargon**

Let's see if we can cut through this jargon. *LocalTalk* is a type of cabling used exclusively for networking Macs and Mac-compatible PostScript laser printers. What's weird about the Mac is that it uses the same port—the printer port—for both serial printer connections (the type used for QuickDraw printers) and LocalTalk connections. The fact is, you can easily create a small network of Macs with LocalTalk cabling—there's nothing else to buy. *Ethernet* is a different, higher-speed, more-compatible cabling standard for networking. In either case, you'll almost always be using AppleTalk as your networking language or *protocol*. *AppleTalk* is the networking protocol that's built into the Mac OS. See Chapter 17, "Networking Macs," for more details on these terms.

# How Do I Hook Up My Printer?

Once you know which printer you have, you're ready to hook it up. At this stage, you need to have your Mac shut down so you can mess around with the ports on the back (or on the side if your Mac is thusly and intelligently designed). You'll need the proper cable for your Mac and any software that came with your printer. Just get that stuff handy and have it ready to install.

You must install according to the type of hardware connections your printer offers.

## *Serial Connection to the Printer Port*

If you've got a QuickDraw printer that hooks directly to the serial port (most inkjets do this), then all you really have to do is plug your printer cable into the printer and then into the printer port on the back of your Mac. Then plug the printer's power cord into the wall.

But what if there's something filling your printer port? If it can be moved, that might be a good idea; if it's a modem or a dock for a personal digital assistant like the PalmPilot, you should probably either connect it to the modem port or get an adapter that will allow you to hook up both the existing device and your printer.

If necessary, you can also plug your printer into the modem port. The only really good reason to do this, though, is if you have another printer or a LocalTalk network connected to your printer port.

## *USB Connection for a Printer*

Newer printers designed for newer Macs (the iMac and other models that include USB ports) are designed to be hooked directly to your chain of USB devices. These connections are usually very simple: You just need to find an available USB port and plug your printer's USB cable into that port. If you have a USB hub (the iMac's keyboard is a hub), you can use a free port on the hub; otherwise, connect the printer directly to an open USB port on the Mac itself.

## LocalTalk Connection for a PostScript Printer

In this case, things are slightly more complicated. A LocalTalk printer can't plug directly into your printer port. You need two LocalTalk adapters or transceivers—one that plugs into the Mac and one for the printer's LocalTalk port—and you'll need some LocalTalk cabling to stretch between the two.

Here's how to connect your LocalTalk network, in a nutshell. With the Mac and the printer shut down:

1. Connect a LocalTalk adapter to the Mac's printer port and another to the printer's LocalTalk port.
2. Connect the phone cable to the "in" port of each LocalTalk adapter.
3. Connect a terminator (included with your LocalTalk adapter) to the "out" port of each LocalTalk adapter.

The terminator, by the way, is just a device that tells your Mac that there are no more connections to look for. When AppleTalk counts things up, it will figure out that there are only two computers connected.

Next, you'll need to make sure AppleTalk is set correctly. AppleTalk has to be active for your Macintosh to recognize that there's a LocalTalk connection in place. AppleTalk is the manager; LocalTalk is the employee. Just like any good manager, you have to wake up AppleTalk to get it to recognize that the employees have arrived for work.

To do this, open the Chooser and make sure that AppleTalk is **On**. Next, open the AppleTalk control panel and ensure that **Printer Port** is selected as the AppleTalk interface. Then you're ready to go back to the Chooser and choose the printer.

If there are other devices connected to the network, you'll need to set things up accordingly. Consult Chapter 17 or see "Can I Share My Printer?" later in this chapter.

With your cabling set up, you can power your Mac and the printer back up. Now keep repeating to yourself, "Turn on AppleTalk," until we get down to the section about software drivers. (Skip this Ethernet stuff if it doesn't apply to you.)

## Last Option: Ethernet Connections

Oh, I'm sure someone has come up with a way to connect printers using filament wire from used lightbulbs, but Ethernet is that last method I'm going to talk about. It works a lot like LocalTalk.

Depending on your Mac, you'll need either an Ethernet transceiver that hooks up to your AAUI port (consult your manual) or twisted-pair cabling that hooks directly into your Mac's Ethernet port (consult your manual). Also, depending on your configuration, you may need to hook your Mac up to an Ethernet hub (consult your manual), or, if you're using transceivers and 10BASE-2 connectors, you can daisy chain your Ethernet connectors together (consult your manual).

Look at that last paragraph again. That's what *other* Mac books look like. Aren't you glad you bought this one?

Actually, you should check Chapter 17 for the low-down on Ethernet networking. If you've got an Ethernet network already brewing, you should be able to print to any PostScript printer that's attached to that network, once you've got the drivers properly in place. If you don't have an Ethernet network, you might consider a LocalTalk connection first.

# Printer Drivers and the Chooser

You're probably saying to yourself, "Isn't this book about the Mac OS? Is this guy just showing up his hardware knowledge for kicks, or does he have a plan?" Well, you see, I had these extra pages, and...

Actually, the type of hardware connection you use can dictate the way you set up your printer in the Chooser. With a QuickDraw printer, you just install the driver, select it in the Chooser, and start printing. With many PostScript printers, you'll have to walk through another step or two.

**iMac Ethernet, and So On**

The iMac (and similar Macs) doesn't have LocalTalk, so you'll need to hook up to a network printer using Ethernet. But what if it's just your Mac and the printer? Get an Ethernet *crossover* cable, which allows you to directly connect two 10BASE-T–based Ethernet devices without a special hub or sophisticated network.

## How Do I Install My Printer's Driver?

I guess I should mention what a *driver* actually is: Printer drivers are just small programs that tell your Mac special things about your particular printer. Every printer is slightly unique, with special features that other printers don't have. So the printer manufacturer writes a small program that tells the Mac how to "drive" its printer.

If you bought an Apple printer or ran the Installer program that came with your printer, chances are your driver is already installed. You can find out by opening the **Apple** menu and selecting **Chooser**. If your printer shows up in the left half of the Chooser, your driver is correctly installed. If not, you'll have to go look for it.

**193**

Otherwise, once everything's hooked up, you'll begin by turning on your Mac and running the installation program that came on a disk with your printer. This should put a printer driver in the Extensions folder on your Mac. (If you're using a popular Apple printer, printer drivers are already included.)

### Manual Install

Can't find an installer? Printer drivers are kept in the Extensions folder inside the System Folder on your main hard drive. If your printer came with a disk that doesn't include an Installer, look for your printer driver on that disk. When you find it, drag and drop it on the System Folder or in the Extensions Folder. Now you'll have to restart your Mac to get it to recognize the new printer driver.

## Installing PostScript Driver Software

If you have a PostScript laser printer, the installation will probably do something different. Instead of adding a driver in the Extensions folder, it'll add a new PostScript Printer Description (PPD) that can be used with the standard LaserWriter driver. These PPDs are stored in a special folder in the Extensions folder called Printer Descriptions.

## Choose It or Lose It—QuickDraw

If your driver is properly installed, it should now appear in the Chooser window. Although the Chooser can sometimes be used for networking connections, one of its main functions is to allow you to visually choose your printer. It's got little icons and everything that make it a breeze to decide which printer you're going to use. With the printer chosen, you can configure it so it actually prints.

To open the **Chooser**, select it from the **Apple** menu.

To select your QuickDraw printer for printing, just click its icon in the Chooser (on the left side). Next, on the right side of the Chooser, tell Mac which port the printer is connected to by clicking on **the printer port icon** or the **modem port icon**. Then it's time to set up your printer driver.

Clicking on the **Setup** button gives you a dialog box that is very specific to your printer. Here's where you may have to choose some specific things about the way you want your printer set up.

Usually there's not a whole lot to configure, unless you're using a "generic" printer driver that can be used with many different printers. If your setup box lets you choose specific information about your printer, then do so. If it doesn't, no problem. (It may offer only Printer Share setup, which we'll discuss later in the chapter.)

Now you can decide whether or not you want your printer to print "in the background." The idea here is this: Background printing allows you to continue working on other documents while the printer churns away. If that sounds like a good idea, click the **On** button under **Background Printing** in the Chooser. Now when you tell your application to print, it will use the Print Manager to print in the background.

Click here to select your printer driver...

...then click the window to tell Mac which port you're using

*Using the Chooser, tell Mac which printer driver to use and where the printer is connected.*

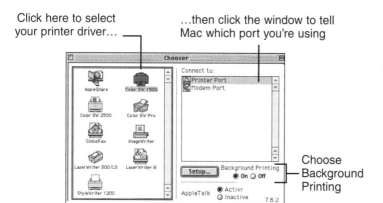

Choose Background Printing

### The Problem You'll Encounter

Here's the one problem you'll encounter when setting up your printer (other than hardware failure, configuration issues, problematic drivers, bad connectors, or cables that have been chewed through by household pets). AppleTalk is on. When you have a QuickDraw printer, you won't be using AppleTalk networking to talk to that printer.

If you're not connected to a network at all, make sure AppleTalk is off in the Chooser. (Click the **Off** button.) If you still have trouble selecting the printer, restart your Mac. If you're connected to a network, you'll need AppleTalk; just make sure it isn't trying to use the same port you just hooked your printer up to. In the AppleTalk control panel, check to ensure that a different port or an Ethernet connection is selected, depending on what your network requires.

Do you need AppleTalk turned on because your printer port is being used for the network connection? In that case, make sure the AppleTalk control panel says "Printer Port," and then use the modem port for your printer connection in the Chooser. Now, no more problems.

## *Choose It or Lose It II—PostScript*

With PostScript printers, the choosing process is slightly different. Instead of finding your printer in the Chooser, select the **LaserWriter 8** driver in the left-hand pane of the Chooser window. On the right side, you should now see your available printers pop up, allowing you to choose a printer to which you are connected. (You may see more than one printer if you are connected to a large network.)

If you don't see the printer you want to use, it may not be configured correctly. In the case of a LocalTalk printer that's connected to the printer port, you need to have AppleTalk turned **on** and the AppleTalk control panel needs to have the **printer port** selected. If you're using an Ethernet connection, you should have the AppleTalk control panel set to **Ethernet**, as discussed in Chapter 17.

If you do see the printer you want to use, select it with the mouse, and then click the **Create** button. This brings up a number of different options. If the choice presents itself, select the **Auto Setup** button. Otherwise, you may be forced to choose a **PostScript Printer Description** file. Click that option, and then locate a PPD for your printer in the Open dialog box. If you can't find one, you'll need to contact the printer manufacturer or check your printer documentation to see if there's a substitute you can use.

You can then click the other LaserWriter options buttons (**Get Info**, **Configure**, and so on) to change the printer's settings to your liking. If you don't feel like doing any more configuring, click **OK**.

## Test the Printer

Once you have the printer selected, your first test toward success is to close the Chooser by clicking its **close box**. More than likely, this will either generate an error message—in which case you need to double-check everything and go through the instructions again—or you'll get a message that tells you the printer was changed and you should select the Page Setup command in any open application. This is the first sign of potential success.

*If you get this message, there's a good chance your printer was selected correctly.*

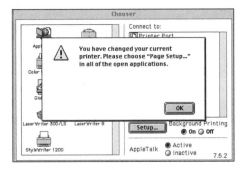

The second indicator that things are going well will be the appearance of a desktop printer icon on your Mac's Desktop. The icon should be full-color without an "X" through it, and it should have a strong black outline. That outline means it's the currently selected printer.

If you've got your printer set up, the driver activated, and your desktop printer icon looks happy, your next step is to try printing (see "How Do I Print a Document?," coming up next). You should get instant feedback letting you know if your printer is humming along successfully or if you're running into trouble. With some printers, the PrintMonitor will appear in the Applications menu allowing you to check the status on currently printing jobs, or double-click the **desktop printer icon** to get more info on the printer's status.

**Ex-Printer**

If your desktop printer is "X"ed out, it probably means the desktop printing software didn't load. Head to the Extensions Manager and make sure the Desktop Printing package is enabled. Also, make sure you didn't accidentally start up with the Shift key held down and then forgot to restart your Mac. Restart and see if the printer comes back.

# How Do I Print a Document?

After you set up your printer correctly, you'll be able to print. If this is the first time you're printing to your printer, or if you have multiple printers, remember to check the Mac's Chooser just to make sure you have things set up correctly. You can also check your desktop printer icons for a black outline to ensure that the printer is selected and ready.

By the way, if you got a message saying you should open the Page Setup menu command in your applications, it's a good idea. This tells an already-opened application that the printer has changed, allowing the application to make any adjustments to page size or other issues that might affect the quality of the printout. Just choose **File, Page Setup**, and then you can click the OK button if everything looks cool.

## Some Last Minute Choices

With a document open and the printer chosen, you're ready to print. Pull down the **File** menu and select the **Page Setup** command. Up pops the Setup dialog box. Here's where you make some configuration choices.

What paper size
should it use?

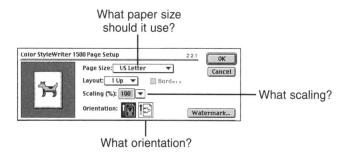

What scaling?

What orientation?

*The standard StyleWriter page setup box. You can choose how the printed page will look here, setting some printer-specific options.*

Next, you're ready to head to the actual print command. Choose **File, Print** from the application's menu. Here's where you make some last-minute decisions.

### Print Orientation

Although this sounds like something you should do with a map and a compass, print orientation is really the process of choosing how a document will be printed: upright or longways. As far as your Mac is concerned, the terms are Portrait (regular orientation) or Landscape (print wider-than-taller, like for spreadsheet numbers). You can choose which you'd like by clicking the appropriate Orientation icon in your Page Setup dialog box. You'll notice that when you change the orientation, the page around Clarus the Dogcow (that little animal in the window there, which is the stuff of legends around Apple) will change, too.

*The standard StyleWriter print dialog box. Here's where you make your last-minute printing decisions.*

How many copies?     What pages should print?

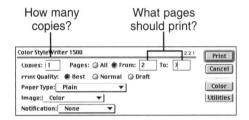

Once you've made all the decisions you're going to make, the time has come to print. Click the **Print** button in the Print dialog box, and your document is off to the printer. If you're printing in the background, you'll see some messages saying that pages are being sent to the printer. Eventually they'll disappear, and the only indication you'll get that something is happening is from the PrintMonitor (in the Applications menu) or from your desktop printer icon.

If you're not printing in the background, you won't be able to get any work done until the printer has finished. Instead, a white dialog box will appear at the top of the screen constantly updating you regarding the status of your print job. That makes the pages come out of the printer a bit quicker, but it's annoying if you want to get some extra work done.

## Using the Desktop Printer

The last few iterations have added a logical little icon to the Mac's Desktop: the desktop printer icon. Instead of menacingly named PrintMonitor and strange crevices of the Chooser for your printer status, why not have a happy little icon on the desktop to help you out with your printer? That's what the desktop printer icon is for.

A desktop printer icon is created automatically in Mac OS 8.5 when you select a printer in the Chooser (assuming that the desktop printing package is properly activated in the Extensions Manager). After successfully setting up your printer, the icon appears on the desktop with a black border indicating that it's chosen.

If you'd like, you can double-click that icon right now to get the status of the printer. Most likely, nothing's happening. But a window will open just the same, showing you what print jobs have been queued in line and what their status is.

Of course, things are more exciting after you've used the Print command to send some print jobs to the printer.

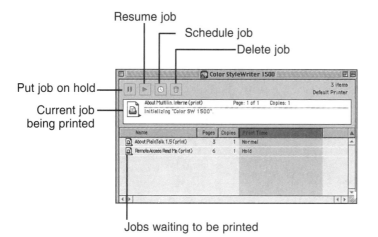

*The desktop printing interface is one-stop shopping for printer controls.*

By the way, when you send a document to be printed, it gets called a "print job" for some reason. Probably harkens back to the days of yesteryear when a computer would output data that then had to be hand-printed by some poor sap with a #2 pencil, a legal pad, and a bunch of time on his hands. That was his job, so the name "job" stuck. (Okay, I made that up.)

## Work that Desktop Printer!

Once you send a job to the printer, the fun is only beginning. The desktop printer icon will change so that it now shows a tiny little document on the front of the icon; that means it has a print job waiting (or currently printing). Double-click the icon to open up the print monitor window.

In that window, you can select any jobs and click the controls at the top of the screen to change the status of the job. Those controls are:

➤ **Hold.** This pauses the printing of the job. If more than one document is in the queue, the held document will be bypassed by other documents that aren't being held.

**199**

➤ **Resume.** This button allows you to put the selected job back in the print queue. It's now scheduled to print again.

➤ **Schedule.** Select a print job, and then click this button to bring up the scheduling dialog box. Choose **Urgent** to put this job at the top of the list, **Normal** to keep it in line (no cutting!), or choose **At Time** and use the entry boxes to choose a date and time for this print job.

➤ **Delete.** Select a job and click this **Trash** button to remove the job from the print queue.

If you don't change anything, the jobs will cycle through as they're completed, moving the next job in line up to the Current Job window while the others wait patiently.

## Easy Printing: Drag to the Printer

There's another reason the printer icon is on the Desktop: You can drag stuff to it like a regular folder icon. Just drop a document on the desktop printer icon, and that document will be printed. In some cases, a print dialog box will appear, so make sure you don't walk right away from the computer. But this is a convenient way to print a bunch of documents without first going and finding their associated applications. Just drag and drop.

## Desktop Printer Alerts

Did your desktop printer icon change so that it shows an exclamation point (!)? That means something has gone wrong or it wants to tell you something; switch to the Finder or click on the desktop printer icon.

# Can I Share My Printer?

Built into every Macintosh is the capability for it to network to other Macintoshes. Just like picking up and dialing a telephone, your Macintosh can call out to other Macs it's connected to and share information. What does this mean to the user? If all the computers and printers are connected correctly, you can have access to any printer linked to the network.

We'll talk more about the whole networking thing in Chapter 17. But we should talk about sharing printers here because this is the printer chapter. (I'm sorry for all the flipping back and forth, but if you'd buy yourself a 50-cent bookmark, this wouldn't be such a problem.)

Anyway, there are actually two ways to give networked users access to your printer. The first way is use an AppleTalk-aware PostScript printer that's hooked up to the network. In that case, you simply choose the printer in the Chooser as I've already described. If it's on the network, others can choose it, too, and set up a desktop printer icon of their very own.

The other way, though, is more interesting. If you have a regular QuickDraw printer that's connected to your printer port—but you have a network connection, like Ethernet, too—you might think that sharing the printer is impossible, because it's not directly on the network. But that simply isn't true!

## Sharing PostScript Printers

If you have an Ethernet network, you already have all the sharing covered. Hook your printer up to your network hub or to your Ethernet daisy-chain, and you're golden. That stuff is discussed in Chapter 17.

But how about two Macs, some LocalTalk cable, and a LocalTalk printer? Huh? You don't want to have to read that whole stupid networking chapter, right?

Here's how to get that second Mac in the mix. You'll need another transceiver for this Mac:

1. Connect the LocalTalk transceiver to the second Mac's printer port.

2. Pull the phone cable (or LocalTalk cable) from one of the other connectors' "in" ports and plug it into the new adapter's "in" port.

3. Connect another phone cable (or LocalTalk cable) between the new connector's "out" port and the original connector's "in" port.

Why this crazy scheme? You must connect LocalTalk devices in a daisy-chain fashion, which means each connection has to continue a chain from one device to the next. In this example, what we've done is a lot like adding a freight car to the middle of a train. The only difference is, our train, or daisy-chain, has to have two cabooses (terminators).

Now, with the chain correctly created you should have what amounts to one long line of LocalTalk cable, connected occasionally through transceivers, with a terminator on each side. Your train is complete. With AppleTalk on and the Printer Port selected in the new Mac's AppleTalk control panel, you are ready to select the printer in the new Mac's Chooser!

## Sharing a QuickDraw Printer

Here's the other kind of sharing. If you're on an Ethernet network and you want to let others select your printer port or USB-based printer in their Chooser, you need to activate Print Share. (A direct-connected printer is often called a "local" printer.) It's easy enough to do.

In the Chooser, select your printer icon. Now, on the right side of the Chooser, click the Setup button. A dialog box appears.

*The Setup dialog box allows you to set up your local printer as a network printer.*

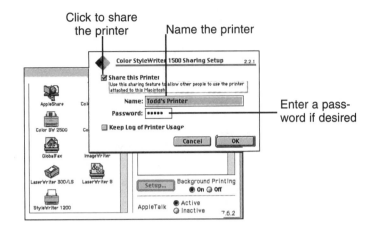

Click to share the printer

Name the printer

Enter a password if desired

## Sharing on LocalTalk

If you have a LocalTalk network installed, you can *still* share your QuickDraw printer. It just needs to be connected to the modem port, because the printer port *is* taken by the LocalTalk connection.

If your printer is capable of being shared, you'll see an option here that allows you to share it. Click the check box next to that option to activate print share. (If you're told that AppleTalk needs to be on, head back to the Chooser and activate AppleTalk. You may also need to set up the AppleTalk control panel to make sure you're properly connected to your network. If you're not connected to a network, there's no reason to share your printer!)

Now you can give the printer a name; this is the name that will appear in users' Chooser. (It'll be the default name provided by the manufacturer if you don't change it. It may be helpful to name it, though, especially on a large network.) After you've named it, enter a password for this printer if desired. You'll need to tell all authorized users this password so they can set up to use your printer.

When you're done, click OK. Your printer is now shared, and other users on your network should be able to choose your printer in their Choosers, setting up a desktop printer icon and everything.

Congratulations! You are now a network-printing guru. Pick up your diploma at the front desk.

## The Least You Need to Know

Before you can print, you'll need to set up your printer—unless there's something really amazing about you that you're not sharing with the rest of us. Setting up a printer isn't too tough to do, but it requires that you know a little about the printer—specifically, is it a QuickDraw or PostScript printer?

QuickDraw printers are usually directly connected to your Mac, using the printer port (the modem port is also an option). PostScript printers are actually networked to your Mac, even if there's only one printer and one Mac; you use LocalTalk or Ethernet, the technologies that allow computers to connect to one another.

Then, with the printers correctly wired up, you're ready to select the printer's driver software in the Chooser. It's just a mouse click. After that, you tell the Chooser where to find the printer and how to treat the printer; you can set various preferences and options. If all goes well, you should be able to print from your applications.

You should also be able to control the printer from a desktop printer icon. Desktop printer icons offer a great interface for controlling your printer's queue, allowing you to move documents around, schedule them for later, or remove them from the queue and not print them at all. (Maybe they insulted you after you'd chosen the Print command.)

Finally, you can share your printer with others. If you've got a few Macs and a LocalTalk printer, you can set up a quickie network to share the printer. If you've got a QuickDraw printer connected directly to your printer port, you can still share it if you happen to be on an Ethernet network.

# Chapter 16

# All About Fonts

---

## In This Chapter

➤ What are fonts, and how do they work?

➤ The different kinds of fonts and which to use

➤ Adding fonts to your Mac

➤ Packing your font suitcase for moving around

➤ Delete your unwanted fonts

---

Choosing fonts for your documents is truly an art form. While some documents can definitely make good with a few extra touches (like this page, with it's pithy, devil-may-care attitude that lulls the average bookstore shopper into a quick sale), you'll find others that go a little overboard with all the cutesy fonts. In this case, the document needs to follow the golden rule of dressing one's self for a party: Back up and take off one accessory. Now you look good.

If your documents just don't quite have the flash and style you need, maybe you should try a new font. What are fonts? *Fonts* are collections of letters, numbers, and punctuation marks with an identifiable typeface. Some fonts, like Times, look like newspaper text, some are a bit rounder like Century Schoolbook, which might be appropriate for a hardback book. Other fonts are just plain and simple, but elegant, like Helvetica.

# What Is a Font?

Technically, a font is a collection of letters, numbers, and punctuation marks with a particular typeface, weight (bold or not bold), and size in plain or italic. However, the word is frequently used to mean a typeface with a particular design, like Courier versus Arial. (Actually, some fonts don't offer full alphabets and punctuation, offering instead a series of symbols or other special characters. Fonts named "Symbol," "Dingbats," or "Wingdings" often fall in this category.)

In the System Folder on your Mac is a folder called **Fonts**. Inside this folder are your font files, which serve two different purposes. First, font files tell your printer how printed text should appear. Second, they tell your Mac how to display text on the screen. (Some font files are found right in the Fonts folder, while others are stored in "font suitcases," which are discussed later in this chapter. They all pretty much work the same; if they're in the Fonts folder, they'll be available in your applications.

When you select a font in your application, the application lets the Mac OS know. If you type a letter, the Mac OS will try its best to display that font correctly. And when you print, the System software will try to tell your printer how you want the font to look. At least, that's how it's supposed to work.

There are three different "kinds" of fonts you might be using with your Macintosh: TrueType fonts, PostScript fonts, and bitmap fonts. Each has its own little quirks, but they're all pretty easy to work with.

**Outline Fonts**

An *outline font* is a font file that describes what the basic shape of a font is to the Mac OS. From there, it's up to the Mac OS to decide how to "fill in" the outline with dots, depending on the point size you choose for the font. An outline font is sometimes called a *scalable* font.

## TrueType Fonts—Don't Worry

Modern Macintosh computers use a font technology called TrueType. (Not always exclusively, but TrueType is the technology built into the Mac OS.) Compared to other kinds of fonts, TrueType is like cable TV: It always looks pretty good. TrueType fonts are very easy to resize because they're *outline* fonts. They're also very easy to manage and they almost never look bad on your screen or on your printer.

If you're using your Macintosh at home and you only print your documents to your printer (instead of taking them to work or something), you should be just fine using TrueType fonts. How do you know if you're using TrueType? If you haven't added any extra fonts to your system, you're using TrueType. All the fonts that Mac OS 8.5 installs are TrueType fonts.

Just about any printer can work well with TrueType fonts, and they come with the Mac OS. If you're already tired of worrying about fonts, just use TrueType.

## *PostScript Fonts Look Great on Paper*

If you own a laser printer, you may be dealing with PostScript. Things can get a little hairy here. PostScript creates great looking printed output, and if you have the correct printer font files installed, there's almost no need to worry about your printouts with PostScript.

But PostScript does some crazy things to fonts on the screen. Why? Because PostScript uses two different font files to get things done. Where TrueType is used for both the screen display and the printed text, PostScript needs separate printer font files and screen font files to work correctly. So if one or the other is missing, you'll see jagged fonts.

---

### Why Doesn't Everybody Just Use TrueType?

From the way I've described it, TrueType sounds like the best font technology out there. And for ease of use, it is. But there are a couple of great reasons to use PostScript, too.

Reason number one: PostScript does more than fonts. TrueType is a font technology. PostScript, on the other hand, is a page description technology. All that means is that PostScript is used for printing both fonts and graphics. To desktop publishers and graphic artists, PostScript is something to swear by. It's incredibly useful for high-end graphics, photos, and other professional printing tasks.

Reason number two: A lot of folks use PostScript. PostScript has been around a lot longer than TrueType, and it's still popular. In major printing houses, pre-press stores, and anywhere else you find professional Mac users, you'll find PostScript. It's so popular, in fact, that most laser printers designed for the Mac feature PostScript technology built in.

So if you've got a laser printer and want to get the most out of it, you'll want to use PostScript fonts. If your printer doesn't support PostScript, or you just don't want to mess with it, stick to TrueType. It's a little easier, and things still look great.

---

### *Why PostScript Can Look Jagged*

If TrueType and PostScript are both outline fonts, why does PostScript .look bad on your screen? The capability to show TrueType fonts on your screen is built into the Mac OS, while the capability to show PostScript fonts is not. This means that TrueType fonts, no matter what point size you make them, always look clean and crisp. PostScript fonts, however, only look good at certain point sizes.

### Smooth Substitution

Actually, there is an important case when choosing the wrong bitmap font *won't* result in jagged text. In some cases, the TrueType and some bitmap fonts will be installed; if a point size other than an available bitmap font is chosen, the TrueType is substituted.

For your Mac to show you PostScript files, the System software has to use something called a *bitmap font* (actually, our third type of Mac font). This is the PostScript screen font, the font that will show up in your document window after you select it in the Font menu. But, by definition, a bitmap font will only show up correctly in certain point sizes. Choose the wrong point size, and your font comes out jagged.

A bitmap font file is a map of all the dots required to create the font at a given point size. Because of this, each bitmap font only looks good at its one, specific point size.

*Bitmap fonts representing their PostScript cousins. Select a point size that's not outlined, and you'll get "jaggies."*

Palatino at 12 point
Palatino at 20 point
Palatino at 24 point ———————————— Some good bitmap fonts

## Palatino at 36 point

## Palatino at 48 point
# Palatino at 72 point |

Some not-so-good bitmap fonts

There's an easy way to tell which bitmap screen fonts you have for a given PostScript printer font. In your Font menu, the outlined point sizes are real bitmap fonts. The point sizes in regular text will be jagged.

So why do bitmap fonts look bad? The same reason photocopies look worse when you enlarge them. A 10-point bitmap font has a certain number of dots that make it look good at 10 points. Enlarge it to 20 points, and those same dots have to fill more space. Now things look jagged.

Remember, though, that your PostScript printer fonts *are* outline fonts. So even if they look bad onscreen, they'll look good on paper.

## *Getting Rid of the Jaggies*

There is a way to avoid jagged edges with PostScript screen fonts. What you need is a program called Adobe Type Manager, or ATM. What ATM does is something similar to what TrueType does. It acts as a go-between for your System software and your PostScript fonts. Whenever an application asks for a screen font, ATM looks at the PostScript font, changes the outline to your point size, and fills it in. Now all screen fonts look great.

ATM is available with the Adobe Acrobat Reader, a freely distributed software package that allows you to read Abode PDF (Portable Document Format) documents. ATM can also be purchased, along with fonts or in similar commercial software packages from Adobe. Once you've got it installed, ATM manifests itself as a control panel that appears in the Control Panels folder in your System Folder.

**Jaggie-Proof?**

Of course, if you have Font Smoothing on in your Appearance control panel, you're not likely to encounter jaggies—at least, not over a certain point size. You may never know what you're missing out on. The only time this might cause a problem is with a true bitmap font (without ATM and with no PostScript printer equivalent) which might *print* jagged. Unlikely, though.

Palatino at 12 point

Palatino at 20 point

Palatino at 24 point

Palatino at 36 point

Palatino at 48 point

Palatino at 72 point

*Ahh, that's better. Same font and point size, but they're no longer rough around the edges.*

The control panel is where you need to make a few decisions to get everything working correctly and efficiently. ATM's control panel is pretty straightforward. Once you turn it on and restart, it will use the printer fonts in the Fonts folder (in your System Folder) to generate screen fonts on the fly for your viewing pleasure. In essence, ATM adds TrueType-like technology (use the same font for screen and print) without forcing you to change from PostScript fonts. Cool?

### Printing PostScript

There's another reason you might want to own ATM. If you have a QuickDraw printer (inkjet or another printer that doesn't include the PostScript language), you can use ATM to print PostScript fonts that look great. Why would you want to do this? In case you need a font not available in TrueType or your work uses PostScript, so you need to at home, too. It's not a bad way to get good-looking printouts from your inexpensive printer.

### Things Change

The original fonts shipped with the Mac were knock-offs of popular typography fonts. Apple gave them somewhat unrelated city names so they wouldn't be confused with the originals: New York, Chicago, Monaco, Geneva, and so on. They were also originally bitmap fonts. These days, Apple still ships those fonts, but in both bitmap and TrueType incarnations. (Double-click the Geneva or New York "suitcase" icons in the Font menu to see both types of fonts.)

## *Bitmap Fonts: One Size Fits All?*

Bitmap fonts were actually the original type of font the Mac used for both the screen and the printer. I've already explained that bitmap fonts are used for the screen font when you display a PostScript font. But they can also be printed if you have any installed.

Just remember that these fonts are not at all scalable. The outlined point size in your program's menu is the only point size at which a bitmap font will look good. Usually, these are standard sizes, like 10 point, 12 point, and sometimes a few others. Stick with these, and things will be okay. Stray at all from these point sizes, and your printouts probably won't look much like actual words!

In fact, that's probably the easiest way to recognized bitmap fonts: They're usually named with an associated number, so you'll see Veritas 12, a bitmap font, versus Courier New Italic, which is likely a TrueType font. (You can also tell all three types of fonts from their icons: Bitmap fonts have single "A on a document" icon, TrueType have a series of "A"s, and PostScript fonts have either really ugly large "A"s, a printer-like font or, well, anything else weird.)

## Moving Your Fonts Around

Hopefully, you won't have to move your fonts around too much. If you're installing new fonts from a commercial package, more than likely they'll find the right place to go on their own. If you install fonts that don't include an Installer program of some kind, it's a fairly simple process. But be careful.

If you're adding your own fonts, take care that you don't leave a PostScript font and a TrueType font with the same name in your Fonts folder. This can cause your Mac to crash or "freeze-up" if it has trouble deciding which to use. You can use both TrueType and PostScript fonts as long as the font files have different names.

# How Do I Add Fonts?

To add a single font, just drag and drop the font file onto the **System Folder icon** (not the open System Folder window). A dialog box appears, making sure it's okay to add this file as a font. Click **OK** to let your Mac know that it's doing the right thing. Your Mac will put the font in the Fonts folder.

Open up that Fonts folder, and you may notice that TrueType and bitmap fonts are in *suitcases*. A suitcase is a special type of folder for TrueType and bitmap fonts on your Mac. It allows you to group similar fonts to make them easier to keep track of and to make it easier to move families of fonts into and out of the Fonts folder.

# Pack Your Own Suitcase

To create a suitcase, select an existing suitcase in your Fonts folder and choose **File, Duplicate**. Rename it something like "Master Suitcase," and then double-click the suitcase to open it. Select all the fonts currently in that duplicate suitcase just like they were files in a regular folder. Drag them all to the trash. Now close up the master suitcase and store it in a safe place other than the Fonts folder. You'll be able to use these as a template when you want to add a font suitcase to your Mac.

To use a suitcase, create a duplicate of your master suitcase and drag that duplicate to the Fonts folder. Name the suitcase according to the Font family you want to put in it: Courier, for instance.

Now, just drag all fonts for that suitcase—both bitmap and TrueType fonts, if you've got

**Font Limit**

Macs have a limit of 128 items in the Fonts folder. That doesn't necessarily mean you're limited to 128 fonts. If you have more, you can use a font management program to move fonts in and out of the Fonts folder. You can also get past the limit by grouping your fonts in font suitcases. A single suitcase (regardless of the number of fonts in that suitcase) counts as one item toward the total of 128.

them—onto the suitcase icon. It's best to group fonts according to their font families, but you could, for instance, create a folder called "Desktop Layout" that groups a bunch of TrueType fonts you use when you're using your page layout program.

# How Do I Delete Fonts?

To delete a font, just open the Fonts folder and drag and drop the font to the Trash. Then empty the Trash. If you're deleting a PostScript font, remember to drag and drop associated bitmap files to the Trash, too.

You can't move or delete font files without closing your applications first. This is Mac's way of keeping you from deleting or losing a font while an application that needs it is still active.

*The font suitcase is a convenient way to pack up your fonts to give you more room for additional fonts or just to send them on a nice vacation.*

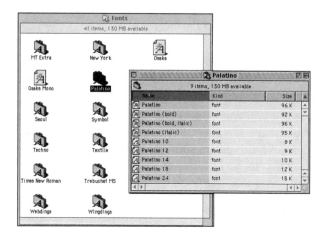

### Before Deleting

Obviously, you should think carefully before deleting any file. But it's particularly important with fonts (and other files in the System Folder) because you can't always anticipate when a program or document might need that particular font. If you want to simply deactivate a font so it won't be used for the time being, drag that font to a folder that resides outside your System Folder. (Create a "Disabled Fonts" folder on your main hard drive, for instance.) Now that font won't appear in the Font menu of any of your applications. If necessary, though, you still have the option of dragging it back into the Fonts folder if it's needed.

Remember, too, that many of the files in the Fonts folder are actually suitcase that have more than one font inside them (usually, but not always, in the same typeface family). If you don't want to delete the entire suitcase, you can drag individual fonts out of their suitcases and to the Trash.

## The Least You Need to Know

There are three types of fonts: TrueType, PostScript, and bitmap fonts. Each of these has its own purposes, although some more so than others. For instance, TrueType fonts, using a technology created by Apple and Microsoft, can be used both on the screen and with a printer. They're pretty good looking and easy to work with. Everybody likes TrueType. It's like the straight-A-high-school-quarterback of font technologies—just wholesome and attractive enough to make you a little queasy.

Bitmap fonts were the original Mac fonts, but now they serve as simple servants to PostScript fonts, which look great in print but not so great on the Mac's screen. (PostScript is what most laser printers—and the graphics pros who love them—use.) The bitmap fonts look good, at certain sizes, on the screen. So when you pick a PostScript font, a bitmap font is actually used to represent that font onscreen. If you pick the wrong size, though, the bitmap font will look bad, too.

Fortunately, all your font troubles will be solved by a program called Adobe Type Manager, so just get it and skip reading the rest of this chapter.

### See the Font

Want to look at a font without being forced to open an application and pull down the Font menu? If you're looking at a bitmap font or a TrueType font, you can simply double-click its icon to see a quick sample.

Fonts can be stored in suitcases and moved around on your Mac, but only under certain circumstances (your best bet is usually at 3:12 a.m. on a Thursday, so set your alarm clock). If you really want to delete a font—and you feel sure it's the right thing to do—just drag it to the Trash. Heck, you might have figured that one out even without a book.

# Chapter 17

# Networking Macs

> ## In This Chapter
>
> ➤ What is a network?
>
> ➤ Using the Network Browser
>
> ➤ Connecting to an AppleShare server
>
> ➤ Turning on File Sharing
>
> ➤ Get on the network from somewhere else

Since the Early Times, Macs have had networking built in. The ironic message, I guess, is that loner, rebellious, creative types that tend to gather around Macs are also collaborators, needing to share data, pass on what they've accomplished, and—c'mon, admit it—gloat a little bit about their achievements.

Well, such gloating—which we'll call "digital gloating"—is easy enough to do. Once you've gotten something accomplished on your Mac that you want to share with your colleagues, you'll want to send it out on the network. Of course, you'll need to know what a network is, first.

And, even if you're not some ultra-swank designer type with a fascinating haircut and a penchant for loudly colored patchwork pants, you're still going to want to know about networking. Small or medium-sized companies can definitely use networks as a way to help communicate, collaborate, and, uh…I can't think of a third one.

In many cases, you're already on a network, and you just need to know the basics, which are, in no particular order:

➤ How do I get my Mac to work correctly on a network?

➤ What's a network?

Let's touch on both of those briefly, after which you'll be ready to hop on the network, whatever that might be, and share your data with comrades.

# What's a Network?

A *network* describes a bunch of computers that are connected by special cabling to one another for the purpose of sharing files and peripherals like printers. With a file-sharing network established, you can place files on other computers that are attached to yours. Likewise, those other computers can access your computer, under some circumstances.

Actually, there are two types of Mac networks you'll encounter. Which one you have will dictate how, exactly, you'll deal with the files that you want to share with your colleagues. Here they are:

➤ *Client/Server network.* This sort of network has one central server computer (or a few of them) that the individual Macs log into. When you share things using this setup, everyone accesses just the server computer and saves their files in shared folders.

➤ *Peer-to-peer network.* In this setup, the network is designed so that you can log into individual Macs in order to share files. For instance, everyone may have a "shared" folder on their Macs where you drop stuff that you want others to have access to. When you need something from a colleague, you specifically access their computer instead of some central location.

Neither of these is the right or wrong way to do things, although each makes more sense in a particular setting. The client/server network is a good idea in large offices where a lot of people need to share the same data. The larger the office, the more likely you are to be able to afford a dedicated computer to act as the server computer.

In a smaller office, peer-to-peer is fine. After all, you're probably mostly working on your own Mac (not accessing mainframe computers in the basement or something), so you only occasionally need to access another computer. Plus, if you only have enough employees or colleagues to count on your fingers, it's not too much of a hassle to log in and out of their computers when you need information. Even in this case, it's a bit better to have client/server, though, because sharing files on your Mac can slow it down and make it less stable. If you can afford it, I'd recommend using a server computer whenever possible.

So which type of network you have depends, in some part, on where you'll find files—that is, are they stored on a central computer or on many computers? It also dictates how much logging-in you'll need to do. Fortunately, whether you're logging into a colleague's Mac or a network server, the process is usually the same.

This chapter will focus more on how Mac OS 8.5 does networking—things like logging in with the Network Browser, discussed in the section "Log In and Browse Around" later in this chapter. But there are some basics of Mac networking you might want to be aware of even if you aren't responsible for putting the network together yourself. If not, skip ahead.

## **Kenny Logs In**

What does it mean to "log in?" By that I refer to the process that your Mac goes through when you tell it to connect to another Mac. You choose the computer with a double-click; your Mac then asks this computer if it's okay for you to gain access, at which point you may have to enter a password. Once that checks out, the other computer will tell your Mac what folders you can have access to. Your Mac may ask you which you want to access. After choosing, that drive or folder appears on your Desktop. You've logged in.

## *The Software of Networking*

For starters, your Mac is likely to use a network protocol called AppleTalk to connect to the different Macs it'll encounter on the network. This is the software part of networking; the protocol is what tells the Macs how to talk to one another. AppleTalk is by far the most popular way to network Macs to one another and to some PC-based servers like Windows NT Server.

But there are other possible languages. If your Mac lives in a sea of PCs, your Mac uses IPX for networking, the Novell Netware protocol. Or if you deal with a lot of UNIX machines, you might be using TCP/IP, which is the networking protocol of choice for UNIX as well as for the Internet. (If you have an Internet connection at all, your Mac is definitely using TCP/IP, at least some of the time.)

On your Mac, there are different control panels that help you set up these protocols. With a typical installation, your Mac will include TCP/IP and AppleTalk control panels; these are used primarily to help you decide how such networking connections will be established. For instance, in the AppleTalk control panel, you'll need to choose the type of network cabling you're going to use for your AppleTalk network connection.

The TCP/IP control panel offers similar choices, although there's a bit more configuration that goes into TCP/IP. Because most Mac owners use TCP/IP for Internet access, we'll discuss it in depth in Chapter 18, "Getting on the Internet."

It's also possible to have two different networking protocols working at the same time; for instance, both AppleTalk and TCP/IP can be working to give you access to your local network of Mac and the Internet at the same time. But how do you know which hardware to pick for what?

*The AppleTalk control panel includes a pull-down menu that allows you to choose the hardware you'll use for your network.*

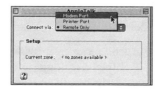

# The Hardware of Networking

Back in Chapter 16, "All About Fonts," I discussed both LocalTalk and Ethernet—the two types of network cabling you're likely to encounter. LocalTalk is slower but easier; it's built into every Mac that has a printer port. LocalTalk networks are usually "daisy chained" together, meaning the network cabling goes to one Mac, then the next Mac, and the next one, on down the line.

Ethernet is faster but can be a little more complicated. You need an Ethernet port or an Ethernet expansion card installed in your Mac. Ethernet comes in two different flavors—10BASE-T and 10BASE-2. 10BASE-2 is something you're less likely to encounter; it uses TV-cable-like coax cabling and can be daisy chained like LocalTalk.

**Times Ten**

There's another standard, called 100BASE-T, that uses the same sorts of connectors and cabling for Ethernet connections but can go up to ten times as fast. You'll need special Ethernet hubs and cards to support 100BASE-T with your existing Macs, but you'll find that new Macs will feature 100BASE-T. The 100BASE-T standard is backward compatible, too, meaning it can hook up to a 10BASE-T network with no trouble.

With 10BASE-T, which is more popular, you need an Ethernet hub. This is called a "star" topology, because each Mac connects to a central hub like the points of a star. (The daisy chain configuration is called a "bus" topology.) Each Mac is connected to the hub that is at the center of all activity. It makes it easy to find glitches, because a cabling problem can only affect the line between your Mac and the hub, not the entire network. With bus topologies (daisy chains), on the other hand, the entire network can go down if there's a problem.

Fortunately, you don't have to worry much about the actual topology of the network to configure your Mac. Instead, the AppleTalk control panel (or TCP/IP or MacIPX, depending on the protocol you need to use) simply makes you decide between LocalTalk and Ethernet. If you're using LocalTalk, choose the printer port or modem port (depending on which has the LocalTalk transceiver connected to it). If you're using Ethernet, just select **Ethernet** from AppleTalk's pull-down menu. If you have more than one Ethernet option, choose the one that is connected to the network.

# Log In and Browse Around

For basic, day-to-day Mac networking, the Network Browser will probably be your point of origin. Actually, the Network Browser is brand new in Mac OS 8.5, so I'm pretty much learning about it right along with you. It's a great short-cut compared to that old bear of an interface we used to have to use: the Chooser.

To access Macs over the network from the Chooser, you open it up and click the AppleShare icon. This brings up icons on the right side of the Chooser that represent the Mac servers that are connected to your Mac and can be logged into. (In this context, a server means any Mac you can log into, whether it's on a client/server or peer-to-peer network.) If your network is organized into different zones, you choose each of those zones separately by clicking the zone name in the lower-left panel of the Chooser.

### AppleTalk On and Off

If your Mac is on an AppleTalk network, you'll need to turn on AppleTalk as well as choose a type of hardware in the AppleTalk control panel. Most likely, the control panel itself will ask you to turn on AppleTalk if it's currently off. If you suspect that AppleTalk is off, though, you can also check in the Chooser, where the AppleTalk on/off buttons live.

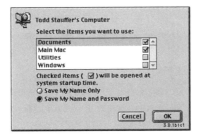

*The Chooser offers a series of steps before you can log into a Mac on your network.*

### AppleTalk Zones

AppleTalk zones are really just named groupings of Macs that network administrators can use to make it clear what servers are meant for what users. For instance, accounting can have its own "zone" (with or without passwords) that's designed to keep Macs in the Advertising zone from display printers that are physically located in Accounting. You can change zones in the Chooser, but you have to do it purposefully, making it less likely that users will log into the wrong network devices by mistake. In most cases, this is a corporate thing; if you're creating a small network, don't worry about zones.

Find the Mac you want to log into, and then double-click its icon. The resulting dialog box asks for your log-in information. Enter it and click OK. Now you may be asked which of the allowed folders you'd like to access. Make your choice(s), and they pop up on your Desktop, ready to use.

To disconnect from a server (if you've been using the Chooser), drag to the Trash all of the volumes from that server that you've placed on your Desktop.

### Two Other Connects

There's another way to connect to some Mac servers: You can use an IP address. If the server software supports a direct TCP/IP connection, you can click the **Server IP Address...** button in the Chooser, and then enter an IP address and click **Connect**. This connection is often a bit faster, too, but you'll need to know that IP number.

Want to log in quickly? The next time you have a particular server volume on your Desktop, create an alias to it. (Highlight the icon and choose **File, Make Alias** in the Finder.) Now, whenever you want to log onto that volume again, just double-click the alias, and you'll be asked to enter your user info.

## Network Browsing Made Easy

With the new Network Browser, though, things are a bit easier and more Finder-like. Open up the browser, and you'll see the different zones available to you. This works very much like List View in the Finder: To see the servers within a particular zone, you can either double-click the zone or just click the small arrow next to that zone to open it up and display the available servers. To see what volumes (drives or folders) you can access on a particular server, double-click the server or just click once on its arrow.

At this point, you may need to log into the server (after all, the server needs to know who you are so it can tell you what volumes you're allowed to see). Once you've logged in, a list of possible volumes now appears. To add one to your Desktop, just double-click it in the browser. Its icon will appear on your Desktop, and the volume's window will open. You're ready to access it.

Click a zone's
arrow to see
available servers

*The Network Browser
makes it a little easier to
see how you're logging in
because it's based on the
Finder List View.*

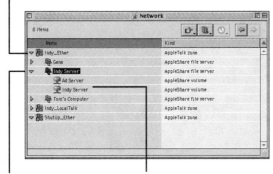

Click a server's
arrow to see
available volumes

Double-click a volume
to mount it on
your Mac's Desktop

### How to Browse

 I recommend using the small arrows; it makes available network servers easier to see, all in one window. But, if you're following the double-click method, you'll notice that this doesn't work exactly like the Finder: Double-clicking doesn't open a new window, it just shows completely new information in the same window. Actually, this works a lot like a Web browser if you've ever used one (see Chapter 19, "Working the Web"). To go back up a level—for instance, if you've just double-clicked a server, are looking at its volumes, and decide you want to head back to the list of server—click the left-facing arrow in the top-left corner of the window. You can click the right arrow to move back down again.

Logging out of a volume does the same thing with the Browser as with the Chooser: The volume disappears from your Desktop. Throw out all volumes for a particular server, and you'll automatically be logged out of that server; you'll need to enter your username and password again.

The Network Browser does some other things, too. For instance, you can double-click a server to show its volumes in a separate window. Experiment with the Network Browser to get a feel for how you best like to deal with your servers and zones. If you've used the Chooser in the past, you won't want to go back after you've seen the Network Browser.

## *Walkthrough: Logging Into a Server*

Just so it's clear, let's do a quick step-by-step on how to log into a server using the Network Browser. To begin, choose the **Network Browser** from your **Apple** menu. With it open:

1. Locate the zone in which your desired server is located and click that zone's arrow.

2. Now find the server and click its arrow to see what volumes are available.

3. You'll likely be presented with a log-in dialog box at this point. If you have a password for this server, choose the **Registered User** button (it's probably already chosen) and enter a **Name** and **Password**. Click **Connect** when you're done. If you don't have an account on this server and the server allows Guest access, you can choose the **Guest** option and click **Connect**.

4. Now in the Network Browser window, the available volumes will appear under the server you just logged into. To mount one of those volumes on your Desktop, double-click it.

5. Once the volume is on your Desktop, you can work with it just as if it were a normal hard drive in your Mac. When you're done with it, though, you can drag it to the Trash to unmount it (or select it and choose **File, Put Away**). Once you've unmounted all volumes from a particular server, that server is logged out; you'll need to enter your name and password again to gain access to it.

# File Sharing: Be Your Own Server

We've discussed peer-to-peer networking already, by talking about how logging into a peer server (that is, another Mac on your network) is very much like logging into a regular server computer. You do both through the Network Browser, following the same procedures. In fact, the only real difference is that a peer server is probably being used by a colleague instead of being dedicated to the job of being a full-time server.

Of course, there's another difference: Your own Mac can be a peer server. To be a full-fledged client/server machine, your Mac would need to be running AppleShare IP or a similar network server program. (AppleShare IP is professional-level server software available for Apple.) And, of course, you probably wouldn't want to check your mail and write your memos on an AppleShare IP machine, because it would be bogged down with the business of being a server computer. After all, the investment in a server computer probably isn't worth it unless you have more than a few Macs logging into it all the time.

But with File Sharing, your Mac becomes a server on a peer-to-peer network. Your colleagues can log into your Mac, copy files out of shared folders, and so on. In fact, your Mac becomes completely responsible for setting up the *network permissions* that determine who can log into your Mac, what their password is, and what they can access. Hopefully, you won't have more than a handful of people logging in at once;

otherwise, your Mac can slow down quite a bit—especially if your Mac is older. But if you need to share files every once in a while, you can't beat File Sharing's price. It's included with Mac OS 8.5.

## Make or Break People

If you'd like to use your Mac as a file server, your first step is going to be deciding who, exactly, can have access to your Mac. You do so by creating new profiles in the Users and Groups control panel. Each user is given a name and a password and, if you like, they can be put together into groups. Later you decide which users and which groups have access to various parts of your Mac's hard drive.

To create new users, open the **Users and Groups** control panel. Click the **New User** button to begin creating a new person. (Well, not literally a new person. That would take considerably more genetic material than we'll be working with.)

The New User window appears. Enter a **Name** and a **Password** for this user. If you'd like the user to be able to change his or her password, leave the **Allow User to Change Password** option checked.

If you've created groups already, you can assign this person to a group by choosing the Sharing item from the pull-down menu. Later, if you'd like to keep this person from accessing your Mac, you can do so by again selecting the Sharing item from the menu. When you're done, click the window's **close box**.

Create as many more users as you'll need to allow permission to log in. If you'd like, you can duplicate users by selecting one, and then clicking the Duplicate button. This allows you to create a user that has the same privileges as the one you duplicated, except with a different name and password. This is especially useful if you've already assigned a user to a particular group, and you want to create another member of that group. (If you haven't assigned any groups, though, duplicating users doesn't give you any advantage. Just create new users.)

You can change the name of a user by clicking once on the name and waiting half a second or pressing the **Return** key. You can edit the user's information and privileges by double-clicking the name.

## Putting Together a Posse

Creating a group gives you an opportunity to set permissions for more than one person at a time. Say you want everyone in the Web editing department to have access to your Web Pages Trial Run folder, but you don't want anyone in management to see it. Well, you can create two different groups: Web Editing and Management (or whatever). Now, when you go to assign sharing permissions in the section "Be Nice and Share," you'll be able to keep everyone in the Management group from seeing what's in that particular folder. You don't have to go through and set separate permissions for each individual manager.

To create a group, click the **New Group** button in the Users and Groups control panel. This brings up a quickie window for naming the group and adding users. Give the group a name in the input box, pressing **Return** when you're done or click elsewhere on the window. Now drag the names of individual users from your Users & Groups window into the New Group window (by now it's been renamed with whatever you called the group, but you know which one I mean). When you're done adding names, click the **close window** on the New Group window.

You've created a group. Just like an individual user, you can rename the group by clicking on its name in the Users & Groups control panel, or you can edit the group by double-clicking it.

*Drag users into the Group window to add them to the newly created or edited group.*

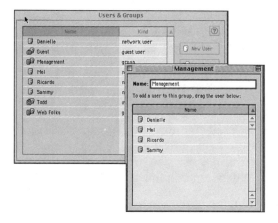

## Allowing Guests to Hang

I know you're on pins and needles waiting to find out about sharing privileges, but I just need to squeeze one more discussion in first. There's one user who's already created and whom you can't delete—no, not yourself. You can delete yourself, if you can convince yourself to do yourself in. In fact, I was referring to the Guest user.

You can't duplicate or delete the Guest. You can try, but you're just wasting valuable energy. What you can do is edit the Guest and allow or disallow guest access.

Guest access means that people can sign into your Mac without having a username and a password. In the right hands, it's a valued tool. But in the wrong hands, it could mean the end of civilization. (But only if you have end-of-civilization data—or any other important, sensitive information—on your Mac that a guest gets a hold of.)

To turn on guest access, double-click the guest user. In the Guest window, choose the **Sharing** item from the pull-down menu. Now place a check next to the **Allow Guests to Connect to This Computer** entry. Close the window, and guests can now connect.

# Turn On File Sharing

You're almost ready to set those elusive permissions. Such power! But first, you need to turn on File Sharing.

You may have a cool Control Strip module or some other fancy way to start File Sharing, but the most obvious way is to open the File Sharing control panel.

Once you've gotten it opened, you'll need to make sure the information at the top of the window is correct. Your username and password should be there, as well as the name you want other users to see in the Network Browser for your computer. (It can be a cutesy name or something simple like Todd's Computer. Not if your name isn't Todd, of course, although there seems to be a decent number of us.)

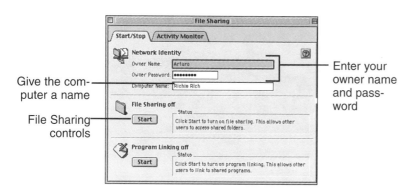

Give the computer a name

File Sharing controls

Enter your owner name and password

*The File Sharing window is also where you enter information about this Mac's owner.*

If all that is squared away, you're ready to start the sharing. Click the button that says **Start** under the File Sharing section of the window. (If it says **Stop,** then File Sharing is already active.) It may take a while when you first start up File Sharing, so be patient.

Next step, permissions.

# Be Nice and Share

Now, finally, it's time to set up your sharing permissions. By default, none of your users except you, the Owner, will have access to any drives or folders on your Mac's hard drive, even if you have File Sharing enabled. First, you're going to specify the disks and folders you want to share with others on your network. You don't do that in a control panel, though. To set up sharing, go to the disk or folder you'd like to share in the Finder. Now select it, pull down the **File** menu, and choose **Sharing** from the **Get Info** menu. (Or you can just open the Get Info window, and then choose **Sharing** from the pull-down menu.)

This results in the Sharing dialog box. Here is where you'll get to decide who's in and who's out. Who is cool, and who is not? It's up to you. Finally, you're the MPIC—Mac Person in Charge.

Here's the deal. In each of the three categories, you're going to have to input the correct answer in order to keep playing. Pull down the menu and choose who gets **Read Only** access, who gets **Read/Write** access, who gets **Write Only** access, and who gets no access. You've got 60 seconds which will be shown only on the clock that the audience at home can see on their screens. You've got to get them all correct, and in order, before the buzzer goes off. Any questions? On your mark, get set… (Sorry. I fell off into game show land again for a second there.)

The Sharing dialog box gives you a chance to determine who gets in and what they can do in a particular folder or drive.

Click to share this drive/folder

Choose the owner

Choose the access type over here

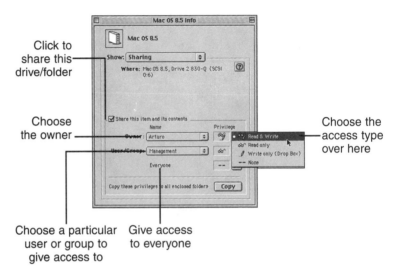

Choose a particular user or group to give access to

Give access to everyone

### Need More Groups

File Sharing is a bit limited in the number of permissions it can dole out; there's no way to squeeze more than one group into that User/Group listing. You can, however, have another set of permissions by adding yourself to a group, and then making that group Owner. Don't worry; it doesn't give everyone else in that group any more special privileges than they already have.

In the Owner menu, you'll probably want to choose yourself, unless you want to allow a foreign leader to usurp control over your drive—perhaps in response to a special treaty you have because your children have wed. Choose a privilege level for the Owner by pulling down the associated privilege menu. You'll see the different privilege levels listed in that menu.

Next, in the User/Group menu, pull down and choose the user or group to whom you'd like to give access to this drive. You can only choose one group to give permission to, so you'll need to included everyone who needs permission in that group. (At this point, you'll probably need to go back to the Users and Groups control panel and put them all in one group if you haven't already.) Choose a privilege level for them in their privilege menu.

Now choose a privilege level or all other registered users. For instance, you might give **Read** access to everyone, but only **Read and Write** access to the Owner and to the **Management** group. Or something like that.

Finally, you need to decide whether or not these privileges should be extended to all subfolders of this particular folder. If they are, you've given your users and groups access to all folders that are enclosed by the drive or folder you're setting now. If not, you'll have to set those others separately.

Close the Get Info window, and you're done. The privileges have been set.

### What the Privileges Really Mean

I might have lost you there talking about the different types of privileges. Maybe you've lived a privileged networking life, and you didn't realize that the rest of us live with virtual limitations. Well, take that digital silver spoon out of your mouth and let me tell you about earning your privileges.

There are four different levels you can set in the Sharing window: None, Read Only, Write Only, and Read/Write.

None means just that: If you have a None privilege, you can't see or use the drive or folder in question.

A Read Only permission means you can access the folder, but you can't save anything to it. A Write Only permission means you can access the folder, but you can't see or read any of its contents. (In fact, you won't be able to tell if it has files in it at all.) You can, however, save a new document in that folder that the Owner can then access. This is sometimes called a "drop box."

Full access is Read/Write privilege, which allows you to treat the network drive or folder as if it were one attached to your own Mac.

# Accessing the Network Remotely

Wouldn't it be nice if you could access the server at work from your PowerBook, sitting in a chair by the beach in Aruba like they do on all those TV commercials? It sure would. Too bad you used all your personal days back when you had that problem with your bridgework and that week you had to keep taking your dog to different vets. Not to mention the fact that Aruba probably doesn't have an island-wide cellular packet switching network for on-the-go Internet access. But it was a nice thought.

**Remote Payments**

Before you can access a server remotely, you'll either need to have AppleShare IP or the Remote Access Server (for individual File Sharing Macs) before you can access the drive remotely. Those both cost money.

You can access the server from the road, though—probably a cramped, artificially cooled hotel room in the heart of Cincinnati. With a phone line, your modem, and the right software on the server-side of this equation, you can dial into an AppleShare server and have the server's drive pop up on your Mac's Desktop. It'll work from home, too.

An AppleTalk Remote connection is the answer here, allowing you to dial into an AppleShare or Apple Remote Access server. It's just like a regular network connection, only you're going to use your Mac's modem to dial the phone and connect over a telephone line to the server. (You don't need any other sort of wiring.) If it's equipped to answer the call, your server will allow you to log in with a name and password. Then you're ready to use the Network Browser.

## Getting Ready for Remote

For a remote access connection to work, you need to first make sure that you've got AppleTalk activated. Open the **Chooser** and click to make sure AppleTalk in **On** (in the bottom-right corner of the Chooser window). Once you've gotten it turned on, close the Chooser by clicking its close box.

A Remote Access connection should work regardless of your AppleTalk hardware setting (in the AppleTalk control panel), but, if you like, you can switch to the AppleTalk control panel and choose **Remote Only**. This has the added benefit of not interfering with your serial ports when AppleTalk is turned on. On a PowerBook (most of which only have one serial port), this can be a major consideration, especially if you want to access the remote server and print at the same time using that port.

**Modem Necessities**

If you haven't already, you may need to configure the Modem control panel before you'll be able to dial out to a remote server. The Modem control panel is discussed in depth in Chapter 18, "Getting on the Internet." That discussion is equally applicable to remote networking.

Now all you need is the correct phone number for dialing in and the name and password you're supposed to use. From there, you're ready to create the connection.

## The Remote Dial-Up Connection

From the **Apple** menu, choose **Control Panels, Remote Access**. This is the control panel used to create a dial-up networking connection. In fact, it's used for all remote connections, which is new to Mac OS 8.5; previous versions of the Mac OS had a separate control panel (called "PPP") for modem-based Internet connections. That's not true any more. This control panel is used for both Internet and AppleTalk.

To use it for AppleTalk, you'll want to create a new configuration. Pull down the **File** menu and choose **Configurations**. Select the **Default** configuration by clicking its name, and then click the **Duplicate** button. Give the duplicate a name ("Dial Work" or something similar) and click **OK**. Now you have a new configuration to edit.

Select that new configuration and click the **Make Active** button. This will switch you back to the Remote Access control panel. Now enter your username and password in the appropriate entry boxes, and then enter the phone number for the server you're calling. If it's a long distance number, enter the entire thing in the entry box.

### Dialing Indirect

If you need to enter special numbers for an outside line, credit card, country code, or similar things, you'll want to use the Dial Assist control panel. Dial Assist is discussed in Chapter 18, and it works the same way for PPP or AppleTalk connections.

Click Setup to
see details

Phone number

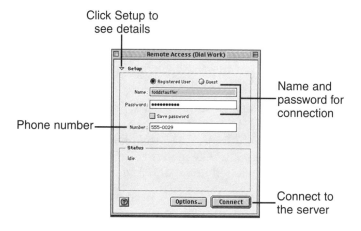

*The Remote Access control panel helps you dial into AppleTalk servers.*

Name and password for connection

Connect to the server

With this information entered, you can likely make the call, and everything will go well. You might want to check a few options, first, just in case. Click the **Options** button to see the Options dialog box.

The first place to head is the **Protocol** tab. On it, you'll find a pull-down menu. If it says Automatic, you should be fine. If you know you're dialing an AppleTalk Remote Access server, you can pull down the menu and choose **ARAP**, which means the connection won't waste any time testing for an Internet connection.

The **Connection** tab can be used for other options, like asking you if you'd like to stay on after a certain amount of idle time. The **Redialing** tab asks you to enter the number of times you'd like the remote number dialed before the control panel gives up on a connection. When you've made your choices, click **OK**.

Now, to connect to the remote server, click the **Connect** button. If you have the modem's volume turned on, you should hear it dialing, then you'll hear the squeal of the modem and, hopefully, the answering modem. After they've noticed one another, the volume should shut off, and you'll see the connect messages on the bottom of the Remote Access window. Finally, you'll see a Connected At: and Connected To: along with some animated level indicators that tell you that your Mac is up and running on the network.

Last step? Switch to the Network Browser and log into your server(s) as usual.

# The Least You Need to Know

A network is a collection of computers strung together by special cabling so that you can exchange files and, sometimes, use peripherals like printers. There are two major approaches to networking: client/server and peer-to-peer. Your Mac is capable of both. If you have a larger office, you may have Mac or PC-based servers you connect to for sharing files. In smaller offices, you may use a peer-to-peer system to log into your colleagues' Macs.

For any network, you need both software and hardware: The software is the protocol, like AppleTalk or TCP/IP, while the hardware is the cabling standard, like LocalTalk or Ethernet. Once you know which you're using, you'll know which control panels to configure, like the AppleTalk control panel or the TCP/IP control panel, and you'll know what to pick in those control panels, like LocalTalk or Ethernet.

With those things set, you can meet the Network Browser. New in Mac OS 8.5, the Browser makes it easy for you to see all the different servers at your disposal. You can log into the servers, choose shared drives and folders, and then move on to the next server. You can also use the Browser's Open/Save-like menus to create favorite servers and log in immediately to your most-used shared drives and folders.

If you want your Mac to be a server in its own right, you'll need to turn on File Sharing, create user and group profiles for anyone who wants to log in, and you'll need to set their privileges on your drive. With all that accomplished, your Mac can show up in other people's Network Browsers.

Finally, if you want to dial into an AppleTalk server remotely, you can do it using the Remote Access control panel—the same one used for Internet access. With the correct phone number, username, and password, you should be able to connect to a remote server from anywhere—even the beach, if you have a phone extension cord that's long enough.

# Part 4
# The Internet and Other Computers

*The mandate from on high tells us that no computer book can possibly be written in the late 1990s without referencing the Internet in a significant way. Fortunately, it's actually relevant in the case of Mac OS 8.5. No matter how you do it, you'll find out how to get your Mac connected, check your e-mail, surf the Web and even create and serve your own Web pages.*

*Plus, you can be proud in front of your friends and colleagues. After you've set up Internet access on your Mac, your life will be completely "buzzword-compliant." Congrats.*

# Getting on the Internet

These days, getting on the Internet is probably equal to just about anything else you might want to do with your Mac—especially in a small office or home office. You might want to write reports, play games, design newsletters, and get some work done, but you also want to get on the Internet. After all, that's what people do with computers.

Why? Because the Internet gives you access to hundreds of millions of other computers that are also connected to the Internet. As a result, you can send electronic mail (e-mail) to folks around the world, or you can view the electronic documents featured on World Wide Web sites of media outlets, companies, and individuals.

After you get on the Internet, you have both an amazing information resource and communications network at your disposal. In Chapters 19, "Working the Web," 20, "Checking Your Mail," and 21, "Building Your Own Web Sites," I'll show you different aspects of the Internet, including browsing the Web, dealing with e-mail, and creating your own Web pages.

In this chapter, though, we focus on first things first: You gotta *get* online if you're gonna *be* online.

# What Is the Internet and How Does It Work?

Saying "I'm going to use the Internet" is something like saying "I'm going to use the international telephone system." It just doesn't mean very much. If you're making an international call, you're using the telephone system, but that doesn't really matter. What matters is the person you're calling.

The same goes for the Internet. Technically, the Internet refers to the networking hardware that connects millions and millions of computers around the world. The Internet is not a particular place or a particular server computer; it is information that's available from literally millions of sources. What's important, then, is not that you're going to use the Internet for the connection, but whom you're going to "call."

## What Can the Internet Do for Me?

Giving your Mac access to the Internet enables it to send and receive electronic mail messages worldwide. You can also access file transfer centers (like downloading on an online service), databases of information, and discussion groups on nearly any topic. You can play games against live opponents 24 hours a day or "chat" with other folks by sending messages back and forth. You also can browse millions of pages of information on nearly every topic known to humankind.

You can also use the Internet for your own personal business. Send electronic messages to clients, the folks in the office, or to your grandkids. Transfer files from your office computer to your laptop while on a business trip. With the right connection, you can even use the Internet for desktop video conferencing by using two Macs, some small video cameras, and the right software. Impressed yet?

## How #1: Use an Online Service to Connect

Are you ready for the easiest way to get Internet access? Use an online service such as America Online. AOL is a popular service for computer users everywhere, with millions of members. It has the added advantage of offering its own content on non-Internet server computers that only AOL members can access, but you can still use a regular Web browser for access to the Internet itself.

In fact, to use almost any Internet program with AOL, you just launch it while AOL is active. You don't have to do anything else special; you can even use the versions of Internet Explorer and Netscape that are included with Mac OS 8.5.

## How #2: Use a Direct Connection

Another way to connect to the Internet is through your work or a school somewhere that already has access. In bigger cities, more and more apartment buildings and small office centers are offering direct Internet access, too. If your building does offer some sort of service, you should talk to your IS department or system administrator about exactly how you can start getting e-mail and access to other Internet applications on your Mac. If you're connected through your local area network, consider yourself lucky: You've got a high-speed connection that's perfect for the latest graphical interfaces to the Net. Heck, you could even run your own server.

## How #3: Get a Personal Internet Account

A great way to get access to the Internet from home is through a dial-up Point-to-Point Protocol (PPP) connection. Essentially, these connections allow your Mac to use its modem as a network service—almost as if you had a networking cable stretched between your computer and the Internet. A PPP connection is limited by the speed of your modem, but otherwise, using it is just like being there.

Think about this point: The Internet is a huge, global network of computers. What's a network again? It's a group of computers connected by wires that allow them to transfer information. Just like telephones are all connected by wires. (I'm ignoring cellular phones.) Unfortunately, you don't have Internet wiring strung along the poles outside your house—at least not in all cases. So, you can't just call the "Internet Company" and have them hook you up.

The next best thing is your phone. Using a modem, you can *simulate* a network connection by using the Remote Access software built into Mac OS 8.5 to call an *Internet provider*. When you call your provider, the software pretends that you're a computer connected to the provider's network, and you are free to use your own computer to roam the Internet—just as if you had a direct connection.

# Getting Yourself a Connection

A lot of home, home office, and small office users connect to the Internet using a modem. In fact, your Mac may include a modem that's built in. Using this approach is a perfectly reasonable solution. You can use other methods, but you have to decide for yourself what option is best. Of course, you'll probably want to know what your options are first, right? There you go again, being responsible.

Remember, an Internet connection is just a network connection to a global network, much like a regular AppleTalk network you could set up in your home or business. Because we can't all stretch a cable to the Internet backbone, though, we need more creative ways to add that connection. They all use TCP/IP, which is the "AppleTalk of the Internet," so to speak.

> ➤ *Modem*   A modem is a small box—or an internal expansion card—that allows your Mac to connect to standard phone lines to transfer data with other modem-equipped computers. Modems can be slow and somewhat unreliable (you may experience the occasional glitch), but using them is probably the cheapest way to get on the Internet, at least for the time being. Top speed for a modem transfer: about 52,000 bits per second or about three to five minutes to download a one megabyte file.

➤ *Integrated Services Digital Network (ISDN)*  If you live in a large city, ISDN may be a good choice for higher-speed access. In this case, your home or office phone lines are actually upgraded to digital lines. (Your current Plain Old Telephone Service—POTS—lines are analog; they transmit sounds, not digital data.) With digital lines, you get a network connection directly to the phone company, usually offering 64,000 to 128,000 bits per second connect rates, or about one to two minutes to download a one megabyte file. Depending on your service, though, ISDN can be expensive; you need a special network connector, the new phone service (sometimes metered, meaning you pay by the minute), and special Internet service access.

➤ *Digital Subscriber Line (DSL)*  This term actually describes a number of similar technologies, including Asynchronous Digital Subscribe Line (ADSL), which you'll hear referred to often. DSL is high-speed access over typical phone lines—provided you're close enough to your local telephone company's switch building and you have high-enough quality wiring in your house. DSL requires a special network box that is usually hooked up to the built-in Ethernet on your Mac (if you don't have Ethernet, you need an adapter card). Speeds start at 256,000 kilobits per second, or about 30 seconds to transfer a one megabyte file. At that speed, service is reasonably affordable—usually about twice the cost of a modem connection. Speeds can get higher, depending on the services in your area and your willingness to pay for the extra speed.

➤ *Cable*  Cable TV companies are getting into the act with a bunch of different approaches to Internet service—although they all involve that cable TV wire that's likely coming into your house right now. With a special converter box, you can hook up your Mac to the cable wire and receive an Internet feed, usually through your Ethernet port. Cable modem implementations vary widely; some may not even support Macs. The ones that do usually offer between 256,000 and 500,000 or more kilobits per second, which would translate into about one megabyte every 15 to 30 seconds. Prices and implementations vary but will likely be competitive when such connections get to your area.

➤ *Somebody else's problem*  Most of these sorts of connections are through a company LAN, your building (office or apartment), or some other service. In these cases, you plug your Mac or your networking hub into an Ethernet wall plug, enter the correct codes and passwords, and you have Internet access. Actually, you're probably using a T-1 or a shared T-1 line, but it doesn't matter. This type is the highest–speed Internet access for most individuals, and pricing varies widely—between $25 and thousands of dollars per month.

So that's access. After you've settled on a choice (if you want one of the high-speed services, you'll probably have to shop a bit and contact your phone or cable company for information), you'll need to pick an Internet service provider.

# Choose a Service Provider

An Internet service provider (ISP) is a company that gives you a pipeline onto the Internet. The company has a direct line to the Internet, and it is willing to sell you a piece of that connection for a price. Choosing a provider is a lot like calling the cable company and saying you want HBO: You call an ISP, get a phone number for your Mac to call and some important information for your TCP/IP control panel, and then you're good to go.

To find an ISP, you can take a number of approaches. Your best plan is probably to ask around locally to see whether you can find an ISP that offers good service and happy customers. You can find ISPs in local newspapers and computing weekly or monthly magazines, or you can just ask around. The easier route is to go with one of the national ISP companies; you can choose from a number of them, including the household names such as America Online. Or you can choose to work through the Mac's Internet Assistant to choose a provider. (EarthLink tends to be Apple's recommended choice.)

At least, this description explains how you go about finding an ISP for modem access, which is the most common way right now. You'll find that Internet service, more and more, is actually being offered by phone companies, utilities, and cable companies, too, which may have their own arrangements. If you want an ISDN or ADSL connection, for instance, you need to contract the special phone service from your phone company and then find a local service provider (which may also be the phone company) that can give you access to the Internet.

The cable company will likely offer the whole shooting match. Cable companies tend to have very controlling personalities; a lot of astrological Tauruses run cable companies.

# The Information You Need to Get

When you create your account, you get certain information from the ISP. This information includes the obvious pleasures such as your e-mail address and, perhaps, the ISP's Web address so that you can visit its Web site. But you need to know a few other things so that you can set up your Internet connection.

For any Internet connection, you need to know these things:

➤ *Type of Address*   Your Mac needs its own Internet Protocol (IP) address so that you can get on the Internet. That address can be assigned in one of two ways: temporarily or permanently. If you get a temporary IP address, then all you have to do is tell the TCP/IP control panel to ask for an IP every time it connects to the ISP. If you get a permanent IP, you need to know the exact four-digit number.

**What's My Number?**

An IP address is a unique location on the Internet. Every connected computer has one, and no two IPs are alike. An IP number is actually four different numbers separated by periods, like 255.255.255.0.

➤ *Configuration Addresses*    If you have a permanent IP, you need to know the subnet mask (usually 255.255.255.0) and the router address (another four-digit IP number).

➤ *Name Server Addresses*    For any sort of connection, you need to know the IP address for the ISP's name server. A name server is a special server computer that provides the convenient service of translating easy-to-remember addresses such as http://www.apple.com/ into their IP number equivalents. (In Apple's case, that's 17.254.0.91, in case you're curious.)

If you plan to use a modem or an ISDN connection to the Internet, you also need to know the phone number for your provider's answering pool of modems, your username, and your password. They are entered in the Remote Access control panel.

Although these modem connections are the slower Internet connections, the fact that they require a password gives you a special bonus: Anyone with a special password for communicating by computer automatically becomes a *secret agent*. (I'll pretend we've never met.)

## Setting Up and Testing

You'll have to figure out all the modem or other hardware on your own; it's too tough for me to worry about. (Most modems just plug into the modem port, while your Mac is off, unless they're already built in. With the modem plugged in, start up the Mac and run any software installers that came with the modem. For ISDN, you hook up the network box to the serial port on your Mac, or you use an expansion card. Then you spend countless days and nights configuring it with help from the phone company, James Dean, and the deity of your choosing. For other equipment, you have to hook up the network box to your Ethernet port with the correct cabling, usually a twisted-pair 10baseT cable.) Sorry, but you're on your own.

What we're worried about in this section are the TCP/IP and PPP (for modem and ISDN) control panels. Ready?

### Tickle Your TCP/IP

The TCP/IP control panel needs to know the nitty-gritty about your Internet connection. You've gathered most of those numbers for just this reason, and you've trained for this event all your life.

To begin, you might want to create a new configuration if TCP/IP is already configured for some reason. To create a new configuration, follow these steps:

1. Choose **File, Configurations** from the TCP/IP menu.

2. Select the **Default** configuration and click the **Duplicate** button. Give the configuration a new name and then click **OK.**

3. Click **Make Active** to activate the configuration; then click **Done** to get back to the TCP/IP control panel.

You have to enter a number of things in the TCP/IP control panel. If you plan to use a modem to connect, choose **PPP** from the **Connect Via** menu. If you're using ISDN, choose the special PPP entry for your ISDN adapter. (You should have installed software that goes with the adapter.) If you're using some other type of high-speed access, you'll likely choose **Ethernet**.

### Internet Assistant

Want to skip all this acronym stuff—the TCP/IPs and the PPPs? Run the Internet Assistant in the Assistant folder on your Mac's hard drive. It asks you most of these questions and sets you up automatically. Then you can refer to this section if you need to transfer settings to another computer or if you run into difficulty.

Choose connection type (PPP, Ethernet) here

Choose how to configure (manually or ISP's instructions) here

Enter an IP (manual)

Enter a subnet mask (manual)

Enter a router address (manual)

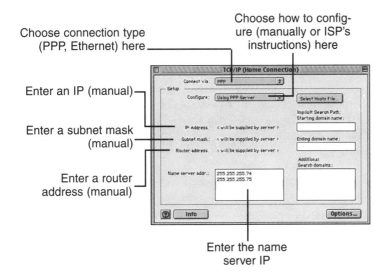

Enter the name server IP

*The TCP/IP control panel is one of the meanest, number-filled control panels on a Mac. Can you tell the Internet was developed by universities and the government using super-computers?*

Next, choose how the Mac will obtain an IP address. If you have a permanent IP, you choose **Manual**. Otherwise, ask your ISP which type of server you'll use. (Many ISPs use a PPP server.)

Now, again if you have a permanent IP, enter that number for the IP Address; then enter the subnet mask and router address, respectively.

Finally, for any sort of connection, enter the IP address for the Name server you plan to use. If your ISP gave you two addresses, just press **Return** after the first one and type the second address.

**Easier Internet**

If you don't have to enter these settings (because you used a more automated system such as EarthLink's or AOL's), try not to feel cheated. That's a good thing. Those services automate this process to make life a little easier for you. You probably don't have to enter TCP/IP info unless you have a local Internet provider (or one that focuses on Windows customers) or you're configuring to work with your company's network.

## Setting Up the Modem

This news just in from the Department of Redundancy Department: For a modem connection, you need to configure the modem. You should already have installed any software that comes with the modem itself, but you still need to set up the modem so that Remote Access knows what it's talking to. Pull down the **Apple** menu, select the **Control Panels** menu, and select **Modem** to open the Modem control panel.

Now, choose the **port** you're using for your modem connection from the **Connect Via** menu; then choose the **modem's name** from the **Modem** menu. If your modem doesn't have an entry, check your modem's documentation to see whether you can substitute a particular modem, or contact the manufacturer to see whether it can provide you with a new Open Transport modem script for your modem. These scripts are stored in the Extensions folder in a folder called Modem Scripts.

Next, decide whether your modem's sound will be **on** or **off** and whether you'll be dialing on a **tone** or **pulse** (rotary) line. Also, if you have a stutter dial-tone on your modem's phone line and you want your Mac to ignore it, click to put a check next to **Ignore dial tone**.

## Dialing for Access

If you have a modem or ISDN-based connection, you need to open your respective PPP control panel next. For a modem, it's actually the Remote Access control panel. For ISDN, it's the control panel that came with your ISDN adapter. (Remember, if you used an automatic dialer setup from EarthLink or AOL, you might not need to use Remote Access.)

In the Remote Access control panel, click the **Registered User** button to enter a username and password in their respective entry boxes. Now, enter the phone number for your Mac to call in the **Number** box. Next, click **Options**.

In the Options dialog box, click the **Protocol** tab. You can leave the entry as **Automatic**, or you can change it to **PPP**, which may help things connect a bit quicker. When you're done, click **OK**.

## Remote Access Options

If you're feeling a bit more daring, you can head into the advanced Remote Access options and change some dial-up behaviors. Want your Mac to sign off after a certain amount of inactivity on the Net? Click the **Options** button in the Remote Access control panel; then click the **Connection** tab. You then see the **Disconnect if idle for** option toward the bottom of the dialog box. Make sure it has a check mark so that it's active, and then enter the amount of time you want Remote Access to wait before it drops the connection.

### ISDN Differs

The ISDN PPP control panel that you use requires a little more setup, but it should feature the same basics: a phone number, username, and password. Check your documentation for other options.

Want Remote Access to dial out and connect to your ISP every time you launch an Internet application (or when you choose Check Mail or a similar command)? Click the **Protocol** tab, and make sure **PPP** is selected from the **Choose protocol** menu. Now, put a check mark next to the **Connect automatically when starting TCP/IP applications** option.

Finally, on the **Protocol** tab, you should see an option for **Connecting to a command-line host**. You may need to activate this option and choose to use a terminal window or a connection script for connecting if your ISP doesn't offer a more advanced method for initiating a PPP connection. Consult your ISP for more information on terminal window or connection script settings.

## Need Help Dialing?

If you're not dialing a local number, if you need to dial special numbers to get out of the office, or if you want to contact ship's security to get a secure line, then you need to open the DialAssist control panel. First, though, you need to change a setting in Remote Access. Choose **Edit, User Mode**. In the User Mode dialog box, choose **Advanced**. You also need to put a check next to the **Use DialAssist** option in the Remote Access control panel.

Now, open Dial Assist. To do so, choose the **Apple** menu, select **Control Panels,** and then select **Dial Assist**. The Dial Assist control panel appears.

You see the picture: You're going to have to figure this out yourself. (You're an Advanced User, right?) I'll give you a hint: Picking stuff from the menus is easy. In many cases, though, you need to edit what's in those menus. To do so, click the corresponding button at the bottom of the window. To enter your credit card number, for instance, click the **Suffix** button, select **My Credit Card,** and then click the **Edit** button. In the resulting dialog box, enter a new name and a number for the card, if you like. Click **OK**, and your credit card number is stored.

Now, don't let this Mac fall into the wrong hands.

241

*Dial Assist helps you dial for any outside lines, credit card numbers, and secret wire-tap blockage services that are necessary for you to get a clear modem connection.*

Enter your current area code

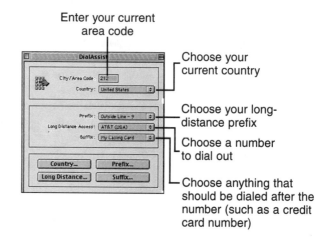

Choose your current country

Choose your long-distance prefix

Choose a number to dial out

Choose anything that should be dialed after the number (such as a credit card number)

## Finally—Testing Your Connection

If you've got a modem or ISDN connection, you can test your connection by opening the Remote Access (or your third-party ISDN PPP control panel) and clicking the **Connect** button. This operation attempts to dial your ISP and get you connected to the Internet. If you see the flashing lights, you are successful.

*A successful Remote Access PPP connection.*

If you have any other sort of connection that uses Ethernet, you should be able to test at any time. (I guess I could have told you this little factoid earlier.) Make sure your equipment is turned on and TCP/IP is properly configured; then launch an Internet application such as a Web browser. If the browser manages to connect, you're on the Internet!

## The Least You Need to Know

Getting on the Internet is probably just as popular as any other reason to own a Mac. The Internet means instant communications, research, news, and entertainment. It's a major reason to own a computer.

To get yourself on the Internet, you need to figure out how you're going to do it. A number of options exist, including using an online service or a special Internet service provider. Then you must decide what hardware you'll use: a modem, a direct connection, or a high-speed remote solution such as IDSN, ADSL, or a cable modem.

Now, you need to shop for your ISP. After you get an account, you need to set up some numbers, passwords, and configuration addresses correctly.

You begin setting up in the TCP/IP control panel; for many configurations, this setup is the only one you need. For modem and ISDN, you also need to configure Remote Access (or a similar PPP control panel). First, you need to configure the Modem control panel; then you can enter the username, password, and phone number for the Remote Access connection. Finally, you can test.

For an Ethernet connection, you usually just have to sign on with a Web browser. For a dial-up connection, open your Remote Access or PPP control panel and click **Connect**.

243

# Chapter 19

# Working the Web

---

## In This Chapter

➤ How the Web works

➤ Surfing basics

➤ Launching the browser

➤ How to search the Internet

➤ Multimedia and plug-ins

---

Along with the popularity of e-mail for sending nearly instant messages, the World Wide Web has played a very important role in the popularity of the Internet. Although "the Web," as it's called, is still a reasonably young entity (its earliest blips on the radar screen occurred in the early 1990s), it has emerged as an important medium in the world of publishing and commerce.

If you haven't yet experienced the Web, you'll probably enjoy yourself—after you find something useful and interesting. If anything is intimidating about the Web, it's taking a virtual machete to the foliage so that you can find what you're looking for.

# How the Web Works

The World Wide Web is a service on the Internet—one of many that includes e-mail, Usenet message groups, Internet Relay Chat, and others. By *service*, though, I don't really mean that anyone controls or provides the Web; instead, the Web is made up of individual server machines that are all designed to use standard protocols for sending Web pages back and forth.

### The Protocol Names

The protocol used to communicate Web data between a server computer and your Web browser is called HyperText Transfer Protocol, or HTTP. (You may have noticed that Web addresses tend to start with http; you'll find more details on that matter later in this chapter.) The language used to create Web pages is called the Hypertext Markup Language, or HTML. It's actually a pretty simple language, as you'll see in Chapter 21, "Build Your Own Web Sites."

On the Internet, the protocol is the thing. It's like the difference between talking on the phone to someone and faxing that person something. Talking requires certain types of equipment (telephone sets), whereas faxing requires different equipment (fax machines).

The Internet works that way on a Mac: Different services such as e-mail and the Web use slightly different protocols for sending data around. If any difference does exist, it's that you don't actually need separate equipment for e-mail and the Web. You do need different software, though.

## The Web Browser's Role and How It Works

The software you use for exploring information on the World Wide Web is called a *browser*; the documents that the browser displays are called *Web pages*. The browser's job is to locate and display Web pages from *Web server* computers on the Internet. You tell the browser an address for a particular page, and it finds that page's server computer, requests the page, and then uses the text, HTML formatting codes, and image files it receives to create and display the page.

This process is almost exactly like loading a word processing document over a network connection. You find the document on a network hard drive, load it using the Open command (or something similar), and it displays in your word processing application. The major difference is that, in a Web browser, you need to use full Internet addresses instead of just filenames.

Back and
Forward
buttons

Home
page

Address
locator box

*Microsoft Internet
Explorer showing a typical
Web page and the ele-
ments you'll find on that
page.*

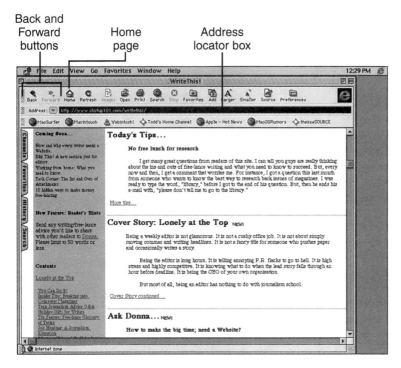

The browser window
(where Web pages display)

Hypertext
link

The browser is a little more than just a document viewer, though; it's also a document
"navigator" or "explorer," helping you move to the next Web page, search for pages,
or change addresses to look at something else. You might notice that my word choices weren't accidental; Microsoft Internet Explorer and Netscape Navigator are the two
most popular Web browsers available for the Mac. You can see why they're named
what they are.

So how do you explore? If you know the page you want to visit, you can enter its
address in the locator box at the top of the window. Enter the entire address; then
press **Return** to send your browser off on its hunt. (You need to have your Internet
connection already established if you use Remote Access or some other PPP control
panel, as described in Chapter 18, "Getting on the Internet.") When the browser finds
that page, it begins displaying the page in the browser window. You can find Internet
addresses just about anywhere—magazines, newspapers, TV commercials,  and so on.

What if you don't have a particular address in mind? The other way to get around on
the Web is by clicking hypertext links. A *hypertext link* is underlined, "active" text
within the document that's designed to take you to a new document of the Web
author's choosing. Usually, a hypertext link takes you to a document on a related
topic.

If you don't like where that link takes you, you can click the **Back** button to move back to the previous page. If you want to move to the new page again, click the **Forward** button. (Some people can be very indecisive.)

The **Home** button should take you directly to a page you've designated as your "home"—usually a page with lots of links and interesting, dynamic things to read, such as a news portal page. Such pages have news headlines, features, links, sports, entertainment, horoscopes, and that sort of thing; often they are like a mini-newspaper you can use as your jumping-off point onto the Web.

### Hypertext: Why It's Called "Surfing"

Ever wonder why Internet propeller-head types call being on the Internet "surfing"? It all begins with hypertext.

Clicking hypertext links is like Web roulette: You never know quite what the result will be. The page you click to may be what you wanted, or it may only partially cover the topic, so you click another link to learn more. That's why being on the Net is like surfing: You catch a wave of information and then move along it to stay with the "break" by choosing new links and trying to continue your info-gathering momentum.

You can do this surfing for fun. For instance, say you're at the CNN sports site reading a page about the American League all-stars, and next to a picture of one of the league-leading batters is a link to the Texas Rangers Home Page. You click that link, and you leave the CNN site; now you're reading about the Rangers organization when you see a link to Arlington, Texas, which is the city where the Rangers are based. Click that link, and suddenly you're reading about a resort town, including attractions such as Six Flags over Texas, which features Warner Brothers cartoon characters. Click that link, and you're at the official Bugs Bunny Web site.

How's that for catching a wave? That's surfing for you. It can certainly be diverting, but it's also an interesting way to learn a lot about related—and, sometimes, not-so-related—topics.

## URLs: The Internet's Address

Not into surfing? You can enter the direct address to a Web page in your browser's address box, but you need to know how. Here's the quick primer on URLs.

The Uniform Resource Locator (URL...I say it like *Earl*) standard is the address scheme used to locate any resource on the Internet. For Web pages, this addressing scheme allows you to directly access any of the perhaps billions of Web pages available to your browser.

An URL is constructed of three different elements:

➤ The protocol name for the Internet service in question: for the Web, that's `http://`

➤ The Web server computer's address, as in `www.apple.com`

➤ The directory and document where that Web page is stored on the Web server computer, such as `support/index.html`

Taken together, these three elements make up a Web URL. For instance, the example creates an URL that looks like `http://www.apple.com/support/index.html`, which goes directly to Apple's Web server computer (`www.apple.com`) and loads a page called `index.html` that happens to be in the `support` folder on that server machine.

In most browsers, you don't have to enter the `http://` part if you don't want to, but otherwise Web URLs are constructed this way.

# Pre-launching and Launching the Browser

Starting a Web browser is just like starting any other application. You just double-click it in the Finder or choose it from the Apple menu or an "App Launcher" that you've created. You need to have your Internet connection active if it uses the Remote Access or PPP control panel, but that's about all the worry you need over starting a browser.(In fact, you can tell Remote Access to launch itself automatically when a browser is activated, as discussed in Chapter 18.)

## Internet Preferences

Eventually, you may want to change a little about how your browser works. Although some browsers have their own Preferences commands, with most modern browsers, these settings are actually stored in a central place: a control panel called Internet in Mac OS 8.5.

You will discover two great things about this control panel. First, it allows you to set your Internet addresses and preferences in one place, which most of your Internet applications can then access on their own. Second, this control panel allows two or more people to share an Internet connection, switching between e-mail accounts, Web favorites, and other preferences.

*The Internet control panel gives you access to universal Internet preferences.*

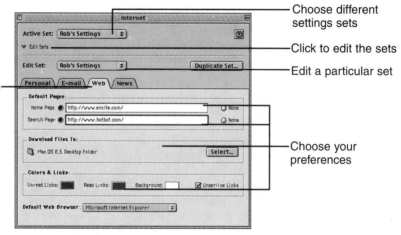

Choose different settings sets

Click to edit the sets

Edit a particular set

Click the Web tab

Choose your preferences

### Download Defined

What's a download? When your Mac is accessing the Internet, it actually copies the Web document and any associated images to your Mac. They're saved in a buried "cache" directory in the Preferences folder of your System Folder. That's a download—when your Mac copies and saves a file from across a network. If you *specifically* download a file other than a Web document— say a shareware program file or an Apple update installer—then that download is stored somewhere on your hard drive where you can get to it. You can set that default folder (or the Desktop) in the Internet control panel. In fact, in most browsers, you can Ctrl+click to select **Save Link To Disk** (or a similar command) from a contextual menu.

You might want to pop this control panel open first and set a few things, although doing so is not absolutely necessary. In fact, this control panel contains only a few different settings for Web browsing, and you may not want to change them until you've explored a bit.

If you want to change some settings, first make sure you're editing the correct profile set. Begin by clicking the **Edit Sets** arrow to show the Editing area. Then pull down the **Edit Set** menu and choose the one you want to use. (If you want a new set, click **Duplicate Set** and give the new set a name.)

Now you can edit the preferences:

➤ *Home and Search Page*   To change one of these pages, just click and highlight the **URL** in the entry box, and type your own URL (or paste it in).

➤ *Download folder*   To change the default folder for downloads, click the **Select** button.

➤ *Link colors*   To change a text link color, click the **color box** and the Color Picker shows up (see Chapter 25, "Apple Extras").

➤ *Default browser*   At the bottom of the screen, you can choose the default browser from the pull-down menu. Here, you choose which browser appears when you click an URL in another program, such as your e-mail program.

## Surfin' Walkthrough

With the Preferences out of the way, how about walking through a quick Web browser session? If you're already comfortable with Web browsing, you can skip this example, but it's a great way to get started if you're not get much of a surfer.

1. To begin, make sure your Internet connection is active. If you use a modem, open the Remote Access control panel and click **Connect**. (This step assumes you've correctly set up a connection in Chapter 18. Of course, the connection can also start up when you launch your Web browser, discussed in Chapter 18.)

2. Start your Web browser. You can either launch the application (probably Microsoft Internet Explorer or Netscape Navigator) from the Finder, or you can pull down the **Apple** menu, select **Internet Access,** and then select **Browse the Internet**. This step starts your default browser.

3. Wait for things to load. If all goes well, your home page will load. (If you haven't set a home page, you're probably looking at the Microsoft or Netscape home pages. These companies feel no shame in a bit of free advertising.) Check out the default page by scrolling around, reading things, and even clicking an interesting hyperlink or two. Remember that clicking the **Back** button returns you to the original page.

4. Enter an URL. Place the cursor in the Address entry box, delete the address that's there, and enter **www.apple.com** or **http://www.apple.com.** Then press **Return** when you're done.

5. The Apple home page should load now. Again, click hyperlinks and experiment. Remember that images can be links, too. Usually, images have a blue border if they can be clicked.

That's about it. Browsing is actually pretty simple. You might encounter only a few other things. Occasionally, you'll click a link for a downloadable file, which brings up a dialog box in Navigator or the Download Manager in Explorer, showing you the progress of the download.

## Multimedia, Plug-ins, and Java

Click some multimedia links, and a *plug-in* loads, too. A plug-in adds some sort of capabilities—such as the ability to play digital movies or sounds—to the browser window. In those cases, you might get a QuickTime movie

**Plug-in Mania**

Plug-ins exist for many reasons and are written by many different third-party developers. Usually, a downloaded plug-in installer puts the files in the right place, but if you need to install a plug-in manually, you just drag the plug-in file to the **Plug-ins** subfolder, usually found in the main Internet Explorer or Netscape folders.

### Java Enabled

If you get a message that Java isn't enabled, you'll want to enable it before you can access a Java-enabled page. Chapter 25 discusses setting up your browser and using Java in general.

playing right in your browser window. (See Chapter 23, "QuickTime and Multimedia," for more details on QuickTime.)

Some links will lead you to a Java-enabled page—Java is a special programming technology that allows the same program to run on all different types of computers. (Usually you need a Mac-specific program to run on a Mac, a Windows-specific program to run on Microsoft Windows, and so on. With Java, you can run the same program on both operating systems.)

Some Web pages include small programs—called Java applets—that run within the Web browser window. Once the page loads, you'll be presented with the applet—often a calculator, stock ticker, ad banner, game, or similar single-purpose program. All Java applets differ, so you need to use the instructions on the page to work with the applet.

### Helper Apps

Sometimes clicking a link attempts to load a "helper application" or an application designed to run the particular file that's been downloaded. If you find you need to edit the helper applications, that Internet Explorer uses, you can do so by opening the Internet control panel and choosing **Edit, User Mode** then **Advanced**. This causes a new tab, **Advanced** to appear in the Internet control panel. Select that tab, then choose the **Helper Apps** icon. Now you can select a type of file and click the **Change...** button to determine what helper application will be used to open a that type of file.

## Mail-to Links

Click some "send e-mail to" type links, and you'll likely open a mail message in your e-mail program. This special sort of link is called a *mailto* link; it can automatically open a new message in your default mail program. In fact, it might even load the mail program if that program is not already running.

You'll need to have your browser set up to handle a mailto link. If you have an e-mail account set up in the Internet control panel, mailto links should work fine. In other cases, you may need to access the Email preferences for your browser and enter a valid e-mail account. In Internet Explorer, choose **Edit**, **Preferences**, then click the **General** entry under E-mail. For Netscape Navigator, choose **Edit**, **Preferences** then select **Identity**.

# Adding Bookmarks and Searching

Two major issues crop up when you finally get used to using your Web browser for good instead of evil. First, how are you going to find cool stuff? Second, if you come across a site you really enjoy and think you might want to visit again, how do you remember it? Well, you'd better have a pad and pencil ready to jot down all those URLs, right?

## Making Note of Your Favorites

Put the pencil down and back away slowly. If you want to remember that URL so you can visit it later using this same browser, you can *bookmark* the site. Basically, this process causes the site's URL to be stored by the Web browser program for later reference.

In Netscape, choose **Bookmarks, Add Bookmark** from the menu while the page is showing in your browser window. Internet Explorer works the same way, but its menu command is **Favorites, Add Favorite**. Now you can pull down the Bookmarks or Favorites menu at any time, choose a bookmark name, and you are whisked back to that page—assuming, again, that your Internet connection is up and running.

## Searching the Internet

You actually already learned one way to search the Internet back in Chapter 4, "Actually, Uh, Finding Things." This is the same song, second verse. Instead of using the **Find** command, you can just go straight to a search page and enter keywords.

The easiest way is to click the **Search** button in the toolbar of your browser program; you should see a magnifying glass or something similar at the top of the browser window. Clicking this button takes you to the default search site. Eventually, you'll learn some of the other methods and decide which you like best, which you can then add in the Internet control panel.

**Uh, Entering Keywords**

See Chapter 4, "Actually, Uh, Finding Things" to learn more about entering keywords for Internet searches.

The following are some search sites to get you started:

- ➤ http://www.yahoo.com
- ➤ http://www.excite.com
- ➤ http://www.hotbot.com
- ➤ http://www.lycos.com
- ➤ http://www.infoseek.com

Each site has a slightly different interface for searching, but most of them make sense. You enter keywords, you click a button, you win a prize (or, at least, you get a listing of related Web page hyperlinks).

# The Least You Need to Know

On the Internet, the Web is the place where all the fun is happening. You're not cool, you're not straight-up, you're not the bomb if you don't have Web access. Hey, I don't make the rules; I simply conform to the letter of each and every one of them.

Here's a rule: You need a Web browser program to browse the Web. The popular ones are Microsoft Internet Explorer and Netscape Navigator. Armed with a browser and a little knowledge, you can start entering Uniform Resource Locators (URLs) and get straight to the Web pages you want to see. Or, if you're feeling a bit more dude-ish, you can surf the Web, clicking hyperlinks to see where they take you.

When you get deeper into the Web, you'll know what sort of a page you'll want to call home. You can enter that preference along with a number of others in the Internet control panel. You can even create different Sets (or preference profiles) for the different folks who use your Mac.

Get used to the Web, and you'll wish you had a way to make a quick note when you like a site. You can do just that—with a bookmark or a favorite. Depending on your browser, you can add one or the other of these features for handy references to the Web site you really like.

Not even sure where to go yet? Check out a search engine (or use the Mac's **Find** command). In either case, you'll be surfing the Personally Satisfying Big Waves of Intelligence in no time flat!

# Chapter 20

# Checking Your Mail

---

## In This Chapter

➤  What is Internet mail?

➤  Setting up for e-mail

➤  Launching and using Outlook Express

➤  Reading and replying

➤  Dealing with attached files and documents

---

E-mail is almost never bills, which is more than I can say about the mail I get from the post office. Although I get plenty of junk mail using either mechanism—whether physical junk letters or electronic ones—e-mail has certainly proved useful for both personal and professional pursuits. Not only is using e-mail a quick and efficient way to communicate with someone across great distances, but in some ways it's actually reviving the personal letter, allowing people to sit down and write what they feel to friends and loved ones.

In this chapter, we'll take a look at what e-mail is and how it works; then I'll walk you through the settings for your e-mail program. If you use the e-mail that comes with Mac OS 8.5, you'll be launching Microsoft Outlook Express, so I'll show you how it works, too.

# What the Heck Is E-mail?

Using the Internet, you can send messages to anyone who has an e-mail address. Using e-mail, then, is sort of like having an intra-office memorandum system for just about the entire planet. If you have loved ones in another part of the world, colleagues you want to keep in touch with, or if you've run to a small island to avoid tax problems, then e-mail is a great, inexpensive way to keep in touch.

E-mail is nearly instantaneous, and it doesn't require you to sit next to your computer all the time. Instead, messages wait in your electronic mailbox at your Internet service provider until you're ready to look at them. When you check your mail, you download the messages to your Mac, where you can then read them.

## How Does E-mail Work?

At the most basic level, an e-mail program is a text editor, like SimpleText. E-mail messages are text documents that can be sent across the Internet from e-mail server to e-mail server. When one is sent to your e-mail server (probably a computer at your ISP or in your company's Information Systems department), the server checks to see what the username is. If the message is addressed to your username, that message is put in your mailbox.

At that point, all an e-mail program (or a "client" as it is usually called) does is access your mail server, ask it whether any messages are waiting in your mailbox, and download them. If you do have any messages, you see them appear in your e-mail program's In Box.

Depending on your e-mail program, you either single- or double-click a message subject in your In Box to read it. After reading it, you can forward the message, reply to it, file it, or delete it. Then you can create new e-mail messages if you like.

You can even attach documents and other files to your e-mail messages and send them along with the e-mail messages. That way, your recipients not only get a note, but also a document or file that they can use on their own computers.

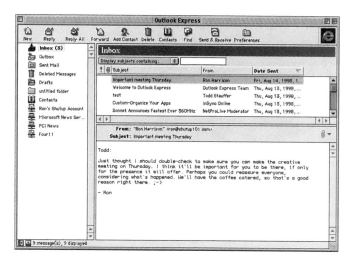

*Most e-mail programs use an In Box/Out Box and a memo metaphor for e-mail. Viewing your messages is pretty much like being at the office every time you sit down at your computer. (Is that a good thing?)*

# What's in an Address?

You don't need one of those automatic metering-stamp things to be able to send an e-mail message, even though they're really cool. You do, however, need to get the address right. Every e-mail user has a unique e-mail address. Usually, your e-mail address is your username, the @ (at) symbol, and your ISP's—or your organization's—domain name. Consider these examples:

**sjobs@apple.com**

or

**tstauffer@aol.com**

I mentioned URLs in Chapter 19, "Working the Web"; a domain name is the part of an URL that references a particular business or organization. **apple.com** is a domain, for instance, as is **aol.com** or **earthlink.net**. The difference between URLs and e-mail addresses is that you're trying to reach a particular person in that organization, so you put his or her unique username plus the @ in front of the organization's domain. Occasionally, you'll find that you send mail to an address like **todd@mail.nocompany.com** (which includes the computer named "mail" in the address), but that's rare. Usually, you just send it to the *user* "at" *someplace* "dot" *com*.

**Hidden Meaning**

Those three-letter endings actually have a meaning; they're used to help identify the sort of organization a particular Net address represents. **.com** is a commercial entity; **.org** is an organization (usually non-profit or political); **.net** is a network provider, usually an ISP; **.edu** is an educational institution; **.gov** is a U.S. government location; and **.mil** is a military base. Other two-letter add-ons are for non-U.S. addresses, such as **.au** for Australia and **.fr** for France. One day, the additional endings we've been promised for years, like **.web**, **.store**, and others, will be added.

# Pre-launching and Getting Started

Mac OS 8.5 comes with yet another Microsoft product for dealing with your e-mail messages: Outlook Express. Although something of a holy war is going on between Internet Explorer and Netscape Navigator aficionados, most people agree that Outlook Express is a decent program for its price—free. It can handle most e-mail tasks efficiently, and it even manages some other things—like dealing with Usenet message groups.

**Internet Setting Blues**

The Internet control panel is brand new in Mac OS 8.5, but its under-pinnings are older. They come from a third-party solution called the Internet Config. Over the past five years, Mac Internet applications have become more and more com-patible with Internet Config, so most of your applications should work with the Internet control panel. Rather old versions (many years) may not recognize the Internet control panel, forcing you to set preferences within the pro-gram itself. (If you're lucky, you won't have to mess with these set-tings at all; they may already be entered for you.)

Let's start at the beginning. Before you start with Outlook Express or another e-mail program, you should enter your Internet settings first. If you haven't already been through the Internet Assistant (or if you want to set up a second configuration), now is the time to open the Internet control panel.

## *Personal Internet Settings*

To set up, edit, or add your e-mail account, you should head to the **Control Panels** menu, where you'll find an entry for the **Internet** control panel. Choose it and make sure the **Edit Sets** arrow is clicked and pointing down to reveal the editing options.

The first thing you need to decide is whether you're going to use a new configuration. If you want to cre-ate a new configuration, click the **Duplicate Set** button, give the new configuration a name, and click **Duplicate**. (You can use the same configuration for all your Internet preferences; just make sure that you're editing the one that's for you, not a coworker, sibling, or significant other. These folks may not *want* their e-mail programs to beep instead of flash.)

If you worked with the Internet Assistant when you first installed the Mac OS, you may already have some of the personal information filled in. The Internet Assistant is the one that walked you through creating or adding an Internet account for your Mac; it's described in Chapter 19.

If none of the personal information is filled in, go for it. Enter your name and your return e-mail address. Note that the return e-mail address is the address that you give out for people to send you messages, not necessarily the address for your ISP account. (The name you enter here will be given out, too, so leave it blank if that's a problem.)

You can also enter your organization's name, if you want it to be included in the identification portion of the e-mail message (called a *header*).

In addition, you can create a signature in the signature box at the bottom of the screen. This signature is included at the *end* of all your e-mail messages and can include your name, e-mail address, Web sites, phone numbers, or anything else you want to divulge about yourself, including favorite quotes, jokes, or whatever. You should keep to four or five lines, but don't be afraid to brag a little bit about what you do for a living, your hobbies, or affiliations. Just remember that this info is attached to all your e-mail messages—including important business messages, if you send any. Make sure your signature is appropriate for those communiqués, too.

## E-mail Account and Server Settings

After you've made your personal settings, you can configure your connection to the ISP (or your company server) to get your mail. You need to have some information handy from your ISP or system administrator at this point.

**Which Address to Give?**

In some circumstances, your return e-mail address may be different from the address you use to check your e-mail. Usually, people use two addresses because they want their e-mail set up that way. For instance, I've established my own domain, mac-upgrade.com, for certain uses. One of my e-mail addresses is answers@mac-upgrade.com. When you send e-mail to that address, though, it actually goes to an account on my ISP's server, like todd@my-isp.net. (That's not the address.) I sign into my-isp.net, but for business reasons, I like to use the mac-upgrade.com account. So, that's the one I use on the **Personal** tab.

Use the text boxes to enter the following information (you can press the **Tab** key to move to the next box):

➤ *User ID*   Your username on the service. It's the part of your e-mail address that comes before the @ symbol.

➤ *Incoming Mail Server*   Often called the POP server, the address you're supposed to use for incoming mail. It's often, but not always, the same as the outgoing mail server. It's also often "mail" followed by a "dot" and whatever your ISP's or company's domain is (assuming your company *actually runs* the mail server).

➤ *Password*   Your e-mail password, which is sometimes but not always the same as your password for the Internet account (for example, what you use in the Remote Access control panel).

➤ *Outgoing Mail Server*   Often called the SMTP server. If your ISP says it has a separate SMTP server, you enter that address here. Often, but not always, it's "smtp" followed by a "dot" and your ISP's domain. It's also sometimes the same as your incoming mail server.

After entering this information, you can click to choose how you want to be notified of new messages. (Not all e-mail programs recognize this setting, but most do.) You can also use the pull-down menu to choose your default e-mail program. If you don't see yours, choose **Select** and use the Open dialog box to find the e-mail program you want to make the default. Click **Open** after you find the e-mail program you want to use. (The default e-mail program is used whenever an e-mail command is launched by another program. For instance, if you click a "mailto" link in your Web browser, it should open in the default application.)

That should do it for settings. Click the control panel's **close box** when you're done adjusting things.

**Advanced Mail Options**

The Internet control panel offers a few advanced options that deal with Internet e-mail. With the Internet control panel open, choose **Edit, User Mode** then choose **Advanced** in the dialog box. A new Advanced tab appears in the Internet control panel. Click the **Advanced** tab and you'll see an icon for **Fonts** which allows you to choose the font for various different situations in your e-mail (and other Internet) programs. Another icon, **Messages**, allows you to enter a "quote" character string and any text you'd like to add to the "header" of your e-mail and/or Usenet newsgroup messages.

## Launching Outlook Express

To start Outlook Express, you can either double-click its icon in the Finder, or you can open the **Apple** menu, select **Internet Access**, and then click on **Mail**. If Outlook Express is your default mail program, it loads at this point.

If you've never launched Outlook Express before, you are asked first whether you want to import saved e-mail messages and contacts from another program. If you've used another e-mail program on this Mac before, you can click **Yes**; otherwise, click **No**. Clicking Yes opens a dialog box that includes e-mail programs currently installed on your Mac. Make sure that a check mark appears next to the one you want to import from, and click **OK**.

With that situation solved, Outlook Express opens and immediately shows you your Internet settings. They are actually the *internal* Outlook Express settings, which offer many more options than the Internet control panel does. Still, if you've set up the Internet control panel, you should have just about everything covered. You can either examine these settings or just click **OK** to move on.

Now you're at the main interface. Notice that it has three different window panes: one for folders, one for the list of received messages, and a third for displaying those messages. To test the interface, click once on the **Welcome to Outlook Express** message. Its text should appear in the lower-right window pane.

# Getting, Reading, and Writing Messages

You've already read at least one e-mail message in Outlook Express—the Welcome message. You're pretty much an old hand, now. All you have to do is click a message's subject in the In Box, and it appears in the message pane. You can also double-click a message to open it in its own window.

After you're done reading a message, you can move it to a folder for safekeeping, if you like. To create a new folder, choose **File, New, Folder** from the menu. A new, untitled folder appears on the left side in the folder list. Type a new name for the folder. Now, you can drag and drop a message to that folder, or you can **Ctrl+click** on the message subject and then choose **Move To** and the folder's name from the contextual menu.

## Message Retrieval

Before you can read messages, you need to retrieve them first. Fortunately, this operation is easy.

Begin by making sure that you're connected to the Internet (through the Remote Access control panel if you're using a modem). If you are, you can click the **Send & Receive** button in the Outlook Express toolbar, or you can select the **Tools** menu, select **Send & Receive,** and then select the option for how you want to send and receive. You can choose **Send & Receive All**, just **Send All**, just **Receive All**, or you can pick a particular account if you have more than one set up. (Of course, you can also set up Remote Access to dial the Internet automatically, as discussed in Chapter 19.)

After you make that choice, the status window appears, showing any waiting messages being downloaded. If you receive something, your indicator of choice (a sound, blink, or dialog box) makes itself known, and new boldface messages appear in the In Box. Click one to read it.

## Want to Reply?

With a message open in the message pane, you can reply by clicking the **Reply** button in the toolbar. (If your message was sent to you and other recipients, you can include them all in your reply by clicking the **Reply All** button.)

Replying to a message this way automatically adds the e-mail address of the sender to your message, puts the prefix RE: in front of the sub-

### Got Two People?

If more than one person has an e-mail account, and you both want to be able to use Outlook Express, you can. Select **File, Change Current User**. You have to go through some setup the first time, but doing so makes using the same version of Outlook Express a pleasure.

ject line, and, according to your preferences, it may quote all or part of the message in the reply. ("Quoted" text appears in the reply by default with a > (greater than symbol) to the left of the text. This symbol reminds the recipient what he or she said in the original message.)

*Sending and replying to messages are similar processes, focusing on the message writing window.*

Which account this message will be sent from

Who the message is to

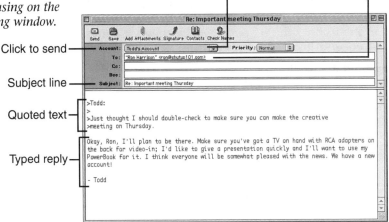

Click to send

Subject line

Quoted text

Typed reply

**Quoting Netiquette**

Note that when I say "cut down" the message, I don't mean to imply that you should edit the actual body of the sender's message so that it might change the meaning of the message. Editing would be bad "net etiquette," or *netiquette*. Instead, all I mean is that you shouldn't quote long passages if you plan to respond to only one or two points in the original message. Instead, quote only the relevant parts of a message; then type your own response.

Now you can type your reply into the Reply window. You can either put your reply above all the quoted text, or you can add your reply after quoted blocks of text so that your reply occurs close to the original thought that you're replying to (see the figure for an example). By the way, feel free to cut down the quoted text so that it includes only the parts of the original message that you're responding to. People like to read their own stuff, but the desire not to read at all is even more overwhelming.

After you're done with the message, you can click the **Send** button to send the message immediately or click the **Save** button to store the message in the Drafts folder. If you send it, a copy of the message is stored in the Sent Mail folder, so you can access it later to remind yourself what you said.

## Creating a New Message

New messages are very much like replies. You can create a new message like this:

1. Click the **New** button, and an empty message screen appears.

2. Choose the account to send from in the pull-down menu. Then enter an e-mail address for the recipient. (If you're using the Contacts database, you can simply

type the first few letters of a stored contact's name. You can open the Contacts database for editing by clicking the **Contacts** button on the Outlook Express toolbar.)

3. Press **Tab** to move to the next windows. Enter e-mail addresses for anyone who should receive a courtesy copy (CC) or a blind copy (BCC). Blind copy recipients are not shown to other recipients.

4. Type a subject line. Press **Tab** one more time, and you're ready to type the body of the message.

That's it. After you're done with the message, click **Send** or **Save** just as you would with a reply message.

### Wait to Send

Would you like your messages to queue in the Out Box, waiting for you to click the **Send & Receive** button before they're sent? Setting up your e-mail this way can save time if you have a lot of messages to write. To do so, you select **Edit, Preferences**. In the Preference dialog box, choose **General**. Then uncheck **Send messages immediately**.

### What's All This Formatting Stuff For?

Did I lie when I said e-mail had to be plain text? Not really. And, yet, you can clearly see that the message composition window gives you controls for adding italics, bold, even colors and alignment. What's wrong with me?

Nothing. These controls allow you to add HTML formatting to your e-mail documents—using the same HTML tags that are used to design Web pages. HTML tags are actually text, too; they're just hidden when recognized by a Web browser or, in this case, an HTML-savvy e-mail program.

So, using these controls is perfectly all right if you recognize one caveat: If you trade e-mail with someone whose e-mail program doesn't support HTML, then <I>your</I> <B>message</B> <H1>may</H1> <a href="index.html">look like</a>nothing but<HR> a bunch of codes to that person.

Want to turn off HTML messages? Choose **Edit, Preferences**; then select **Message Composition**. Click the **Plain Text** button under **Mail sending format**. See Chapter 21, "Build Your Own Web Sites," for more details on HTML codes.

## 263

## Sending Files to Others

I've already mentioned that e-mail is all in text only, right? So how could you send something like, say, a sound file through e-mail? As an attachment.

You attach files and documents to e-mail messages just as you might attach a resume to a cover letter you're sending through the mail. With e-mail, though, the process is a bit more complicated. Because only text can be sent through e-mail, the document or file needs to be translated from binary format (computer language) into plain text. This translation is done by way of a process called *encoding*.

What's important about encoding is that you need to pick the method you use to encode according to what sort of computer your recipient uses. You have these choices:

➤ *BinHex*   This method is the Mac standard for encoding attachments.

➤ *Base64, MIME, AppleSingle*   Pick one of these methods if you're sending to a Windows or DOS-based PC; most newer Mac programs can handle them.

➤ *uuencode*   This method is best for sending to UNIX machines, although most computers can handle this one.

Which method you choose depends on whom you're sending the message to. To make your choice, select **Edit, Preferences** and choose **Message Composition**. Use the **Attachment encoding** pull-down menu to choose the type best suited for your message.

**File Size**

Don't forget to consider the file size of any attachments before sending them. Large files can take very long to upload and just as long for your recipient to download. Also, consider that your ISP may limit the size of files that can be transferred via e-mail. Check the ISP's rules documents or your terms of service agreement.

To add an attachment to an e-mail message, click the **Add Attachments** icon in the toolbar. An Open dialog box appears. Navigate to the file you want to attach and click **Add**. You can add as many files as you need to. After you've added them, click **Done**. The waiting attachments line up along the bottom of your e-mail message, ready to be sent.

## Receiving Attached Files

If a file is attached to a message you've received, a small paper clip appears next to the subject of the message in the In Box. Also, a small blue paper clip icon is highlighted in the message pane. (Actually, it is just more blue than usual.) It's a pull-down menu, just in case you couldn't tell. Click on the paper clip to pull down the menu, and then choose the name of the attachment. Outlook Express tries to find a "helper application" that can open or display the attachment. If it can't, it asks you whether you want to save the attachment on your hard drive. If you do, click Yes. A Save dialog box then appears, allowing you to save the file.

A lot of attachments you receive will likely be compressed. Compressing files using a program such as StuffIt Lite or StuffIt Deluxe from Aladdin Systems (or the Windows standard, PKZip) is a good idea before sending them over the Internet because compressed files travel more quickly. They're smaller, after all. Compressed files cannot be used until they're decompressed. If you suspect you've received a compressed file (especially if it has .sit or .zip appended to its name), then you should drag it onto StuffIt Expander, a freeware program designed to expand many sorts of compressed files. StuffIt Expander is installed along with the Internet portion of the Mac OS 8.5 installation.

To expand some types of compressed files, you need another shareware program called DropStuff with Expander Enhancer. It adds to StuffIt Expander's capabilities, as well as allows you to create your own stuffed files. If you don't have DropStuff with Expander Enhancer, you can find it online anywhere you can download Mac files. Try `http://www.aladdinsys.com/` or `http://www.macdownload.com/` on the Web.

**Don't Accept Attachments**

If you weren't expecting an attachment, not saving, decompressing, or otherwise working with it might be a good idea. Unsolicited attachments are a breach of netiquette. (You should always ask someone before sending an attachment unless that person has stated somehow that it's okay.) Some unsolicited attachments could be virus infested or otherwise damaging. Stay away from strangers.

# The Least You Need To Know

Electronic mail, or e-mail, allows you to send memo-like messages to nearly anyone in the world who has an e-mail account. E-mail programs are basically text editors that know how to sign onto your ISP's mail server and look for messages. If you have any, they are downloaded and shown in the In Box, where you can single or double-click the message (depending on your mail program) to read its contents.

To send a message, you need to understand a bit about e-mail addresses. They're similar to the URLs discussed in Chapter 19, except that these e-mail addresses are designed to reach an individual. So, you generally take the domain part of the URL (like **apple.com** or **aol.com**) and add the username plus @ to the beginning. Typical e-mail addresses, then, are like **sjobs@apple.com**.

To get started sending and receiving, you head over to the Internet control panel, where you can enter a number of settings, including a full name, e-mail information, and choices on how you'll be notified of new mail and which program to use as your default e-mail application.

For many, the default e-mail application will be Outlook Express, which comes with the Mac OS for free. It's a pretty good program. You can launch it by finding its icon on the hard drive (probably in the **Internet** folder under **Microsoft Internet Applications**), or you can choose the **Apple** menu, select **Internet Access,** and then click **Mail**.

With Outlook Express launched, you're ready to check for messages and download them to your In Box, all accomplished simply by choosing the **Send & Receive** button. You can click a message to read it and click **Reply** to reply to it. The message is automatically quoted for a response. You can edit the quoted text to taste and then type your own message. When you're ready to send, just click the **Send** button, and the message is off.

To create a new message, click **New** in the toolbar. Then enter an e-mail address, subject line, and your thoughts. You can even attach documents and files to your e-mail message and send them along, too. You just need to pick the right encoding format for the sort of computer that will be receiving the attachment. Retrieving attachments is even easier; it just takes a bit of intimacy with a paper clip.

# Build Your Own Web Sites

Back in Chapter 19, you saw some of the magic and mystery of the World Wide Web. I bet you were thrilled. I bet you were intrigued. I bet that, even for only a split second, you wondered if maybe you could do something like that.

Well, I'm here tonight to tell you that you can.

Actually, creating Web pages really isn't that tough, although you might be a little surprised at how backward it still is. You enter silly codes and have to format things like you're using a word processor from one of those PCs in the early 1980s. (Assuming you've been around that long. I hear that kids born during the Reagan Administration are going to college these days.)

Your Mac can do something else, too: It can serve those Web pages over the Internet. Using a technology called Web Sharing, your Mac can actually become a Web page server computer. The only caveat: You can't have a typical dial-up Internet connection. (Or, if you do, you'll have to change things often.) You can still use a modem, but you'll need a special account.

There's another reason to use Web sharing, though. If you have an office of Macs and they happen to be using TCP/IP networking, you can use Web Sharing to share files between your office mates. Or in a pinch, you can use Web Sharing to show a colleague or friend something over the Internet—a digital image or what have you.

Don't worry; I'll show you.

# Web Pages and Web Sites

I've been talking about Web pages quite a bit through these Internet-related chapters. Web pages are documents that can be read by Web browsers; they're stored out on the Internet and are given particular addresses, called *URLs*.

The other thing that's interesting about Web pages is that you can create them. In fact, you wouldn't know it just to look at a Web page, but it's really just a text document.

*A Web page is a text document that includes instructions for how the Web page should be displayed.*

A Web page can be created in SimpleText, BBEdit Lite, or any number of Plain Text editors. In fact, you can even create Web pages in word processing programs (if you're careful and follow the instruction card located in your seat-back pocket, under the tray table). Web pages use *HTML*, the *Hypertext Markup Language*, which is really just a series of codes that describe a page: things like making text <B>bold</B> or <I>italic</I>. It's really pretty easy.

You'll remember also that a lot of what goes on with the World Wide Web includes the use of links, which help you get around from page to page. These *hyperlinks*, as they're called, are what connect pages to one another. But what if you're talking about Web pages that are all linked together, even though they're served by the same computer? That's a *Web site*.

So if you're getting serious about Web design, you'll probably be putting together your own Web site: a bunch of pages linked together covering different topics, times, interests, and so on. But why do this? Maybe you have a business or a hobby that you'd like to publish info about on the Web. I, for instance, being into Macs as I am, have a site called Mac-Upgrade.com that's all about adding things to your Mac.

Another great reason: intranets. An *intranet* is sort of the opposite of the Internet. It uses Web browsers and HTML documents, but it's really designed for internal use at a company or organization. With an intranet, you use Web tools to create an internal, company-wide Web, which can publish information like Human Resources forms, product release updates, company meeting schedules, and, perhaps, a database of current problems, customer service answers, or similar features. Highly sophisticated company intranets can include interactive parts that allow employees to use message boards and chat sessions to communicate among themselves using their computers.

From our perspective, it's a simple matter to create a basic intranet or Internet presence using Web technologies and an AppleTalk or a TCP/IP network. You'll start by creating Web pages, and then you'll get them online.

# Creating Web Pages

There are entire books dedicated to the subject of creating Web pages (I've written a few of them), so, obviously, this can get a bit complicated. But it's possible to discuss the bare minimum in just a few pages and get you started with Web page creation.

The best part is that a lot of the explanation required for getting Web pages on the Internet focuses on the servers and uploading. If you

> **Easier Creation**
>
> You can also find programs that make Web creation easy—programs like Claris Home Page or Adobe PageMill. Because those programs aren't included with Mac OS 8.5, and that's what this book is about, we'll focus on a more basic way of building Web pages using SimpleText.

have a direct connection to the Internet or a static IP address from your dial-up ISP, all of that is behind you; you can use your Mac to serve up pages.

First, let's take a quick look at creating the pages. All you'll need for this exercise is SimpleText, a bottle of water, and a little time. If you work quickly enough, you can turn this muscle-building exercise into an aerobic workout as well—just remember to keep yourself hydrated.

# The Web Page Template

Every Web page has a certain structure. Each has a "head" and a "body." The head of a Web page is where the title of the page is entered—for our purposes, it really isn't much more than that. (In a Web browser, the title appears in the title bar of the browser window. You, as the Web designer, have control over that title.) The body is where pretty much everything else will be entered.

In SimpleText, enter the following in a blank document:

```
<HTML>
<HEAD>
<TITLE>Title of Page</TITLE>
</HEAD>
<BODY>
</BODY>
</HTML>
```

That's your Web page template. Let's talk about a few things.

First, all of those bracketed words are called HTML *tags*. HTML is a "markup" language, meaning it's not really programming as such; instead, it's simply a way to augment an existing text document. If you sat down in SimpleText and typed a memo, the Gettysburg Address, or—even better—some content for a Web page, the HTML tags are there to tell things to the Web browser. Stuff like "Make this Bold!" or "This is the Title of the page."

There are two sorts of tags: *container tags* and *empty tags*. Container tags have two bracketed commands: one to begin and one to end. An example is bold text, which uses a <B> tag to begin and a </B> to end. Anything between the two tags is bold text. In fact, all container tags work pretty much this way; you begin without a "/" mark, but the ending tag is the same, just adding the "/". <HTML> and </HTML> is another example of a container tag; this one defines a document as an HTML document. Everything between the two tags is supposed to be interpreted by the browser as part of the document, just like everything between the <BODY> and </BODY> tags is supposed to be shown within the browser window.

The other type of tag is an empty tag. This is only one bracketed command, and it's different because it doesn't act on text like all container tags do. Instead, it does something on its own, like add an image <IMG SRC="graphic.gif"> or a horizontal line <HR>. There aren't as many empty tags, but they're pretty significant for nice-looking Web pages.

# Entering Text on Your Page

First things first. With your template created, jump up to the "Title of Page" text and enter a meaningful title for your page between those <TITLE>,</TITLE> tags. That will be the title for the Web browser window when somebody views this page.

```
<TITLE>Typing Exercises You Can Try</TITLE>
```

Now you're ready to enter some text. You do so between the <BODY>,</BODY> tags; that's the only way to get the text to reliably show up in the browser window. To begin, just type something for your page. Don't worry about tags yet.

There are, however, a few rules about typing in text on Web pages. First, spaces and returns on the keyboard don't matter. That's right—not at all. Only one space between words will be noticed by the browser, and hitting the Return key doesn't do anything as far as the browser is concerned, except make the HTML codes easier for you to read. For instance, consider the following typed within the <BODY>,</BODY> container tag of an HTML document:

```
Now is the time for all good people to come to the aid of their party.
<HR>
Now is the time
     for all good people
to come to the aid of their party.
```

(Remember, the <HR> creates a horizontal line.) In both of these cases, the text will look exactly the same when it's shown in the browser. The browser will disregard both returns and extra spacing.

In fact, this is the exact opposite of the way IRS forms work.

The reason for this is simple: The browser uses special tags to denote paragraphs and ends of lines. You also use special tags to distinguish between regular text and text that needs to be spaced a certain way.

The paragraph container is <P>,</P>. When you type text between these two tags, the lines will be properly spaced and rendered. The line break tag is an empty tag: <BR>. For text that should be rendered *exactly* as you type it, use the preformatted container <PRE>,</PRE>. Here's a look at each of those examples in action:

```
<P> Now is the time for all good people to come to the aid of their
party.</P>
<HR>
Now is the time<BR>
     for all good people<BR>
to come to the aid of their party.<BR>
<HR>
<PRE>
Now is the time
     for all good people
to come to the aid of their party.
</PRE>
```

*On the top, a paragraph example, then line breaks (notice that spaces still aren't registered), and then preformatted text, which usually defaults to a different font in Web browsers.*

Most of your text will be created between paragraph tags, so you should get used to using them around most everything you write. That way, you'll get attractive spacing and easy-to-read pages. Plus, your Web browser won't complain or improperly render the page because you have unattached text floating around.

While you're typing this paragraph text, you might consider some of your text augmenting options. Use the following tags if you like: <B>bold text</B>, <I>italic text</I>, <TT>teletype, monospaced text</TT>.

# Getting "A Head" with Your Document

Looking at this page printed in this book, you see the exact basic elements you find on a basic Web page. There are headings, paragraphs, callouts, and figures. There's bold text and italic (occasionally). There are bulleted and numbered lists.

Web pages work the exact same way. Using different tag combinations, you can create all these different elements that help organize a page.

For most text, as I've said, you'll need to put it within a <P>,</P> container. But there are a few instances where this isn't so important. One of those cases is the headings and subheadings of your document page. These use their own container tags, called *headings*. They look like <H1>,</H1>; the numbers run from 1 to 6, with 1 being the largest heading and 6 being the smallest. Heading tags also act as paragraph tags (with a carriage return on either side of the container tags), so there's no need to put them inside a paragraph container.

```
<H1>Getting 'A Head' With Your Document</H1>
<P> Looking at this page printed in this book, you'll see the exact
basic elements you'll find on a basic Web page. There are headings,
paragraphs, callouts, and figures. There's bold text and italic
(occasionally). There are bulleted and numbered lists.</P>
<H2>Organize Your Page</H2>
```

```
<P> Web pages work the exact same way. Using different tag
combinations, you can create all these different elements that help
organize a page.</P>
```

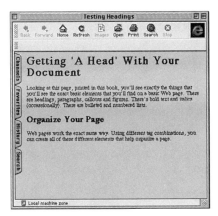

*Headings are used to break up paragraph text and organize the page.*

Aside from the mythical "Organize Your Page" second-level heading, you can see how Web page design and textbook creation aren't so different from one another.

## Adding Your Lists, Checking Them Twice

There are two types of lists you can create with HTML (with a few permutations that I'll taunt you with but refuse to discuss in this book). They are the bulleted lists and the numbered lists; in HTML, they're called the unordered and ordered lists, respectively.

Lists are enclosed with container tags: <OL>,</OL> for numbered (ordered) lists and <UL>,</UL> for bulleted (unordered) lists. The empty tag <LI> is used to begin each line item within the list.

```
<H3>Rules for Horror Movie Basement Scene</H3>
<P>The following are the instructions for a typical ascension-to-
one's-death in a horror movie involving a
(haunted/disturbed/paranormal) house's basement.:</P>
<OL>
<LI> Open the door.
<LI> Find the light switch. Ascertain that it doesn't work, even
though power has clearly been cut to the entire building.
<LI> Grip baseball bat..
<LI> Proceed into darkened basement anyway.
<LI> Trip, but don't fall, on third step.
<LI> Look wrong way when audience discovers killer behind the furnace.
</OL>
```

**273**

Like heading containers and the <PRE></PRE> container, lists containers don't need to be enclosed in paragraph container tags; the Web browser will put carriage returns before and after the <OL>,</OL> tags.

## Adding Images to Your Pages

Images are pretty easy to add and a great idea because they tend to spruce up a Web page nicely. There are some things to remember, though. Images need to be in GIF or JPEG format, meaning you might need to use a graphics conversion tool to work with images you create in some Mac programs. (Mac programs tend to work in the Mac-native PICT format, although most popular graphics applications can easily convert to GIF or JPEG.)

**Images Size**

How do you make small images? Cropping them in one way: The smaller the physical image, the less storage space the file will require. You can also use fewer colors; many programs have the capability to save images in 256 of thousands of colors instead of millions. Finally, use compression options. GIF is good for images you create that use text, lines, and geometric shapes, while JPEG format is best for compressing photographic images.

You'll also need to save your images with the filename extension **.gif** or **.jpg** as appropriate; the Web works with these little filename extensions the same way that MS-DOS does. Finally, Web images should be rather small in file size so that they transmit more quickly to modem-based users of your Web site.

The <IMG> tag itself is an empty tag (it has no closing tag) that's fairly easy to use. All you have to do is know the URL to the image you want to include. That's right: Just like Web browsers, your Web page uses URLs for things like links to pages and graphics that are supposed to be included on the page. Remember: An HTML document is a text-only document that gives the Web browser instructions. In this case, the instruction is, "Find this image either on this server's hard drive or on another computer on the Internet and place it here in the document."

In most cases, you'll use a *relative* URL. If the image is stored in the same folder (or the same online directory) as the document file you're creating, you can just use the filename, like **image.gif**. After all, there's no other information the Web browser needs. If the image is in a subfolder, like a folder called **images**, the relative URL would be **myimage/image.gif**. The full <IMG> reference includes the SRC attribute, which is where you give the image files location.

```
<H1>Welcome to my Web Page</H1>
<P>Thanks so much for visiting. Sorry I haven't updated things in a
while, but I've been away in Bermuda! Here's a snapshot from my
trip:</P>
<IMG SRC="beach1.jpg">
<P>Like it></P>
```

This results in an in-line image, which means simply that the image will appear exactly at the place in the text where you place it. If you place the image tag in-line with the text, it will appear at that exact point in the document.

```
<P>I just got back from the beach. <IMG SRC="beach1.jpg"> Isn't it a
pretty spot? </P>
```

You can also cause the image to be a "floating" image, meaning that text will wrap around it like an image in a magazine layout. To do that, you use an **ALIGN** attribute with either **RIGHT** or **LEFT** as the value.

```
<IMG SRC="beach1.jpg" ALIGN=RIGHT>
<P>I just got back from the beach. Isn't it a pretty spot? We got
quite a deal on the hotel room since a good friend works for one of
the airlines. It was a lot of fun, with plenty of dancing, music every
night and amazing meals!<P>
```

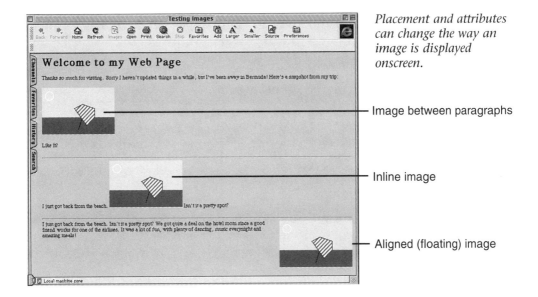

*Placement and attributes can change the way an image is displayed onscreen.*

Image between paragraphs

Inline image

Aligned (floating) image

One last thing: What will users see if they can't see images? Because Web browsers run on all different sorts of computers, you can't suppose that all your users have a graphical browser; they could be using text terminals at the library, for instance. Or they may have images turned off so they can browse more quickly with a slow modem. For those folks, you'll need to include the **ALT** text, which displays an alternative text description when the image itself can't be shown.

```
<IMG SRC="image.gif" ALIGN=RIGHT ALT="Picture of My PowerBook">
```

**Separate File**

This is important, and I always get questions on it from new Web designers, so I'll repeat myself here. An HTML document is a text-only document. It does not contain image files. Instead, it includes instructions to Web browsers in the form of tags. One of those instructions, the <IMG> tag, tells the browser to find the image located at a particular URL and add it to the Web page it's creating. If that IMG uses a relative URL, the image file itself needs to be separately available at that location. If a tag in the current Web document says **<IMG SCR="image.gif">,** you also need a file called **image.gif** in the same folder as the Web document, or you'll get an error.

# Creating Your Hyperlinks

After you've completed the text and images on your page, you'll likely want to link to something—after all, that's the advantage of having a Web site, right? Creating links is like combining an appearance container—like Bold or Italic—with the image tags that reference URLs. After all, you have to change some text to make it underlined and blue, so you'll use a container. But it needs to access a URL, so you'll be entering that, too.

The hyperlink tag is actually called the *anchor* tag, and it's represented by the letter "A" as in <A>,</A>. The anchor tag almost always has the attribute **HREF**, which means "hyperlink reference." That's where you put the URL. Like images, URLs can be relative (for example, **products.html** or **products/powerbook.html**), or they can be absolute URLs (for example, **http://www.apple.com/products/powerbook.html**).

```
<P>I just bought a new <A
HREF="powerbook.html">PowerBook</A>! Let me
know if you think it's cool. It has a full 14"
screen, <A
```

```
HREF="http://www.apple.com/products/dvd/">DVD</A>, high-speed
processor, removable Zip drive and it runs Mac OS 8.5. I'm loving
it!</P>
```

Remember that a URL that is simply the name of an HTML document, like **product.html**, tells the Web browser that that document can be found in the same folder as the current document. If that URL appears in a document called "index.html," then "product.html" should be found in the same folder. If it's in a subfolder, include the subfolder's name, and then a slash "/" as in **products/powerbook.html**.

The <A> tag can be used around images, too, turning them into hyperlinks:

```
<A HREF="powerbook.html"><IMG SRC="powerbook.jpg"></A>
```

**276**

## Saving Your Web Document

As with images destined for the Web, HTML documents must have the proper file-name extension. (Because not all computers on the Internet are Macs, we have to use this system as a least-common denominator for files.) With HTML documents, that ending is either **.htm** or **.html**. It's up to you.

If this page is the main page for your site, it should be named **index.htm** or **index.html**. With most Web servers, a page called "index.html" will be automatically loaded if the user doesn't enter a particular page name for the URL. For instance, entering **http://www.apple.com/** and **http://www.apple.com/index.html** give you the same result.

If you've been creating your document in SimpleText, choose **File**, **Save** or **File**, **Save As** (if you've already been saving the file) and give the file a name in the Save dialog box. Remember the filename extension. Then click the **Save** button.

If you'll be using the Mac's built-in Web sharing, you can save the document to your Web Pages folder on your main hard drive. Next, you'll set up Web sharing, which is covered a bit later in the chapter.

## Loading Your Page and Creating Intranets

With the page saved, you can load it in your Web browser to check it out. Instead of entering a URL, choose the **File**, **Open File** command from your browser's menu. Now use the Open dialog box to find your page. When you do, click the **Open** button, and you should be able to see the page you've created. (You can also drag a Web document icon from the Finder into the Web browser's window to open and view the page.)

Want to share your Web pages with coworkers in your company? If you're all connected via AppleTalk, you can just place your Web pages in one of your shared folders on the network; you might want to use File Sharing to allow access to your Web Pages directory, for instance. Both absolute and relative URLs should work, assuming your users have TCP/IP access, too. (If they don't, only relative URLs will work correctly.)

Once other networked users find your page, they can do the same **File**, **Open File** trick to load the page from your hard drive into their browser.

**Sophisticated Intranets**

You may also be able to convince your network administrator to turn on TCP/IP access within your company's network, even if you don't have external Internet access. That creates a true intranet, allowing coworkers to access your machine using a static IP address. More on that in the Web Sharing section that's coming up.

## Transfer to Your Site

Even if you're not using Web sharing, you might want to use the Web Pages folder and organize your folder in the same way your files will be organized when you upload them to your ISP's file server. That way, you don't have to rearrange things or change URLs.

If you're not using Web sharing on your Mac, you're probably using space on your ISP's host computer. To do that, you have to use an FTP program (like Fetch) that's designed to transfer files over the Internet. Your ISP will have to tell you exactly how to login, what directory (folder) is yours on the Web server, and what your username and password are.

### Copy the Contents

Note that I didn't copy the actual Web Pages folder; that would create another subfolder for my URL. (In the example, instead of **http://www.shutup101.com/todd/**, my URL would become **http://www.shutup101.com/todd/web pages/**.) Fetch and similar programs should allow you to select all the files within one folder and copy them into another folder on the Web server, using the FTP "Put" command.

Once you have those things figured out, though, you can connect to the Web server using a program like Fetch. Then, hopefully, your site is arranged the way you want it in the Web Pages directory. That will allow you to simply select all the files and subfolders, then upload them directly to the Web server. (In Fetch, there's a **Remote**, **Put Folders and Files...** command that makes this easy to do.) Now your relative URLs should still work because none of the filenames or subfolders have changed.

## Using Web Sharing

Have you gotten to thinking about this Web thing and decided that the life of an ISP must really take the cake? Ever really thought about it? There is adventure, cunning, dazzling glitz, and glamour—all because you, among all your fellow Earthlings, control the server. And you can tell regular users what to do.

Well, that power is now yours (assuming you have permission from your ISP, that is). With Web Sharing and a static IP address, your Mac can become a Web server, too. All you have to do is flip a switch in the Web Sharing control panel. That (and a few weeks worth of emails and a couple hundred bucks) will have you in the server driver's seat in no time.

## What's with This Static IP, Already?

I know I keep mentioning this. When you have a regular modem-based Internet account, usually your ISP doesn't give your Mac a permanent IP address. Instead, it assigns your Mac an IP address right when you connect the Mac to the ISP and get on the Internet.

What this means, though, is that your Mac will have a tough time being a server, because its address will change all the time. It's like being the reluctant star of an episode of *America's Most Wanted*: If you keep changing addresses every few days, it'll be tougher for people to find you.

So you'll need to request a static IP address from your ISP. If you use a modem, you'll likely have to pay a bit extra for a static IP, but it'll be guaranteed to be yours. (You may also have to pay for a dedicated modem line, which would be required to keep your server available at all times.) If you use a direct connection, as in an Ethernet connection, you likely already have a static IP address. This is the address you'll give out to people whom you'd like to invite to your Web site.

## Set Up Web Sharing

Armed with your static IP, you're ready to begin Web Sharing. You should have already saved your Web site in the Web Pages folder on your Mac's hard drive—that's the default folder for Web Sharing. Now, with your Internet connection active through Remote Access or through your Ethernet connection, you configure the Web Sharing control panel:

**Not Just Numbers**

You can see where Web hosting from your Mac can get expensive—paying for dedicated lines and what-not. What's worse is you'll have to pay even *more* if you don't want to tell people to visit your site at **http://255.255.255.255** or some such address. To get a name associated with that number, you'll have to enlist your ISP's help. They'll help you register a domain name (http://www.whateveryouwant.com/) and get it working properly with your IP number. Again, though, it'll cost some green.

1. From the **Apple** menu, choose **Control Panels** and then **Web Sharing**.

2. The Web Folder should be Web Pages; if not, you can click **Select...** to choose the folder. The Home Page should be None, or you can click **Select...** to choose a home page in your Web Pages folder. (If you're using a page called **index.htm** or **index.html**, it will automatically be used as the home page.)

3. Choose **Give everyone read-only access**. This will keep all visitors from uploading things to your Mac.

4. Click the **Start** button. After a moment, the dialog will change to say **Web Sharing On**, and you'll see your IP address (and any associated domain names) at the top-left of the control panel in the **My Address** section.

That's it. Now Web sharing is active, and you can tell friends, neighbors, and customers to start visiting you at the address that appears in the **My Address** section.

## *Web Sharing Security*

Remember, turning on Web Sharing gives the entire Internet access to your Web site. You can control your Web security by using File Sharing profiles (as discussed in Chapter 17, "Networking Macs") by selecting the Web Pages folder in the Finder and selecting **File**, **Sharing**. That will let you set permissions for your Web server. You can choose to let them:

➤ Read (download) pages without a password, but not write (upload) anything to the directory. This is a typical Web server setting.

➤ Read or write pages without a password. This is rarely recommended, because it allows anyone on the Internet to write files to your Mac. That probably won't be a problem, but it does allow for the possibility of a malicious visitor who uploads a virus-laden or otherwise distasteful file. It also means visitors can change your pages.

➤ Read pages without a password, but write files only with a correct username and password. This is good if you have others that help you maintain your Web site, or if you want to allow some people to send you files over the Internet.

➤ Read pages only with a password. This makes it a "members-only site."

**Web Security**

Using Web Sharing, your users can't access anything else on your Mac except the contents of the Web Pages folder and any subfolders. This means it's important to avoid one thing, though: Don't create an alias in that folder that points elsewhere on your Mac. That could give Web visitors access to other parts of your Mac over the Internet. Also, if you don't use File Sharing on this same Mac, you might consider using Sharing Setup to give *no* users access to any part of your hard drive *except* the Web Pages folder.

And so on. Actually, there are a number of different permutations, but you hopefully get the general idea. Basically, you want to keep in mind who might access your Web site and how good you feel about that, because accessing your Web site ultimately means they're getting (usually limited) access to your Mac over the Internet.

Once you've changed the Sharing setup for the Web Pages folder, make sure you choose **Use File Sharing to control user access** in the Web Sharing control panel.

# The Least You Need to Know

Once you get used to the World Wide Web, you might start itching to create your own Web pages. It's actually not that tough. All you need is SimpleText and a little learnin'—which I'm rarin' to give ya.

HTML documents use two different types of tags—container tags and empty tags—to mark up a regular text document. This markup is really just instructions to a Web browser, telling it what text should be bold, where it should put horizontal lines, and what URL it should use to find an image file.

Once you've created your HTML document, you can save it to the Web Pages folder on your main hard drive if you intend to use the Mac's built-in Web Sharing capability. Or you can use an FTP program to send the file up to your ISP's Web server computer.

Web Sharing works a lot like File Sharing for local networks, except that it allows you to share with the entire Internet instead of just your office mates. Web sharing requires a static IP address (unless you want to tell people your IP every time). Once activated, you can share the contents of your Web Pages folder with the rest of the world. (You'd better put on a clean shirt.)

# Part 5
# Cool Mac Stuff

*Now, you'll dig into the guts of the fun stuff in Mac OS 8.5. This is way beyond the basics, although you can still easily grasp onto these concepts and enjoy extending the power of your Mac.*

*After reading these chapters, you'll be able to share documents and disks with those same Microsoft Windows-based friends and colleagues. You'll also be able to play, record and edit your own digital movies. And, you'll gain experience working with Mac audio, speech technologies, and a few interesting add-ons like the Apple System Profiler and Java applets. You are officially beyond cool!*

# Deal with DOS and Windows

Many times, you'll hear that Macs aren't compatible with DOS and Windows, the operating systems used to run nearly 90 percent of personal computers in the world today. In fact, many people go so far as to say that's the Mac's biggest problem—that it uses Mac OS instead of Windows for day-to-day computer control tasks. I have to disagree because I think the Mac has its strong points, making it the better OS for certain tasks and certain users. You might agree with this opinion as well, although reading this book does not obligate you to that opinion. (You do have other ethical obligations, though, like running out and buying two more copies of the book and giving them as gifts.)

Also, the original premise is somewhat inaccurate. Although the Mac OS—out of the box—can't run applications specifically designed for Windows, that doesn't make it completely PC-incompatible. The Mac can deal with DOS floppies and other removable media, for instance. Pop in a disk, and it shows up on the Desktop. Mac can also read DOS and Windows documents and load them into a Mac application, if you have the right translators. And, with a little help from third-party programs, the Mac can even run Windows applications right there on the Mac's screen. In a way, using a Mac is almost like being a secret agent; with a Mac, you feel like you've broken the code when you pop in a PC disk. So, don't worry about compatibility. You've got it covered, 007.

# Using PC Removable Media

Some first-time Mac users (or experienced, PC-only types) are surprised when they learn about this capability: the Mac OS can pop a PC-formatted disk right onto the Mac's Desktop, no questions asked. This capability goes a long way toward compatibility, which is actually a one-two punch. After you get the disk on your Desktop, you can access it. Your next problem is working with the documents on that disk, which you can do through file translation. That topic is covered in the next section.

### PC Terminology

Sorry for the delay, but these terms need to be placed in context, or I'll lose *myself* in all this other-worldly jargon.

Intel is the popular maker of chips that run Microsoft operating systems. (In Bond parlance, Intel is the evil "Goldfinger," and Microsoft is the deadly "Jaws.") Often called *PCs*, these computers were once referred to as *IBM-compatibles* because IBM made the first models. These days, you're more likely to hear *Intel-compatible*.

Such computers usually run operating systems from Microsoft including the now aged *MS-DOS* or just *DOS* operating system, which was text-based, not graphical like the Mac. *Windows 95* and *Windows 98*, which are the progeny of DOS, still share some elements in common with it, such as the disk formatting scheme (disks can be read by any of these operating systems interchangeably). Windows is much more graphical, however, making the experience of using a Mac and a Windows-based PC similar.

With this information in mind, you'll see these terms in this chapter: *PC* refers to an Intel-compatible machine and anything that works with Windows, DOS, and PC hardware, such as a *PC diskette*. *DOS* refers to files (such as a *DOS word processing document*) that work with any Microsoft OS, and *Windows* refers to something that works only with Microsoft Windows in a graphical mode (such as *Windows long filenames*).

## *Getting PC Disks on the Desktop*

For now, let me talk a little about PC disks. I've mentioned before that disks have different formats for different operating systems. A Mac-formatted disk is different from a PC-formatted disk, for instance. With the Mac OS, though, the capability to read those PC-formatted disks is built in. In fact, assuming you have your Mac OS extensions enabled (you haven't started with the Shift key held down, for instance), all you really have to do is pop the PC-formatted disk into its respective drive (floppy, Zip drive, CD-ROM), and it appears on the Desktop.

*Here's a PC Zip disk that's been inserted in my Mac's Zip drive.*

Using PC disks in a Mac is a trick that gadget guru "Q" would be proud of. This capability is all thanks to the File Exchange control panel that comes along for the ride with the Mac OS 8.5 installation. File Exchange knows how to read PC-formatted disks and helps you get them to appear properly.

To work with the disk, you simply double-click its icon as you would any disk or disk. Its files appear in a window on the Desktop. In Mac OS 8.5, you even see the longer file names used by Windows 95 and Windows 98; otherwise, you may see short or slightly odd names (with three-letter extensions such as .txt or .doc). Seeing these extensions may not be very comforting, but it means you're looking at DOS files.

## File Exchange: The Heart of It All

You shouldn't have too much trouble getting PC disks to appear, but if you do have trouble, the indicator can be a little confusing. If you pop in a PC disk, and the Mac doesn't recognize it, the Mac may respond by saying "This disk is unreadable by this computer. Do you want to initialize the disk?" This message means erase and format, by the way, which is something you probably *don't* want to do if the disk has any important DOS/Windows documents or files on it. Click **Eject** to get out of this harrowing situation. (Now, smooth the wrinkles in your Armani suit.)

What's happened? Most likely, File Exchange has been disabled. Either you started with the Shift key pressed as the "Welcome to Mac OS" message appeared, or you need to enable File Exchange in the Extensions Manager. See Chapter 14, "Stuff That's Buried in the System Folder," for more details on the Extensions Manager.

Get File Exchange enabled and restart. Now, try the disk again. You should have better luck getting it to appear on the Desktop. After you get it there, double-click as usual to get started.

## Working with Unsupported Disks

Most removable sorts of disks—CDs, floppy disks, Zip cartridges, and so on—are pretty easy to get working with your Mac. Some others may not be as cooperative. If you come across a PC disk that you can't seem to mount to the Desktop for some reason, and you have File Exchange loaded, you can still do something.

Open the File Exchange control panel, and click the **PC Exchange** tab. Now, click the **Mount Now** button. With luck, this operation mounts any PC disks that have been installed in SCSI-based external drives. It it doesn't, you need to see whether your drive manufacturer offers a special system extension for showing PC media on a Mac's Desktop.

# Translating DOS and Windows Files

After you get your PC disk to show up on the Desktop, you'll probably want to access those files, right? It's like you've broken into the enemy's special briefcase, and now you need to take microfilm pictures of the secret plans. Well, in some cases, you don't need to do too much. The DOS/Windows document may work just fine if you open it in the correct program.

Many DOS/Windows documents can be read directly by a Mac application—usually if they're similar versions across platforms. For instance, Microsoft Word 98 for Macintosh can read files created in Word 97 for Windows. Similarly, the Mac version of FileMaker can read FileMaker Pro databases written in the Windows version, Photoshop for Mac can read Photoshop for Windows, and so on.

If you're trying to load a document, and you have the Mac version of the Windows application used to create the file, then you should have no problem using it. If you do have problems, contact the application developer to see whether it offers a translation tool, an upgrade, or something else that will allow your version to read the Windows file. (For instance, Word 4.0 for Mac can read Word 97 files, too, if you install a translator that's freely available from Microsoft's Web site.)

## *How to Load a DOS/Windows Document*

The easiest way to get Windows documents to load in their Mac counterparts is to use that Mac application's **File, Open** menu command. In most cases, these applications have a translation menu built into the Open dialog box, where you can tell the Mac application how it should translate the file. Select the file in the Open dialog box, and then choose its format from the pull-down menu.

Another way that may work is to drag and drop the file onto the application's icon. Depending on the application, this operation may cause it to examine the file for its file type and attempt to translate it.

The last way to translate the file is to try double-clicking it. Often, this approach doesn't work because DOS/Windows files don't have the same information in them as Mac files do, so the Mac OS is often stuck. This situation is sort of like you've encountered a booby-trapped timer and don't know the code. In that case, the Mac OS asks you what application it should use, and it tries to remember that information. But what happens if the application you choose isn't working correctly with the document? At this point, you need to reach into your utility belt.

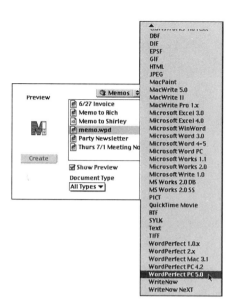

*In the Open dialog box of many applications, you can find a menu that allows you to choose from what format a document should be translated.*

### Know the Code

Mac files include extra information—called *meta information*—that's embedded in the file itself. For instance, a Mac file can tell you what its file type is (TEXT, for instance) and what application created it (SimpleText or BBEdit). Therefore, even the same sorts of files can be automatically opened in different applications if their *creator codes* are different.

DOS/Windows files use a slightly less robust system—the three-letter extension at the end of a document's name. This extension tells an OS what the file's file format or creator program is. This system is less robust because the codes are determined by the application's authors, not any central authority, so they can duplicate one another, be changed by users, and may not always suggest the correct application.

## The Nefarious PC Exchange

The code cracking—actually, it's called *extension mapping*—goes on the File Exchange control panel. Your Mac needs to know which PC filename extensions (those three-letter combos) need to be associated with which programs. If necessary, you can map it out for your Mac.

289

Open the File Exchange control panel, and choose the PC Exchange tab. At the top of the window, you can choose when PC Exchange kicks in; by default, it always tries to help you open PC files. You can turn off **Mac PC Extensions to Mac OS file types on PC disks** to keep the Mac OS from attempting to help you with PC files that are on PC-formatted floppies, Zips, and other removable media. Turn off **Open unmapped files on any disk using mappings below**, and PC Exchange no longer attempts to help you with any file translation tasks.

I assume you want to leave File Exchange on most of the time, though. Every once in a while, though, you might want to change a relationship or add a new one. To change an existing one, highlight the PC extension in question and click the **Change** button. Up pops a window full of applications you can choose for that particular extension. Select the application you want to load files with that extension from now on, and then click **Change**. Your change is registered.

*Changing and adding extension mappings are pretty much the same procedures.*

Enter the extension letters (if necessary)

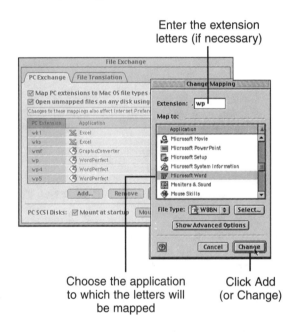

Choose the application to which the letters will be mapped

Click Add (or Change)

To add a new mapping, make sure the PC Exchange tab is selected and click **Add.** In the Extension entry box, type the three-letter extension. Next, select the application name that you want associated with that extension, and click **Add**. Now, when you double-click a PC file with that particular extension, it is loaded in your chosen application.

# Running Windows Applications

Although this isn't strictly a talent of the Mac OS itself, I thought I should mention that the Mac can actually run Windows and DOS programs, too, if you want it to.

This is best done with Mac OS 8.5 and a rather new Power Macintosh (preferably based on a G3 or higher processor), but some other Mac models can handle it.

What you need is emulation software, which is an extra program called SoftWindows or RealPC (written by Insignia, `http://www.insignia.com/`) or Virtual PC (written by Connectix, `http://www.connectix.com/`). All these *emulation* programs allow you to run Windows programs.

*SoftWindows allows you to run almost any sort of Windows application that you want, right on top of your Mac.*

In the case of RealPC and Virtual PC, the application pretends to be a Pentium-class Intel-compatible computer. Therefore, when you start the program, it's actually capable of doing just about anything a PC can do. Of course, it uses the Mac's screen and its connector ports, but it runs PC software. With RealPC, you get just MS-DOS, which is fine for many game players. Virtual PC comes with your choice of Microsoft Windows versions: Windows 3.1, Windows 95, or Windows 98.

SoftWindows is a similar program, but it emulates Windows itself on top of the Mac; it doesn't emulate the underlying PC. The difference? Not much, except that SoftWindows works a bit better with business applications written specifically for Windows.

# The Least You Need to Know

A fully decked-out Mac can almost be more Windows-compatible than a Windows-compatible computer—which surprises some people. True, the Mac OS isn't designed to run Windows programs natively, but you can add that capability as a feature. In the meantime, the Mac OS does help you quite a bit with file translations and getting access to PC media.

Pop in a DOS-formatted floppy and, most likely, the contents appear on your Desktop. The process is usually just that easy, thanks to a control panel called File Exchange. Zip disks and similar removables should work, too. If you come across a DOS disk that doesn't proceed carefully, don't erase it! Instead, try to mount it from the File Exchange control panel.

After you get the disk on the Desktop, you can launch the PC documents you find. You can do so in a few ways: You can load the document using the application's **File, Open** command, or you can drag the document to the application's icon. You can also try double-clicking; if that approach doesn't work, you need to go digging in the File Exchange control panel again.

Let me add one last point: Your Mac *can* run Windows and DOS applications. You just need some special software, available at better Mac stores everywhere.

# QuickTime and Multimedia

It took me forever to figure out what, exactly, QuickTime was. Not that I didn't know a little about it; its most obvious characteristic is that it allows you to play digital movies on your Mac. In fact, without QuickTime, you can't play such movies unless you're using a special application and a special document format created by some other company. I learned this the first time I ever double-clicked a QuickTime movie file.

But QuickTime is also more than that. It's actually an underlying technology for dealing with all sorts of cool things—video, sound, and images—all of those things that are lumped together when we talk about "multimedia." So you can work with images and sounds, in addition to movies, if you like. Or you can bring all three together. In the same way, this technology allows programmers to easily add video, audio, and image manipulation to their programs. That's how, for instance, a program like SimpleText—designed for basic text editing—can also happen to play QuickTime movies.

And QuickTime is also a file format. Using a QuickTime-enabled application, you can open, save, and close QuickTime documents. Again, these documents can have images, video, and sound co-mingled within the same document.

Oh—and, finally, *QuickTime* is a catch-all word that Apple uses to discuss a bunch of technologies that have to do with gaming, 3D, and other things. There's QuickTime VR, QuickDraw 3D, GameSprockets, RAVE, and others.

# What Does QuickTime Mean to Me?

This sounds like an elementary school essay. "Well, QuickTime is important because it is part of the government of our Macs, which makes it so we can go to school, and our little brothers can annoy us."

There are really three different issues you should concern yourself with when it comes to QuickTime. In no particular order (aside from the obvious order on this page), those issues are:

**The Hard Way**

The hard way to find out if QuickTime is properly installed is to hop over to the Extensions folder (or the Extensions Manager we chatted up in Chapter 14, "Stuff That's Buried in the System Folder") and take a gander. Do you see lots and lots of QuickTime extensions? (QuickTime installs quite a few.) If you see them, and they're properly activated, you're probably ready to work with QuickTime.

If you still don't think QuickTime is properly installed, run the QuickTime installer again from inside the main Mac OS installer on your Mac OS 8.5 CD-ROM. That'll teach 'em.

➤ *Making sure QuickTime is installed.* QuickTime as a "technology" manifests itself as a ton of little extensions in the Extensions folder. With Mac OS 8.5 and QuickTime 3.0 or greater, there are two really easy ways to figure out if QuickTime is properly installed. First, is there a QuickTime commercial on your desktop? If so, QuickTime 3.0 is probably installed correctly. Second, double-click a QuickTime document (either that advertisement or something else you may have lying around or on CD-ROM). If you get a splash screen that seems to be selling you something, that means you've got QuickTime 3.0 or higher properly installed. (I may be lying if Apple's decided against this approach someday in the future.) Another way to tell if QuickTime is installed is to watch for a series of QuickTime icons on the Mac OS startup screen as your Mac starts up (they tend to be orange and green with a big "Q" in most of them).

➤ *Playing QuickTime movie files.* The QuickTime document format is referred to as a "movie." In fact, you create a QuickTime movie even if the movie you've created is only sounds. Seems odd, but it's really pretty simple: We just call QuickTime documents "movies" for no particularly good reason. If your movie has no video, it's an audio-track-only movie. Anyway, these movie files need to be played. That's often accomplished through the MoviePlayer application, although any program that's QuickTime-enabled can play them. That includes SimpleText, the Scrapbook, Microsoft Word, Macromedia Director, Netscape Navigator—tons of programs.

➤ *Editing QuickTime.* Actually, editing QuickTime movies and sounds is simple—at least, what I know about editing QuickTime movies and sounds is simple. Unfortunately, you'll need to spend a little extra money for the privilege. You'll also need to remember that QuickTime movies can be difficult to edit, because they're actually four-dimensional, even though they're represented on a two-dimensional screen that's being rendered using binary math. Just remember that. (I'm kidding. QuickTime movies are very easy to edit.)

QuickTime is the underlying technology for some cool programs; it lets you play movies—even movies that have only audio tracks—and it includes technology that allows you to edit those movies. What more could you ask for?

## Other QuickTime Technologies

QuickTime also includes some other technologies that can affect movies and multimedia. Some of them are more related than others, but, these days, Apple sort of lumps them all together. They include the following:

➤ *QuickTime VR.* This technology allows for virtual reality movies within MoviePlayer. Using special programs, artists and programmers can take enough images in a 360-degree circle, and then paste those images together to create an all-around panorama. Then, using the MoviePlayer, you can "walk through" that panorama.

➤ *Streaming Technologies.* These technologies and compressors make it possible for you to receive QuickTime movies and soundtracks—which tend to be very big Internet hogs—over the Internet in a timely fashion. Streaming means you don't have to wait for the whole movie file to download before it starts playing.

**Sprockets and Drivers**

A quick glance at your Extensions Manager should tell you if you have game sprockets installed: You'll see the Input Sprocket, Network Sprocket, and similar files. Most of the time, these files are installed along with games that use them, so you won't need to worry too much about them. What should you worry about? Drivers for your game controllers. Check the included disks, CD, or Web site of the manufacturer of your joystick and see if they have Input Sprocket drivers. That should improve your gaming experience quite a bit, especially with newer Mac games.

➤ *QuickDraw 3D.* QuickDraw 3D does a number of things, but most importantly, it's a method for creating 3D objects on your Mac's screen. This can be for sophisticated design and animation purposes, or it can be for gaming and "edutainment" (educational games). Most people worry about QuickDraw 3D in two different cases: When you want to view a 3D object and when you want to accelerate games or 3D creation. We'll talk about both instances.

➤ *GameSprockets.* GameSprockets are bits of OS that Apple has written to help game developers—stuff like how to interact with joysticks, how to get on the Internet, how to draw 3D on the screen. That way, programmers can focus a bit more on important stuff like how to make a WERT-class fighter fly straight and shoot sideways.

## The QuickTime Extensions

Let's cover this one quickly. If you've recently installed Mac OS 8.5, you probably have all of the QuickTime files properly installed in the Extensions folder. If someone has been moving things around in your Extensions folder, though, here are the files that need to be in the Extensions folder for QuickTime to work properly:

QuickTime

QuickTime MPEG Extension

QuickTime Musical Instruments

QuickTime PowerPlug

QuickTime VR

Sound Manager

You should also have the QuickTime Settings control panel in your Control Panels folder. You should note that the Extensions Manager doesn't organized QuickTime as its own Package, instead including it in the basic Mac OS 8.5 package.

For QuickDraw 3D, you'll find that it is part of its own package. If you choose **View**, **As Packages** from the **Extensions Manager** menu, you should be able to activate or deactivate QuickDraw by simply clicking the **check box** next to the QuickDraw 3D package icon.

# Working with QuickTime Movies

If you've got QuickTime properly installed, movies usually aren't a problem to get running. Your first try should be to simply double-click the movie file and see if that does the trick. If not, you can open the MoviePlayer and choose **File**, **Open** to get that movie set up and ready to roll. (Need to find MoviePlayer? Try the QuickTime folder on your main hard drive. If it's not there, try the Apple Extras folder.)

With the MoviePlayer onscreen, you're ready to work with your movie. (Feeling like a Hollywood director yet? Er...okay, how about the kid that sits next to the projector in the local UA?) The MoviePlayer's controls are pretty straightforward; they should look a lot like a VCR's.

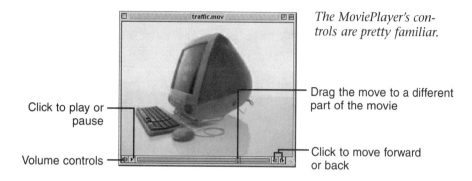

*The MoviePlayer's controls are pretty familiar.*

Click to play or pause

Volume controls

Drag the move to a different part of the movie

Click to move forward or back

To start playing a loaded movie, click the **Play** button; you can click that button again to **Pause** (notice that the button changes its look). The **Reverse** and **Fast Forward** buttons can be used as you would expect. Notice also that the progress bar at the bottom of the movie shows you how far you've gotten into the movie. In almost all cases, you can drag that little **slider box** around to change your position in the movie.

You'll find other controls in MoviePlayer, too, hidden up in the menus. To change the size of a movie's playback screen, choose **Movie**, **Double Size**. You can play with the other commands in the **Movie** menu, like **Get Info** and **Show Copyright**.

Frankly, I've had more fun than this, but not with any digital movie-playing tool.

## QuickTime Virtual Reality

QuickTime VR is an offshoot of QuickTime that allows for the creation of virtual reality panoramas. These can actually be pretty cool, allowing you to "walk through" scenery changes and spin around to view an entire 360-degree image at once. You still use the MoviePlayer application; it's just that the controls change slightly. When you load a QuickTime VR movie, you won't need to worry about the play and forward/backward controls. Instead, you're controlling things with the mouse.

Use the mouse pointer for control

*The MoviePlayer changes a bit to accommodate a VR movie; now you'll use the mouse to move around.*

297

There are really two different types of QuickTime VR movies: a panorama and an object. (The figure shows an object, the iMac.) In a panorama, you use the mouse to move through images that look like a 3D vista of some sort. In an object movie, you'll rotate the object using the mouse. It's a little different.

You'll see a few different cursors when you're moving around in a QuickTime VR movie. Generally, you can click and hold the mouse button, and then move it left and right to rotate within the current view. If you see the mouse pointer turn into an **arrow pointing forward**, click once to move further "into" the virtual world. If you need to move backward (or "exit" a particular spot), move the mouse pointer to the very edges of the screen until you get an **Exit** option. To work with an object in the movie (sometimes you can "pick up" objects and rotate them), point to the object with the mouse. If the pointer changes to a **circle**, you can click to work with that object.

## Web-Based QuickTime

You'll find that a lot of the QuickTime movies you want to view are found on the Web. Sometimes they're large files—be warned—and it can take a long time to download them to your Mac, especially if you have a basic modem connection to the Internet. Still, if you're interested in watching QuickTime movies in your browser window, you'll need to have the QuickTime plug-in appropriately installed.

The Mac OS 8.5 or QuickTime installer should do a good job of making this happen for you; these days, the plug-in installation is pretty automatic. If, for some reason, QuickTime doesn't seem to work in your browser window, head to that browser's folder and look for a folder called Plug-Ins. In that folder, there should be either a copy of or an alias to the QuickTime plug-in. If there isn't one, you should either re-install QuickTime or create an alias of the plug-in file and drag it to the browser's Plug-In folder. (You'll likely need to restart the browser after doing this.) If you can't find the QuickTime plug-in, try the QuickTime folder on your main hard drive or use the **File**, **Find** command in the Finder.

With the plug-in installed, you can view movies directly in the browser window. Note that this works only if the Webmaster wants it to; they'll need to enter special HTML codes on their page to get the QuickTime movie "embedded" in the Web page. Once that's done, though, you'll get a MoviePlayer-like box within the browser window.

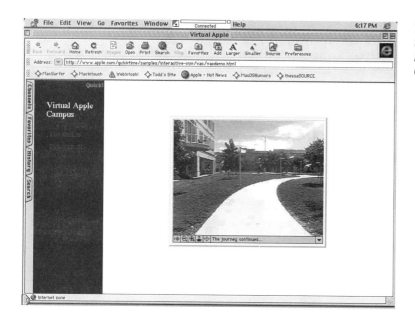

*The QuickTime plug-in turns part of a Web browser window into a QuickTime movie player.*

The controls are pretty much the same—assuming you need to use them. In most cases, embedded QuickTime movies will start themselves after enough of the movie has been downloaded (so that the movie doesn't have to stop and wait for the rest of it to download).

# Edit QuickTime Movies

The first step toward editing QuickTime movies is to pull out your wallet. Apple charges for the privilege, requiring you to upgrade to the QuickTime Pro edition if you want to do any editing in MoviePlayer. (You can also edit QuickTime movies in many different commercial applications, too.) If you have the Pro version of MoviePlayer, though, it's actually quite simple to piece together movies and create different effects.

## Combining Two Movies

The easiest way to edit your movies it to cut and paste. For instance, to drop one movie into another movie, simply click on the first movie

**Ordering Pro**

You can order the professional version of QuickTime 3 (or higher), which includes the fully featured MoviePlayer, from Apple's Web site at **http://www.apple.com/ quicktime/**. You can actually pay online and receive a code that enables the pro version in your current QuickTime installation.

*Note:* Indications at press time are that you can receive a QuickTime Pro license and code if you simply register your version of the Mac OS online by visiting Apple's Product pages at **http://www.apple.com/ products** on the Web.

to make it active, choose **Edit**, **Select All**, and choose **Edit, Copy**. Now go to the second movie, place the slider bar where you want the new movie's parts to appear, and then choose **Edit**, **Paste**. Assuming the movies are the same size (in pixels or inches), everything should come together nicely.

*The Pro version of the MoviePlayer has more options that allow you to edit QuickTime movies.*

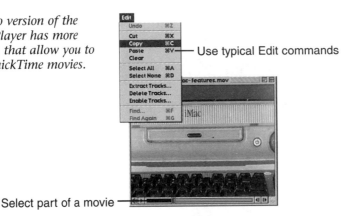

Use typical Edit commands

Select part of a movie

Oh, how do you select parts of a movie? Place the slider at the beginning of the part you want to select. Then hold down the **Shift** key and move the slider to the end of the selection in the movie. That part of the slider bar becomes blackened, showing you that part of the movie has been selected. Now you can choose **Edit, Copy** as described.

You can cut and paste other multimedia elements into your movie document, like PICT images and text. In fact, creating titles and section screens within your movie is simple. Try this:

1. In SimpleText or a similar program, create some styled text for your movie's intro screen.

2. Select all of the styled text and drag it to the desktop. This should create a text clipping.

3. Switch to MoviePlayer and place the **slider box** so that you're at the beginning of the movie.

4. Drag the text clipping into the MoviePlayer window.

Now not only is the text added to the movie, but it's resized to fit properly, giving it very much a movie title look. It's a great idea for any sort of credits or other information.

## Adding Sound to the Movie

QuickTime movies can have different *tracks* or parts of a movie that can be playing at the same time as other parts. For instance, you can have a soundtrack that plays at the same time as the movie. In fact, because QuickTime movies can be just sound with no picture, you can combine two different movies—a sound movie and a video movie—to create a single movie with both picture and sound. Here's how:

1. Open both the sound movie and the video movie in MoviePlayer.
2. With the sound movie's window selected, choose **Edit**, **Select All**.
3. Switch to the video movie. While holding down the **Option** key, choose **Edit.**
4. In the **Edit** menu, choose the new command, **Add.**

That's it. You've just added an audio track that will play while your video flashes by. Cool, eh? Of course, you can select parts of an audio track by holding down **Shift** and moving the slider button. And if you need to get the sound track out of an existing QuickTime movie before you can add it to another one, that's easy, too. Just load the movie in MoviePlayer, and then choose **Edit**, **Extract Tracks**. In the **Extract** dialog box, select the track you want to pull out of the movie and click **Extract**. Now you'll have a new movie with only that one track.

Obviously, you can let things get as complicated as you need. MoviePlayer isn't exactly a full-featured movie editor (which would allow for cuts, transitions, and special effects, not to mention better control over adding sound and text), but it's great for basic movie editing if you're just starting to play with a video camera and a Firewire or AV-equipped Macintosh.

**Advanced MoviePlayer**

Not that there isn't a whole lot more you can do in MoviePlayer, too. Apple's documentation is pretty complete; see **http://www.apple.com/ quicktime/information/** on the Web. They've got instructions for special effects, text overlays, and a lot more.

## Saving Your QuickTime Creation

You save in the normal way: Choose **File**, **Save**. There are some other options to take into consideration when you're saving a movie, though.

First of all, the Save dialog box will ask you if the movie should be saved **normally (allowing dependencies)**, or if MoviePlayer should **make movie self-contained**. A self-contained movie will include everything needed to play that movie on any QuickTime-enabled Mac or PC. With dependencies, the movie will take up much less space but will likely not work anywhere but on your Mac. (Basically, it's leaving other files you've used—sound movies or text clippings, for instance—on your Mac where it found them instead of pulling them into the movie file itself.)

**Saving Small**

The best Web movies are small in size and in file size so they can be downloaded. In fact, the best way to save your movies for the Web with the MoviePlayer Pro version is to choose **Edit**, **Export**. In the resulting dialog box, click the **Options** button, which allows you to choose some options for how your movie will be saved and com-pressed. Click the **Settings** buttons to see the different compressor options. (Check out Apple's QuickTime Web site, **http://www.apple.com/ quicktime/**, to learn more about the compressors.)

If you're saving your movie for the Web, remember to use an eight-letter name and a three-letter exten-sion (for example, **mymovie.mov** or **ourtrip1.mov**) so that PCs can use the file as easily as Macs can.

# The Least You Need to Know

Computer industry pundits are always looking for the next "killer application" that will justify higher-performing computers and new software titles. That might just be QuickTime and digital video editing, which are just beginning to really see popularity on more typical consumer machines. The latest version of QuickTime makes things even easier.

QuickTime means many different things. It's a tech-nology, a file format, and a bunch of different exten-sions that need to be in your System Folder. This includes some files that don't quite seem related, like the QuickDraw 3D and Game Sprockets files used for 3D rendering and gaming, respectively.

With all of QuickTime's extensions installed correct-ly, the first thing you'll want to try is using MoviePlayer to play back a QuickTime movie and allow you to watch it. With the correct files in the right places, you can even watch QuickTime movies from within your browser's window.

Finally, using the QuickTime Pro version, you can edit your own movies. There are plenty of interesting tricks, including edits for adding sound, piecing together two movies, and adding text for the credits. Then you save the movie, with special consid-eration if you'll be sending your movie out over the Web. And cut!

# Chapter 24

# Get Mac to Talk and Sing

---

### In This Chapter

➤ Types of Mac Sound

➤ Digital Sound Settings

➤ Getting Your Mac to Speak

➤ Getting Your Mac to Listen and Obey

---

When Steve Jobs introduced the first Mac in 1984, he pulled it out of a rather large bag by the handle (Macs had carry bags back then) and put it on the table. Once it was plugged in, started up, and had gotten past the smiley face, it introduced itself to the crowd with a happy "Hello" on the screen. But it did something else, too. It spoke, saying, "Hello. Welcome to Macintosh. It sure is nice to get out of that bag."

The crowd was pleased.

A lot has happened since then, including the Macintosh becoming perhaps the premier computing platform for audio and video production, as well as a popular choice for creating multimedia, television, and other media endeavors. All of that takes sound capabilities, which the Mac offers in spades.

You'll also find that something else has carried over since that original Mac press conference: an interest in computer speech. Built right into Mac OS 8.5 are both Text-to-Speech and speech recognition technologies. Ever had a one-sided conversation with your Mac in the past? Maybe it's time it started talking back. (If it doesn't start talking and you don't stop, you could have a family intervention on your hands. Trust me.)

# Types of Mac Sound

There are really two types of sound that the Mac can deal with, although I want to discuss three different sound-related technologies. (Not to mention four calling birds and five golden rings.) The two types of sound are digital sound and MIDI. The three sound technologies are digital sound, MIDI, and speech.

Macs can be used to record sounds, as you may have already found if you got busy creating your own alert sounds back in Chapter 9, "Banish the Boring Mac!" Doing so can be a rather exact science; in fact, people have been known to make actual money by specializing in the art of getting sounds in and out of Macs. This sort of sound is *digital* sound, because you're recording the sound to your Mac's hard drive by representing its sound waves as digital data: ones and zeros.

### PlainTalk What?

The PlainTalk microphone is the only microphone Apple recommends for the microphone port on the back of nearly all Macs. (Some Macs have RCA jacks: red and black jacks for the left and right channels of an audio signal, but most have a single stereo mini-plug adapter.) The reason for this is simple: The microphone jack is actually a line-level input, meaning regular microphones won't work, only special line-level microphones or devices with line-level outputs, like a stereo receiver/amplifier. If you want to use a more typical microphone, you'll need to plug it into a stereo receiver, and then use the line-out ports on that receiver to connect to the Mac (probably using a Y-connector from your local Radio Shack or similar place).

This is different from MIDI (Musical Instrument Digital Interface) technology, which allows your Mac to control electronic instruments. Instead of recording sounds, like a tape recorder, MIDI allows your Mac to record notes in a special notation, turning Mac into something more along the lines of a player piano reading mechanism. Using MIDI, your Mac can store notes, chords, instruments sounds, sustain lengths, and so one, and then play them back through MIDI-compatible equipment.

Then there's speech technology. This is where the Mac doesn't really record anything; it just listens or speaks as the case may be. With text-to-speech technology, your Mac can speak out loud pretty much any text on the screen. You may have already encountered this phenomenon if you've installed Mac OS 8.5 and left a dialog box on the screen for any length of time. (After a while, the Mac will say, "Alert…" and read the dialog box message.)

Speech *recognition* can also be installed along with Mac OS 8.5. In this case, you can get your Mac to listen to you speaking, and it will respond to commands. While the speech technology in the Mac OS is somewhat limited, you can create your own commands using aliases and AppleScripts. It's fun, and, supposedly, Apple is improving it. For real speech dictation, you'll need another application, though.

# Recording and Working with Sounds

Let's start by focusing on digital sound. This is where you turn your Mac into a recording studio, with you playing the role of the important music producer. (You'd better open your shirt a few buttons, get some more necklaces, and prepare to be much more pessimistic.) Ready?

For serious recording, you'll want to get special equipment: microphones, pre-amps, mixing boards, PCI sounds cards, and maybe a dose of talent and skill. Not that you don't have those things, mind you, but they can be pretty expensive for the novice. Especially the skill part. Oh, and you should sound-proof your apartment or basement, whichever is appropriate.

For less serious recording, all you'll really need is to properly set up the Monitors and Sound control panel. You'll also need some sort of sound-in source, like a PlainTalk microphone, a built-in CD-ROM drive, or a home stereo system connected to the sound-in port on the back of your Mac. Then, finally, you're ready to boogie.

Before you can record (but after you've chosen a device you're going to record from), you'll need to head to the Monitors and Sound control panel. It's there that you'll find the nexus of the Mac sound universe.

Okay, so it's just a few slider bars. "Nexus" sounds cooler.

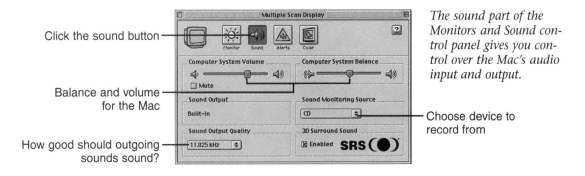

Click the sound button

Balance and volume for the Mac

How good should outgoing sounds sound?

*The sound part of the Monitors and Sound control panel gives you control over the Mac's audio input and output.*

Choose device to record from

Some of this stuff was already covered in Chapter 9, including the volume and balance sliders; they work just like they might on your car stereo or home stereo or office stereo or walkman. So let's talk about the slightly more weird stuff:

➤ **Sound Output.** Here you can choose where sound is supposed to head out of the Mac. If you have a special sound card installed in one of your Mac's NuBus or PCI slots, for instance, you might want to choose that card for sound output. Often you won't have much choice: **Built-in Sound** is often the default, and it means sound will be sent out via the "speaker" port on the back (or side) or your Mac. (If you have no speakers attached, you'll hear the sound through the Mac's built-in speaker or speakers.)

➤ **Sound Monitoring Source.** This menu is where you'll choose the device your Mac should listen to when you're ready to record. This can be the microphone, internal CD-ROM (playing an audio CD, I'd imagine), a line-in device (like an external stereo system), or some other device you've installed in your Mac.

➤ **Sound Output Quality.** Here you set the quality level your Mac should use when playing recorded digital sounds. The higher the number, the higher the level: 44.1 KHz is considered CD-quality; 22.05 KHz is about FM radio quality (or a little worse). Your setting should also match the quality level at which a particular recording was made. If you hear hissing or some other odd sound while listening to a digital audio recording, you might try changing this setting.

**Karaoke Mac?**

MIDI is actually pretty popular on the Internet. You can download lots of MIDI files that are songs that someone has played and recorded on their own keyboard or in a MIDI program. Using a MIDI player program, you can play them on your Mac. That will use the QuickTime library to play the MIDI song through your speakers. Or you can use MIDI player software to play the song on a keyboard synthesizer or similar instrument.

If you find a song you really like, you can build your own karaoke system. Plug a microphone into your home stereo, hook your stereo up to your Mac's microphone port, select **Sound In** as your monitoring source in the **Monitors and Sound** control panel, and then play a MIDI song. While it's playing, use the microphone and sing your brains out!

Once you have these set correctly, you're ready to record. As shown in Chapter 9, you can record using the Alerts section of the Monitors and Sound control panel. More likely, though, you'll want to record sound using a special program designed for the task.

# Making MIDI Music

Again, this one is going to fall a little outside the scope of this book, because MIDI programs, MIDI adapters, and MIDI instruments are all things you're going to need to get for yourself. Usually, you can get a MIDI adapter that attaches between your USB or serial ports and MIDI instruments, like keyboard synthesizers. Using programs on your Mac, you can play music on the synthesizer and have your Mac keep track of the notes you're playing. Then you can edit the music on your Mac and send it back out to the synthesizer for perfect playback. With the right controllers, lots of instruments, and good MIDI software, you can eventually put together a nice little orchestra in your basement or studio.

But I'm not going to tell you how to do that. The one thing I *will* tell you is that one big chunk of MIDI is built right into the Mac: the QuickTime Musical Instruments library. In essence, this makes it easy to turn your Mac into a MIDI instrument on its own. That means that just about any MIDI application can play back music through your Mac without an instrument attached, as long as the QuickTime Musical Instruments extension is present in your Extensions folder.

# Get Your Mac to Talk and Listen

Would it be convenient to have your Mac read your e-mail to you? Read Web pages or documents? It's possible. In fact, it's pretty easy. All you need are two things. You need to have Text-to-Speech turned on in your Speech control panel, and you need to have an application that's capable of implementing text-to-speech.

At the same time, you can get your Mac to listen to you speak, too, and respond to your commands. That happens in the Speech control panel, too.

## Mac Reads!

What's Text-to-Speech? It's technology added to the Mac OS that takes text—like, in SimpleText—and turns it into speech. The computer says what it sees. It's a little weird, but don't say that around your Mac. It may be sensitive.

Different settings
from this menu

*The Speech control panel lets you set a variety of talking and listening options for your Mac.*

First, the settings. For Text-to-Speech, the settings are pretty basic. If you have the Speech control panel open and working, you have all of the Speech extensions correctly loaded. In that case, Text-to-Speech is already active. If not, you'll need to pull down the **Apple** menu, choose **Control Panels**, **Extensions Manager**, and then make sure the following files are activated:

➤ Speech control panel

➤ Speech Manager extension

➤ Macintalk Pro or Macintalk Espanol extensions

Of these last two, only one of the Macintalk engines is required for Text-to-Speech to work correctly, according to Apple. You'll likely use Macintalk Pro, unless you want your Mac to speak in Spanish. Also, not shown in the Extensions Manager, you'll need Macintalk's voice files installed in a special Voices folder in your Extensions folder.

If you were forced to activate one or more of these extensions and control panels in the Extensions Manager (if they didn't have an "X" next to their entry, but you clicked to put one there), then you'll need to restart your Mac before Text-to-Speech is enabled.

To begin, open the Speech control panel. To choose a voice for your Mac, pull down the Options menu and select Voice. Now select a voice from the Voice menu—they all have names that suggest what they're going to sound like. To test a voice, click the small speaker icon next to the Voice menu. You can use the slide to change the rate at which it speaks—changing the rate slightly might make it sound more or less natural.

To begin, open the Speech control panel. To choose a voice for your Mac, pull down the **Options** menu and select **Voice**. Now select a voice from the **Voice** menu—they all have names that sort of suggest what they're going to sound like. To test a voice, click the small speaker icon next to the Voice menu. You can use the slide to change the rate at which it speaks; changing the rate slightly might make it sound more or less natural.

Do you want the Mac to speak alert boxes out loud? You can decide in the Speech control panel. From the **Options** menu, choose **Talking Alerts**.

Now put check marks next to the options you want activated. The **Speak the phrase:** option lets you choose what the voice will say to represent the "!" exclamation point in the alert box. (It can say "Halt," "Alert," and similar things.) Use the slider bar to determine how long your Mac will wait before it starts speaking the text. (This assumes you want it to speak when you're not looking at the monitor, for instance. If you see the alert, there isn't too much point in having it speak immediately.) If you empty both check boxes, Talking Alerts is no longer enabled.

Finally, you're ready for some speech. In a speech-enabled application, find the **Speak Text** command and select it. (SimpleText is a good place to start if you're just experimenting. The command is **Sound**, **Speak All**.) Now sit back, close your eyes, and allow your Mac to tell you a story.

## Mac Can Hear!

How about if your Mac could hear and obey your commands? You don't even have to rub its sides and say the magic words. This speech recognition thing sounds pretty exciting, right? Right?!

Well, it's okay, although the real action comes when you add dictation programs to your Mac. The built-in technology is cool, but the basic Mac OS speech recognition is only for moving around a bit in the Finder; unfortunately, you have to buy different software if you actually want to dictate to your Mac and have it type what you say.

For any type of speech, you'll need a PlainTalk microphone, and you'll need to have the microphone chosen as the sound-in source in the Monitors and Sound control panel. You'll also need to make sure you've installed the Speech Recognition software. Speech Recognition isn't installed by default, so you'll need to launch the Mac OS Installer and perform a custom install to activate speech recognition.

To turn on speech recognition, choose **Speakable Items** from the **Options** menu in the Speech control panel. You'll see an option to turn on Speakable Items. Click **On** to activate it. With a check in the **Recognized 'OK' and 'Cancel' buttons** option, you can say "OK" and "Cancel" out loud to respond to dialog boxes in any application.

Now a little box pops up complete with your Mac's new face. When you speak, the computer will hear and respond—assuming, of course, you say the computer's name correctly. You set that name back in the Speech control panel: Choose **Listening** from the **Options** menu. Put a check next to the method you want to use to get the computer's attention. (You can either click a key or say a name like "Computer.") If you choose **Keys toggle listening on and off**, you'll need to say the computer's name when you give it a command, but you can use the key shown in the dialog box to get the Mac to start or stop listening to you.

Close the Speech control panel and begin speaking.

*Here's your Mac's character, who responds when you speak commands.*

What do you say? You begin by saying the computer's name, and then you ask a question or issue a command, like "Computer, what time is it?" or "Computer, open the Chooser." Both of these should work.

You can find the possible commands in a menu on your **Apple** menu called **Speakable Items**. There you'll see all the possible commands your Mac can respond to.

You can also add commands. With the Speakable Items folder open (it's in the System Folder), you can do one of two things. You can create an alias to an application, like ClarisWorks, and give the alias a name like "Open ClarisWorks." When you give that speech command ("Computer, Open ClarisWorks"), it'll launch that alias, which, in turn, will open ClarisWorks.

Second, you can create AppleScripts that do things; for instance, an AppleScript that chooses the print command in an application. Create the AppleScript, save it in the Speakable Items, and then name it "Print This Document" or something similar. When you're ready, invoke the command "Computer, print this document" and see what happens.

**Faces and Aliases**

Two things. First, you can change the character your Mac uses to speak back to you; choose **Options, Feedback** in the Speech control panel. Second, you should be able to say "Open..." followed by any program name in the Apple menu. So you don't have to add absolutely every one of your applications or utilities to the Speakable Items folder if it's already on the Apple menu.

# The Least You Need to Know

There are three basic uses for sound on a Mac: You can record sounds digitally, you can use the MIDI language to control musical instruments, and your Mac can talk and listen using speech technologies.

Digital sound is your Mac's way of recording sounds to its hard drive—almost as you would record sounds to a cassette or minidisc recorder. To do this, you'll need to correctly set your Monitors and Sound control panel so that you have the right sound input device chosen and some other options are in order. Then you'll need to use a sound recording application and get to it!

For MIDI, you'll need special controllers, special electronic instruments, and MIDI software. In fact, there isn't much at all I can tell you about MIDI, except that QuickTime includes a MIDI extension that makes it possible for your Mac to act as a MIDI instrument and play back any MIDI songs you create or download.

The Mac can also read text on the screen and even respond to your speech commands if you have a microphone hooked up. Use the Speech control panel to turn on one or both of these features. Want SimpleText to read to you? It's a lot of fun.

# Other Mac Applications and Technologies

Mac OS 8.5 offers some other tidbits I thought you might find interesting—stuff that either sits in a corner waiting for you to come play or the occasional interface doo-dad that pops up when you least expect it. Let's take a quick look at some of those little extras that Apple includes in various places around your hard drive.

Please note that, while Apple has a folder called "Apple Extras" that's installed on your hard drive, that's not what I'm talking about exclusively. What's covered in this chapter are technologies that you'll use all the time while you're doing things with your Mac applications—things like the Color Picker and some of the small programs and desk accessories in the Apple menu. Plus, we'll talk about Apple's Java Runtime, which is in the Apple Extras folder but is used in many different situations.

## Extras in the Apple Menu

We discussed the Apple menu at length in Chapter 5, "Getting Things Done," but I punted on a variety of the little programs that appear there. Why? Because I thought it'd be cute to have them all gathered here, in this chapter, where they could stay together forever. Plus, they're all things you don't *have* to use if you don't want to.

These files aren't particularly related, either, except that you'll find them all on the Apple menu you when pull it down. Also, these applications are all actually *saved* in the Apple Menu Items folder in the System Folder. While most of the icons in there are aliases, these happen to be the full application. So don't drag them to the Trash if you're going to need them later. If you do, you'll have to re-install them from the Mac OS CD-ROM.

## AppleCD Audio Player

This little application is designed to let you work with an audio CD that's been put in your Mac's CD-ROM drive. While (most of the time) audio CDs will simply fire up and start playing, you can pull down the **Apple** menu and choose **AppleCD Audio Player** to get control over that audio CD.

In the CD Player, you can use the typical-looking CD player controls to move forward, back, and pause the playback. You can also separately control the volume with the volume slider bar. Likewise, as with many physical CD players, you can shuffle the CD songs or program certain songs to play.

**Control Strip CDs**

You can also use the CDStrip module to control audio CDs from the control strip. Look for the shiny CD icon in the control strip; that's where you'll find quick and convenient controls for playing audio CDs.

Click the small arrow, and the rest of the interface opens up to reveal all of the song tracks on that CD. Here you can edit the name of the CD, names of the songs, or double-click a track number to head directly to that track. Changes are automatically saved; the CD player can tell when you re-insert that particular CD and will respond with your names and labels. You also use this interface to program your songs; with the **Prog** button selected, you can drag and drop tracks to rearrange them.

## Apple Video Player

If your Mac has video digitizing capabilities, you'll find that you have an Apple Video Player entry on your Apple menu. This launches the Apple Video Player, which automatically displays the image being sent to it by the video inputs on your Mac. (Your Mac may also have come with other software that offers more advanced editing.)

You can use the video player as is (especially if you're just using it to watch a video input or television feed), assuming you have the cabling correct for video watching. You can also use the **Controls** from the **Windows** menu to pop up a little remote control for your video window. The icons on the right side of the Controls window allow you to switch between video capture, video setup and video playback modes. Use can use the capture controls, for instance, to capture QuickTime video or still PICT images from your video feed. Once you capture a movie, you can use the MoviePlayer application to play it back and use MoviePlayer Pro to edit it. (See Chapter 23, "QuickTime and Multimedia," for more on MoviePlayer).

## The Notepad

The Notepad is simply a convenient way to keep track of ideas, notes, URLs, or anything else you need to jot down quickly. I like to use new Notepad for important text that I use over and over again; for instance, boilerplate copy that I tend to use when replying to e-mail messages. If I'm planning to send e-mail to 20 different companies requesting PR kits, I'll build the first paragraph and put it in the Notepad. Then, whenever I write another one of those notes, I simply highlight the text on the Notepad, drag it to the document window, and start working with it.

The Notepad interface is simple. Just type as you would any document. To change pages, click the curled-up page corner at the bottom of the Notepad window. You've got eight pages to work with, but a lot of space on each page, so it isn't too limiting. If you want more pages, choose **File**, **New Note** from the menu, and you'll get a new page.

**Notepad File**

The Notepad data file is located in the System Folder in a file called Notepad File. If you need more than one Notepad, duplicate this file (**File**, **Duplicate**), and then rename it and save it in the Apple Menu Items folder. (Or save an alias to it in the Apple Menu Items folder.) Now you can choose that file (for example, "Phone Notes") instead of the Notepad application icon when you want to add notes to that particular notepad.

## The ScrapBook

The ScrapBook is another place where you can store things if you like. In this case, though, you'll probably want to use it to store image files and QuickTime documents, both of which the ScrapBook can handle. That way, you can quickly get to images and movies you use often in your documents or presentations. An example might be your company's logo. Instead of finding it on your hard drive so you can launch the logo file, copy it and paste it into a document; you can simply store it in the ScrapBook, and then copy and paste (or drag and drop) when the desire hits.

The ScrapBook works with simple copy and paste; you can also drag and drop images or text into ScrapBook. Copy the image, movie, or styled text out of the document where it was created (or where it currently resides). Choose the **Apple** menu icon and then **ScrapBook**. Now, choose **Edit**, **Paste**. The object you copied and pasted should appear at the *end* of the series of items in the ScrapBook.

## Stickies Notes

Do you have sticky notes plastered to the front of your monitor? What if you could plaster them on your Mac's desktop, too? It's built right in.

Choose **Apple** menu, **Stickies**, and you'll see a couple of notes that explain how Stickies work. They're easy enough to use; just choose **File**, **New** to create a new sticky, and then type your note. You can keep hundreds of different notes on your screen if you want to (as long as your Stickies application has enough memory). Realize, though, that Stickies work slightly differently from regular Mac document windows. Following are the differences:

➤ *No scrollbars.* You scroll sticky notes by clicking to place the cursor in the note, and then use the arrow keys to move around.

➤ *Auto-saved.* Notes that appear on the screen are saved automatically; you don't have to do anything special. You save only notes you no longer want to display onscreen.

➤ *Don't close.* Clicking the close box will allow you to close the sticky from the screen and ask you to save the file. If you choose to save, it's saved as a regular text document for SimpleText. Once you close a sticky, you can't get it back as a sticky; you'll have to re-create it from the text file.

**Stickies File**

For the sake of balance, I'll let you know that Stickies create a file in the Preferences folder (in the System folder) where the Stickies info is stored. If you ever need to move your Stickies to another Mac, copy that file to the new Mac's Preferences folder, and you've got 'em.

I use a lot of sticky notes, usually as reminders I never check until it's too late. Still, I find them invaluable. My best tip for folks who use sticky notes a lot is this: On the first line of your sticky, give it a good, descriptive title. Now click the windowshade box (you'll need to hold down the **Option** key to get the windowshade box to appear) or double-click the title bar to minimize the window. Now you can have a whole lot of notes on your screen at once and still see what they're all for. Then just open up the notes when you need to edit or read them.

# The Apple System Profiler

With Mac OS 8.5, Apple includes a very powerful program designed to help you do a little troubleshooting and—more to the point—help you when you're talking to Apple's or other vendor's customer service folks. You can use the Apple System Profiler to get all sorts of info about your Mac, including information about attached peripherals, extensions, and control panels, and even what sort of processor your Mac has.

To open the Profiler, pull down the **Apple** menu and choose **Apple System Profiler.** The Profiler appears onscreen; open to the System Profile tab that shows you many different things about your Mac.

To check out other parts of your system, click one of the tabs at the top of the window. You can find out what drives and devices are attached to your SCSI chain (**Devices and Volumes**), what startup files are enabled on your Mac (**Control Panels** and **Extensions**); you can even check out what **Applications** you have installed on your Mac and how many different **System Folders** you have installed.

Perhaps the most complicated of the tabs is the **Devices and Volumes** tab, which allows you to get another, deeper level of information about the devices connected. Aside from showing you what SCSI ID numbers are currently in use and what drive technologies—IDE or SCSI—are being used, you can get very specific information about a particular device by clicking the small **down-arrow** next to each device entry. That will alter the window to show you information about the drive's formatting, size, percentage used, and more. It's very handy.

Different device "buses"
and subsystems

Click arrow to reveal more info

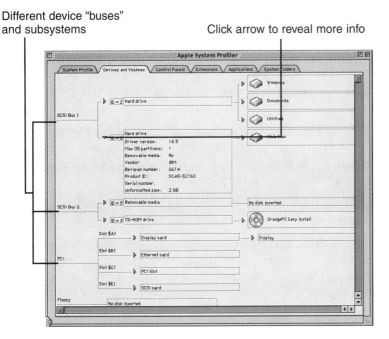

*The Apple System Profiler can be used to give you in-depth information about nearly any device attached to your Mac.*

If you'd like a report you can view and print, choose **File**, **New Report**, and then check off the items you want reported in the **New Report** window. Click **OK** when you're ready to have the report generated. You can then Save or Print the report.

# How Mac Java Works

Maybe you've heard a lot about Java, and you've wondered what the hype is. Well, lend me your ear, friend. Java is a programming language developed by the Sun Corporation. A lot of people like it because it's reasonably new and it works a lot like many of the programming languages that programmer's are accustomed to, except it's a bit more intelligent in some areas.

There's another part, too: Java programs can be written in the Java language, and then run on top of nearly any operating system out there. You can run the same program on UNIX, Windows, Mac, and so on. That's quite a step, because most programs are designed to run only on one OS, requiring a rewrite to be useful on another.

## *The Java Virtual Machine*

For Java to do this, it needs a little help. The Java Virtual Machine (JVM) works as a sort of emulator in which Java applications run. When a Java application says, "Show the user a button," the Mac JVM knows how to display a Mac-style button while the Windows JVM knows how to display Windows-style buttons.

Of course, things have to be as confusing as possible in computing, so there are actually a number of virtual machines available for the Mac OS. Most of them are written by the same folks who bring you Web browsers: Microsoft and Netscape. Symantec has also contributed a JVM, as has Apple. In fact, these days Microsoft and Apple work together on their JVM.

Apple's version is called the Mac OS Runtime for Java (MRJ). Aside from sounding like Julius Erving before he got a Ph.D., MRJ is also the basis for running Java applications on your Mac. You'll find some of MRJ hanging out in a subfolder of your Apple Extras folder called Mac OS Runtime for Java (of all things!).

## *Java and Web Browsers*

Many people associate Java with Web browsing, because one popular use for Java is writing small *applets* that can run on Web pages—usually card games, stock tickers, weather forecasts, and that sort of thing. Java isn't only about browsers, though, as you'll see in the next section.

In this section, though, Java is about browsers. If you'd like to view and use Java applets when you come across them on the Web, you'll need to have your browser properly configured to deal with Java. Netscape Navigator tends to work with its own JVM, so there isn't too much to worry about there. You can control if Netscape loads and runs Java applets, though. In Navigator 4.0 and higher, choose **Edit**, **Preferences**, and then choose the **Advanced** category. Click to check or uncheck the check box next to **Enable Java**. Click **OK** after you've made your decision.

There's an extra step in Internet Explorer, because you'll need to choose the JVM to use if you plan to enable Java. In Internet Explorer 4.0 and above, choose **Edit**, **Preferences**, and then choose the **Java** category. Now click the check box at the top of the window to **Enable Java**. To choose your JVM, pull down the **Java virtual machine** menu and make your selection. Click **OK** when you're done.

If you have Java enabled, there's nothing else you need to do to work with applets on the Internet; if a particular Web page features a Java applet, it will load and run automatically.

## Running Java Programs

Although associated with the Web, Java is more than that. If you like, you can run full-fledged applications using Java. All you really need to do is double-click a Java application to get it running. If the MRJ is correctly installed, your Java application will start up like any other.

If you have a Java applet (not a full application) you'd like to run, you can do that, too—only this time you'll need the Apple Applet Runner. You'll find it in the Mac OS Runtime for Java folder. Double-click the Applet Runner to start it up, and then use **File**, **Open** to open and run Java applets.

Full-fledged Java applications don't need to use the Applet Runner. Instead, you can simply double-click the Application's icon, and it should fire right up. The only thing you'll probably notice about the Java application is that it can look slightly different from a typical Mac OS application; sometimes the buttons, icons, or screens can look a little odd. Remember, Java applications are designed to run on any computer that supports Java. That means the same application will work in Windows, the Mac OS, and on UNIX, without changing a thing about it.

*Formula One for Java is a full-fledged application written in the Java language; it can run just as easily in Microsoft Windows as it does on the Mac OS.*

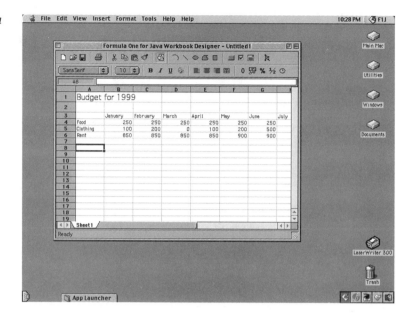

# Picking Your Colors

You really can't go *directly* to the Color Picker; it's not an application or a control panel, but it's still very important in many different Macintosh applications. Most times, when you're called upon to pick a color in an application, you'll be using the Color Picker. (If you'd like to see it, you can access it through the Appearance control panel. Click the **Appearance** tab, then pull down the **Highlight Color** menu, and choose **Other**. The Color Picker will appear.)

*The Color Picker isn't a program; it's an interface element, similar to the File Open dialog box. Programmers can add the Color Picker to their own applications.*

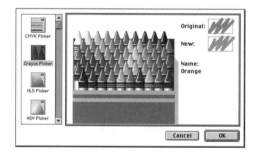

The Color Picker offers you many different sophisticated ways to pick colors, including the CMYK, HLS, and HSV pickers. If you're a color wizard, publishing maven, or professional artist, you may know what all that means. If not, though, you

**318**

may enjoy my favorite color picker: **Crayon Picker**. Select that one, and you can choose colors as if you were choosing crayons from one of those large boxes with the sharpener in it.

You may also find that the RGB (Red, Green, Blue) color picker or the HTML color picker makes sense for you. Which you use doesn't really matter, though. Just click to select the picker you'd like on the left side of the window, and then choose the color on the right side. Sometimes, you'll use slider bars, sometimes you'll use numbers, and sometimes you'll point and click. It's fairly easy—experiment.

Once you have the color you need, click **OK,** and you'll be whisked back to your application, with the color in tow. The application should then know what to do with it.

# The Least You Need to Know

You'll find that the Mac OS drops a few orphans in different places on your hard drive—programs and technologies that have no specific place in every application but might find a place in your heart.

On the Apple menu, you'll find some fun, little remote controls; it's a little like digging between the cushions on your coach. The AppleCD Audio Player and Apple Video Player are both a good time for Mac owners with a hi-fi, AV setup. Others on the Apple menu include the Notepad, ScrapBook, and Stickies, all of which can help you get a little better organized. In fact, you may find you use each of these every day to make things go just a touch smoother as you work.

One other Apple menu application is the Apple System Profiler—a great tool for taking a look at the innards of your Mac. You'll find it helpful when troubleshooting external devices and when you're wondering about your Mac's components, but the real convenience kicks in when you call an Apple support line. You'll be able to tell them most of what they need to know.

Heard of Java? It's a programming language that happens to work on almost every OS out there. With it, you can run applets in your Web browser and full-fledged applications on your Mac. All you need is the Mac OS Runtime for Java and some preferences settings.

Finally, there's the Color Picker. If you're ever in an application and you need to choose a color, you'll meet the Picker. My personal favorite is the crayons picker, which lets you pick colors with names like Raw Sienna and Warm Marble. But there are plenty of more sophisticated ways to pick colors, too.

# Part 6

# Keep Mac Happy

*It's often heard that Macs are reasonably trouble-free, well-behaved, and easy to maintain. And that's true, within reason. The fact is, any computer engineer is a complex combination of high-caffeine cola, meat-sauce pizza, and a few too many all-nighters. When you stop to consider who's putting these computers together, maybe it's not so far-fetched that they break every once in a while.*

*I don't even want to know what you'd think if you stopped to consider who, exactly, is writing this book.*

*In these chapters you'll see how to give a Mac first aid (unplug before giving mouth-to-mouth), how you can deal with persistent bugs, and what sort of maintenance routine you should be performing on your Mac's software to keep it healthy.*

# Chapter 26

# Dealing with an Unhappy Mac

## In This Chapter

➤ When your Mac doesn't start

➤ Emergency procedures

➤ First Aid for your Mac

➤ Exploratory surgery

➤ Erasing your hard drive and starting over

Macs are great, but they can have problems. Most of the problems you'll encounter will be software issues—things that probably can be fixed or worked around. Occasionally, you may come across something that actually has to do with the Mac's hardware, but such problems don't happen too often.

I like to look at Mac maintenance the same way I look at the lifeguards on *Baywatch*. (Maybe that's a bad example.) What I'm saying is, you need to perform First Aid— you've got to get your Mac up and on its feet—before you can dig deeper to figure out what's really going on and causing trouble.

That's what this chapter is about...*Baywatch*. (I've got to stop doing that.) In these pages, you'll see how to wrest your Mac back from the grip of death, set it upright and in its locked position, and begin the long, arduous process of getting your hair back into place.

Smile. You're a huge star in Brazil.

# When Your Mac's Got a Wee Case of Death

Say that you've got your Mac powered up and the monitor seems to be on, but you're getting an odd little icon on the screen. Instead of a happy Mac telling you all is well, you've got a Sad Mac icon or a blinking disk drive icon. Something has gone wrong; now it's up to you to find out what.

When you find out, you'll probably approach the problem using some of the common tricks of the Mac troubleshooting trade, including re-blessing System Folders, booting from CD-ROM drives, and zapping PRAM. Ready?

## The Sad Mac Icon

The Sad Mac icon often indicates a hardware problem. Although you don't have to run your Mac down to the Mac shop for repairs immediately, this icon may suggest that something to do with a connector, internal card, RAM module, or similar computer component has gone wrong.

One way you can be almost sure that the Sad Mac is telling you about a hardware problem is if it shows up without much of anything else happening—like the Happy Mac showing up or your Mac changing to the "Welcome to Mac OS" screen. In this case, the first thing to do is to try restarting the Mac. You may have to throw the power switch or punch the reset button (check your Mac's manual). Sometimes, after a restart, the Sad Mac clears itself up, and you don't have further problems.

If you continue to see the Sad Mac, then you may have a problem with the RAM or upgrade cards you've installed in your Mac. If you've just been working with an upgrade, then take things apart and see whether you can do a better job of installing whatever it was. If you haven't just been upgrading—and you don't think anything traumatic like dropping the Mac or getting a power surge has taken place—then you may have a software problem.

If you see the Sad Mac due to a software problem, it's likely caused by something similar to the problems that cause the flashing "?" issue. So, troubleshoot as if a "?" is the problem. How do you troubleshoot that? Hold on, now. I was just going to tell you.

## The Flashing "?" Problem

Usually, a little disk icon accompanies this flashing "?" giving it at least a bit more meaning. The point is that your Mac can't find its startup drive. It could have this problem because somebody has grabbed it and headed for the hills. A more likely scenario, however, is that something is slightly wrong with the System Folder on your startup drive.

So what can go wrong? First, you may have a System Folder with a corrupt or missing System file. When you have this problem, the System Folder can become "unblessed," which is a cutesy way of saying that it's no longer an active System Folder.

*A blessed System Folder has this icon; an unblessed System Folder has a regular, plain vanilla folder icon.*

Of course, other problems could affect your hard drive as well, including a problem with other System files (including some sort of corruption), SCSI problems, cabling issues, heat, hard drive failure, or something similar. You could even have a problem with PRAM, which I'll discuss in a moment. For now, let's begin with what to do with that blinking "?" of yours.

**No "?" Too**

You might encounter this problem without a flashing "?" too. I've seen external drives that don't start *and* they don't show the "?" leaving you to wonder what exactly is wrong. Go ahead and troubleshoot as shown in this section.

## Start from Another Disk

Your Mac should attempt to find a good System Folder on all attached drives if it can't find one where it expects it to be—usually on the main hard drive. If your Mac can't seem to get started without a little help, then you can try restarting from a Mac OS CD-ROM. (If you have a non-Apple Mac OS clone computer, you may need to start using the original CD that came with that Mac.)

To start from a CD, open the CD-ROM drive and place the Mac OS CD in the drive tray. Then close the drive and restart your Mac. It should find the valid System Folder on that CD-ROM and start the Mac OS. If it doesn't, try restarting again, this time holding down the letter **C** on your keyboard immediately after hearing the startup chime.

If you can't get the Mac OS to start from the CD that way, try holding down ⌘+**Option+Shift+Delete** until the Mac finds a valid System Folder.

## Re-Bless the System Folder

After you start with the CD, you can then run Disk First Aid on your main hard drive to see whether it can find the problem. (Disk First Aid is a disk-fixing tool found on the Mac OS CD-ROM. It's also discussed later in this chapter.) As an alternative, you can clean-install the Mac OS and try to start over again with your hard drive.

If your problem is that the System Folder on your hard drive is unblessed (it has a regular folder icon), then you can attempt to "re-bless" it before trying a clean installation. You can also "re-bless" the System Folder by dragging the System file back into the System Folder itself, if you dragged it out somehow. If you can't find the System file, use the **Find** command in the Finder to locate it.

If the System file *is* in the System Folder, but the folder is a regular-old-lookin' folder, then you can still try re-blessing it. Drag the System file out of the System Folder (to the Desktop, for instance), and then drag it back into the System Folder. Check the folder icon. Is the System Folder blessed now? If it is, great! You should be able to restart.

## Still Doesn't Start? Zap PRAM

If your Mac still doesn't choose the right drive, or if you never got past step one and the CD-ROM thing didn't work, then you should try two things. First, you should disconnect *any* external SCSI devices and start again. SCSI just loves to create problems like this.

If that trick doesn't work, you can try zapping PRAM. Parameter RAM is a small portion of static RAM (fed by a small battery on the logic board to keep it working) that holds many different settings on your Mac—some of the stuff you set through control panels and the Chooser. If data in PRAM becomes corrupt, all sorts of weird things can happen.

**Lip-Reading Mac**

Try not to curse your Mac for being troublesome if you happen to have either a microphone or one of those infrared ports built into your Mac. Remember what HAL did to the crew of the Discovery in *2001: A Space Odyssey*? Want to wake up from your cryogenic sleep chamber only to find that you're...dead?

In fact, zapping PRAM is sort of a last ditch, catchall solution to many different Mac problems. If you can't figure out the problem, try zapping PRAM. It doesn't do too much harm. Here's how: Restart your Mac. Right after you hear the startup tone, hold down the keys ⌘+**Option+P+R** until you hear the startup tone at least two more times. Now, PRAM has been zapped. Sit back and see whether your Mac starts. If it doesn't, restart one more time, this time following the instructions for starting from a CD.

# First Aid for Your Mac's Disks

Startup trouble could be the symptom of a hard disk problem that's affecting the Mac's ability to get data loaded and dealt with. This problem doesn't have to be a hardware problem; that is, the hard drive doesn't have to be wearing out or something. It might be a software problem.

Part of the Mac OS's job is to manage all the files that get created and saved to your hard drive over the course of time. Eventually, you'll run into a snag. Either a file will become corrupt (usually as a result of an application crashing or the Mac OS hanging), or the file system itself can become corrupt. For that reason, after a crash, Mac OS 8.5 runs Disk First Aid automatically.

If you're having trouble that hasn't required such a restart, however, you can still run Disk First Aid to see how things are going. (In fact, running Disk First Aid periodically as a precaution is not a bad idea.)

You can find the program on your Mac OS installation CD-ROM or in the folder called Utilities on your hard drive. Double-click the **Disk First Aid** icon to launch the program.

With the Disk First Aid window open, you can see that using it is actually pretty easy. In the top of the window, choose the drive you feel needs a bit of checking up. Then click the **Verify** button if you just want to test the drive or **Repair** if you want to both verify the drive and test it. (Frankly, I don't see much reason not to do both, but you may come up with one.)

After you start the program running, a progress bar appears in the lower-left corner, and messages pop up in the **Review instructions and results** window pane. Problems pop up in red.

**PRAM Woes**

Not too much bad will result from zapping PRAM, although you'll find that some settings change. For example, AppleTalk, which defaults to On in the Chooser, may change; General Preferences might change; your Startup Disk returns to the default; File Sharing settings may change; and a few others. For a few days after zapping PRAM, expect a little odd behavior that you might need to fix by reselecting a setting or two.

Click the
drive to test

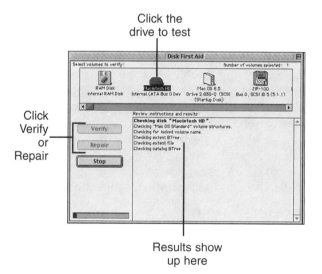

Click
Verify
or
Repair

Results show
up here

*Disk First Aid is Mac's built-in tool for fixing software-based hard drive problems.*

Running Disk First Aid takes a few minutes, but it likely doesn't need your help, so you can grab a good book, run over to your SoloFlex, or do whatever you need to do. Come back after a few minutes or a few hours, and you'll see that Disk First Aid has completed its mission, ready to quit or check another disk. With luck, your problems will be over.

### File a Report

You can save the report that Disk First Aid creates while it's checking your drive. Why? So you can see any patterns of behavior if you happen to be running into chronic problems. Choose **File, Save Results** to save the report.

# Exploratory Surgery: Drive Setup

Another utility called Drive Setup is included with Mac OS 8.5; this one is really designed to allow you to *initialize* a hard disk, which means erasing it completely, laying down a new file system, and starting from scratch. Initialization is a last-ditch approach to problems, but it is one solution. First, though, you should try some other approaches.

Drive Setup can help you with a few maintenance tasks. Let me add one caveat, though: Drive Setup can't do too terribly much with the current startup disk. You may have to use the Startup Disk control panel to change to another drive that has an active System Folder, or you may need to boot from the Mac OS 8.5 CD-ROM to get the best results when dealing with your startup drive.

### Apple Only

Realize that Drive Setup is really meant only for Apple-brand disk drives. It probably won't allow you to use it with other drives—at least, not for initialization—but if you do use it with non-Apple drives, you could cause more harm than help. Any internal drive that originally came with a Mac is an Apple drive in this context, even if it was manufactured by a different company.

## Drive Setup Quick Fixes

If you're having trouble getting a drive to appear on the Desktop (its icon is missing), the problem occurred likely because the drive didn't *mount* for some reason. This problem may have various causes, some of which are software issues that can be fixed with a program such as Disk First Aid. Unfortunately, you can't fix a disk if you can't see it. So, you can use Drive Setup to attempt to mount the disk.

Here's how to get started. Open Drive Setup. In its main window, you should see every drive that's connected to your Mac, including any that may not be mounted. To mount a particular drive, select it in the window, and then select **Functions, Mount Volumes** from the menu.

If you find that your problem is that the disk needs to be turned on or warmed up, you can try choosing **Functions, Rescan the Bus** after the drive is ready to be noticed by your Mac.

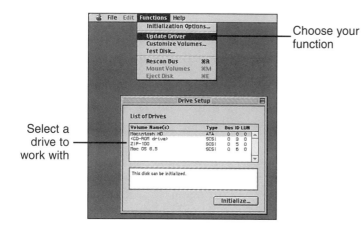

Choose your function

Select a drive to work with

*Drive Setup is a powerful but slightly dangerous utility. Don't accidentally initialize a drive; if you do, you'll wipe all the data off it.*

For Apple drives, you can also use Drive Setup to update the driver software for the drive—that's the software that speaks to the Mac OS at the lowest levels of computer insider chat. Updating it is pretty much always a good idea. To update the driver, select the drive in question, and choose **Functions, Update Driver.**

## The Cosmo Quiz for Drives

Need to see whether your drive can pass the test of longevity? Is the relationship between your data and your drive rocky for a reason? You can use Drive Setup to perform a rather low-level test on the disk itself to check for physical imperfections and errors that could be affecting your drive's capability to save data cleanly. (These bad sections of the disk are then mapped so that the OS can avoid saving to them.)

What would make you suspect this problem? If you have chronic problems with saving—you seem to have corrupt files in a number of different programs, documents, or other files—your problems could have to do with a bad part of the hard drive itself. That problem alone might make the testing worthwhile.

To test the drive, select it and then choose **Functions, Test Disk.** You then see a dialog box that warns you of the dangers and allows you to click **Cancel** to recover with dignity. If you're certain you want to go through with this process, click Start.

**Testing Safety Precautions**

This testing process is a pretty dangerous one. Ideally, your data is safe, but a lot of testing and data movement are going on. If power to your Mac is interrupted or something similar happens, you could lose a lot of important data. Before performing a test like this, I advise you to make a complete backup.

## *Your Initialization Options*

The final Drive Setup task you can accomplish is formatting—or initializing—the drive. This task is called *initializing* because you're getting ready to set up the drive as if this were its initial go-around. You'll be erasing all the data, putting down a brand new file system, and getting ready to reinstall the Mac OS or whatever else you've backed up from this drive. If that's what you really want to do, then so be it. Fire up Drive Setup and choose the drive you want to initialize. Now, choose **Functions, Initialization Options**.

First, you should see two different formatting options. You can click to place a check mark next to either of these choices. What do they mean? A Low level format means the Mac does more than just sweep away the existing file system; it also tests the drive and maps out bad sectors so that they're not used in future saves. This option is a great idea, but formatting a drive this way can take a very long time.

You can also choose Zero All Data, which simply writes zeros to every single storage bit on the drive, meaning it completely wipes the drive free of the data that was on it. This choice is best if you don't want anyone to be able to use a format-recovery utility to see any data you may have stored on the machine. It also takes much longer than a typical initialization, though.

Click **OK** if you chose either of these options or **Cancel** if you didn't.

## *Partitioning and Formatting*

Now, you're ready to initialize the drive. With the correct drive name still selected in the Drive Setup window, click the **Initialize** button. You then see the Initialize dialog box, which is meant to verify that you really want to *destroy all the data* on the drive you've selected and lay down a new file system. Check this three times before proceeding.

You should also consider whether you want to partition the hard drive into separate "virtual" drives. Each virtual drive appears on your Desktop with its own name and icon, even though it's part of your current drive. You simply take a portion of the available storage and give it a new name.

For instance, I have three icons that represent one drive on my Mac. My 4 GB drive offers a decent amount of space. So, I split it up three different ways: one portion for my SoftWindows stuff, one for documents, and one for utilities. Splitting up the drive makes things a little easier for me to organize because I'm managing a lot of files.

If you've decided to partition your drive, click the **Custom Setup** button. In the Custom Setup dialog box, you can choose the number of partitions and the type of file system you'll be putting on each.

### Block Sizes and Mac OS Extended Format

Another good reason to partition a drive *is block sizes.* On a drive formatted with the Mac OS Standard format (also called HFS), you will find a fixed number of blocks (about 65,000) per drive. No matter what the size of the drive, it has only that many blocks. The larger the drive, the larger the blocks. Unfortunately, you can save only one file per block, so even if the file doesn't fill the block, you can't save another one there.

The result: You waste a lot of space on a very large drive. So, partitioning the drive into smaller virtual drives—each with its own 65,000 blocks—means you waste less space on the hard disk as a whole. The best results are at about 512 MB of virtual drive; 1 GB partitions are probably more realistic for today's drives though.

As an alternative, you can use Mac OS Extended format, also called HFS Plus, when you format your hard drive. Mac OS Extended format offers many more allocation blocks, meaning the size isn't as constrained as before and the drive is used more efficiently.

The downside to Mac OS Extended format is that it isn't backward compatible; Macs running Mac OS 8.0 or earlier cannot read a Mac OS Extended format drive. If your Mac isn't on a network, that shouldn't be a problem. If you do use your Mac—or the disk in question—with other Macs, you should consider this fact before formatting in Mac OS Extended format.

Also, realize that some earlier hard drive utilities—such as Norton Utilities 3.5—are not compatible with Mac OS Extended format and shouldn't be run on such a drive. Check to make sure before you use your disk fixing utility.

Choose the number of partitions you want from the **Partitioning Scheme** menu. (ProDOS, incidentally, is the formatting scheme for Apple II series computers, just in case you need to save Apple II data on your Mac—perhaps for use with an Apple II emulator program.)

In the **Volumes** pane, you can select each partition individually by clicking it with the mouse. A little box appears at the bottom of each partition, allowing you to resize it. You can also enter an exact size for the selected partition in the **Size** entry box.

Next, select each partition individually. Then, from the **Type** menu, choose the sort of format the partition—Mac OS Standard (HFS) or Mac OS Extended (HFS Plus)—should use.

With all your choices made, click the **OK** button.

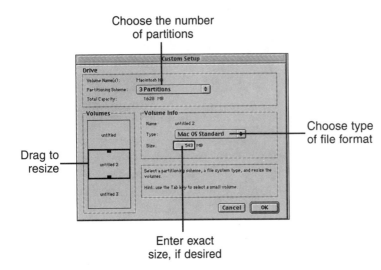

Choose the number
of partitions

*Partitioning isn't tough,
but it isn't for the faint of
heart, either. If it isn't
making much sense to
you, you might want to
just skip it and format the
whole drive as one*

Choose type *partition.*
of file format

Drag to
resize

Enter exact
size, if desired

## Erasing Everything on Your Hard Drive

With all your choices made and everything set to go, only one last task is at hand. Click the **Initialize** button. The initialization begins, and the drive is erased and ready for new software—maybe even a brand new installation of the Mac OS. But this process takes awhile. In the meantime, go watch a movie on TV, read the paper, or take the dog for a walk. You deserve a break after all these decisions.

## The Least You Need to Know

Life can be pretty traumatic when a Mac seems to have fallen and can't get up—especially if you have little blinking icons on the screen that don't seem like they can possibly be good signs. And they're not. But they do mean something, and they make for a good place to start troubleshooting.

Using your Mac OS CD-ROM, you can get your Mac started again, at which point you have some tools to help you fix that drive, including Disk First Aid and Drive Setup. Run Disk First Aid, and you may find that your problems are solved. Or you may need to dig a little deeper.

Using Drive Setup, you can head in for exploratory surgery. You can install a new disk driver, mount the drive if necessary, and perform a low-level test on the media. If things aren't looking good, you may need to format the drive.

The Mac OS includes tools for formatting and partitioning the drive. You need to choose between Mac OS Standard and Mac OS Extended format and then create your partitions and choose how serious of an initialization you want—regular, low-level, or zero out the data. Then erase everything on the drive, and you're ready to start over.

UH-OH...

# Chapter 27

# Fixing Mac Errors

## In This Chapter

➤ Crash, Error, or Freeze: Why?

➤ Squashing Bugs, Rooting Out Corruption

➤ Finding and Resolving Conflicts

➤ How About That Internet?

And they said that Macs didn't crash. (Whoever said that hasn't used one in a while.) In fact, all computers crash, and, especially, nearly all computer programs crash every once in a while. In large part, OS makers like Apple and Microsoft don't focus on making the OS work so that programs don't crash; they spend more time making it so that if an application does crash, the OS can recover from it gracefully.

Mac OS 8.5 does that better than any OS so far. Many, many application crashes will recover nicely to the Finder, allowing you to keep working or restart the Mac, fire up the offending application, and start again where you left off.

Crashing and error messages aren't the norm, however, so we should concern ourselves a bit with the question, "Why is Mac crashing?" or "Why is a particular application crashing?" Troubleshooting those answers can lead to answers that make your computing experience that much more enjoyable. Let's take a close look at what the different sorts of crashes and errors are, and then we'll examine how best to troubleshoot them.

# The Types of Software Failure

There are four types of failures you're likely to encounter while working with your Mac: error messages, crashes, hangs, and freezes. The symptoms of each of these are different, and you deal with them differently, as well. Often, the type of failure that occurs will sometimes give you an idea of why you're having the trouble and what you should do about it.

Here's a quickie description of the four failure types and how to recover from them:

➤ *Error message.* This sort of failure may be accompanied by the application quitting, and it may not, but it gives you a message that something is wrong—ranging from something basic like "Out of Memory" to something a bit more cryptic like a "Type 11 Error." My favorites, though, are the painfully obvious error messages like "*The Program* Unexpectedly Quit." I can tell. You usually recover from an error message by clicking **OK** in the alert box, saving your data, and quitting the program. You can then either restart the program or restart your Mac (to be safe).

➤ *Crashes.* These failures mean the program itself quits or disappears without an error message. (An "unexpected quit" sort of fits in both categories.) With some error messages, you get a chance to recover and save your data before quitting; with crashes, that doesn't happen. Instead, the program simply quits, sometimes without a warning. There usually isn't anything to do after a crash except save data in your other applications and restart your Mac.

➤ *Hangs.* This sort of failure means the program has become caught in a logic loop. It's constantly waiting for something, calculating something, or otherwise working to no end. You usually can't recover from this and save your data, although you might be able to quit the program and save data in others before restarting your Mac. In this case, the first thing you should do is wait. An apparent freeze might just mean your Mac is running slow, not frozen. (Especially if you see any sort of activity at all.) Next you should try pressing the **Esc** key and waiting. If that doesn't work, press ⌘+"**.**" (period). If none of those works, you can Force Quit by pressing ⌘+**Shift+Esc** and clicking the **Force Quit** button. This may work, or it may result in a freeze.

➤ *Freezes.* This last type of failure affects the whole Mac. A single program may have crashed, but it managed to affect other programs or the Mac OS itself with the crash, forcing your entire computer to freeze. (A freeze's most tell-tale sign is usually a mouse pointer that won't move.) You can't quit to the Finder or save any data in programs. Once you've determined this is a freeze (and not a hang, which has similar symptoms, except that you can usually move the mouse pointer), your only recourse is to restart your Mac by pressing **Ctrl+⌘+Power key**, pressing the reset switch on your Mac, or turning the power switch off and on again.

So those are the types of software failures and ways to get out of them. Once you've experienced a failure, though—or maybe after you've experienced the same failure once or twice—it's time to begin to concern yourself with the reasons for the crash. Why did this happen? (Or why does it keep happening?) That points you to the three different reasons for crashes: corruption, conflicts, and critters.

Okay, critters are really "bugs," but I couldn't come up with another "c" word for bugs. Crustaceans? Creepy-crawlers?

### Just Plain Slow

Sometimes your Mac may seem to have hung or frozen when, in fact, it's just doing something very slowly. This is especially true if you're copying files over the Internet or over a network. One tell-tale sign is if you see left- and right-facing arrows (or other blinking icons) in the top-left corner of your Mac's screen, on the toolbar right next to the Apple icon. That means network activity is taking place, and your Mac may not actually be hung up. Just wait patiently, get a cup of coffee, and see if things don't right themselves.

## Bugs

Let's take the last one first. Bugs are really nothing more than mistakes; they're problems in a program that haven't been fixed, probably because the programmer doesn't realize they're there. Usually, these bugs cause the program to act strangely (or poorly) under certain circumstances, after you've performed certain things in order, or when you do something in particular. Say you choose the **File**, **Print** command in an application, but the print dialog box doesn't show up. That's usually because of a bug—a mistake—in the program itself. The same might be true if elements don't align correctly on a page, the program doesn't correctly save a file, or if the program just doesn't do what it's supposed to do.

Because bugs are internal mistakes in a program, there really isn't much the typical user can do—except not use that particular command or stop using the program. Usually, the best plan is to wait around until the company that writes the program releases a bug fix or an updated version of the program that solves the problem. You might try calling that company's customer service line to make sure they know about the problem and see if they can suggest any workarounds. Or you can take some of the advice (later in this chapter) on upgrading and using the Internet to find solutions.

## Conflicts

Errors and crashes can result from two programs—or one program and the Mac OS—not getting along very well. It could be because the programs are trying to do the same thing, it could be that they both are trying to access the same part of the Mac OS or a particular peripheral, or it could be that the two of them just have strong personalities.

Actually, you'll often find that the more pronounced conflicts occur between a program and an extension to the Mac OS; sometimes an older program conflicts with a new Apple extension, or sometimes programs conflict with a non-Apple extension. This is especially true if the extension dramatically changes how something works in the Mac OS; for instance, an extension that speeds up the Mac or doubles RAM can often cause conflicts.

The way around conflicts is usually not to run both programs, extensions, or other problem files at the same time. Sometimes you'll just toss one out or replace it; other times you can remember to just keep them on opposite sides of your Mac.

We'll talk about conflict management a little later in this chapter.

**Memory Fragmentation**

Getting a lot of out-of-memory errors? You may actually be experiencing a different kind of corruption: memory fragmentation. Just as some problems happen to files because your Mac is writing to the hard drive a lot, your Mac can have the same problems after it has been running for a while, especially if you've been launching and quitting a bunch of programs. After a while, memory can become fragmented, resulting in less memory that's available to applications. (This can also be more insidious; some programs don't work well with RAM and can hog it, causing problems.) The solution: Restart your Mac. If the out-of-memory errors are related to memory fragmentation, they'll disappear.

## Corruption

The third reason you'll see errors is deeply rooted in the Mac OS's file management system: corruption. This usually refers to corrupt files, and it usually happens when the Mac gets interrupted while it has a file open or it's trying to write to a particular file. In fact, some other sort of crash can often lead to corruption, which then leads to crashes. It's like the endless single-sided Moebius strip, except this one keeps you from getting any work done at the office.

Viruses—self-replicating programs that attach themselves to your applications and documents—can also cause files to become corrupt. If you suspect a virus, see the section "Does My Mac Have a Virus?" later in this chapter.

Once a file becomes corrupt, it can cause an application to crash when the file is accessed. For instance, a corrupt document can incorrectly signal to an application that the "end of file" has been reached, even though the application doesn't have all the data it needs. The result might be a crash.

There are two good ways to tell if corruption is affecting your applications. First, it's likely corruption if your application crashes when accessing a particular document—say, every time you try to load a particular memo. Second, it's likely that corruption has set in if you're experiencing problems in related programs; for instance, crashes in many of your Internet programs. This can be caused by a corrupt Internet preferences file.

## Rooting Out Corruption

This might be tough for the muckrakers outside Tammy Hall (I know, I need to get out more), but rooting out corruption on your Mac isn't quite as tough. You have two different tools at your disposal.

The first tool you can use is Disk First Aid. Run it as described in Chapter 26, "Dealing with an Unhappy Mac," and then rinse and repeat if necessary. (I'm kidding.) Disk First Aid is good at fixing the Mac file system and, sometimes, repairing corrupt files. You'll find that tools like Norton Utilities and TechTool Pro can do the same things for you.

The second tool you can use is your noggin'. If you feel that a certain file is crashing your application, try not using the file for a while. If you feel that your problem is a certain application's preference file, open up the System Folder, then the Preferences folder, and drag the offending file out to the Desktop. Now run the program and see if things get any better. If they do, you can throw out the preferences file. If they don't, you might want to put that file back.

## Does My Mac Have a Virus?

There's a lot of talk about computer viruses out there. Could that be what's affecting your Mac? If you're a frequent downloader (you get a lot of stuff off the Internet) or if you share files and disks with other computer users, you're at risk for viruses. Computer viruses, like biological viruses, are easier to catch if you're milling about with others all the time. A virus can be transmitted by pretty much any sort of media—floppies, CD-ROMs, removable media disks—as well as over network lines.

A computer virus is simply a program designed to replicate itself. It does this by attaching itself to other files. Sometimes viruses are harmful on purpose—attacking your Mac filing system and trying to delete files. Others cause problems accidentally by attaching to important programs and causing them to behave erratically.

**Throw Away Preferences?**

In nearly every case I've encountered, Mac applications don't mind if you need to toss their preferences files; they'll just make another one when launched. You may lose some settings in your application, but if you suspect corruption, that's a small price to pay. Want some other files to throw away? In many cases with Web browsers, clearing the "cache" or throwing away cache files (also squirreled away in the Preferences folder) can solve a lot of problems. The same thing can be true of any "temporary" files left over after an application crash—like a temporary file in your e-mail program's folder that is part of an aborted download. Temporary files can also affect other applications like word processors and spreadsheet programs. One trick is to use the Find command in the Finder to look for the word "temp" and include hidden files and folders. You may also find temporary files in a folder called Rescued Items in the Trash after a crash.

Symptoms of a virus attack include the inability to save or load files, files that are missing, and unwarranted disk or network activity (for instance, drives are being accessed a lot, but you're not doing anything).

If you find yourself at risk, you can buy anti-virus software that periodically scans your hard drive and any floppy disks you insert for viruses. There are a number of these programs available online or in retail stores. The best of these programs run all the time, checking new floppy disks when you insert them and alerting you to abnormalities, but they may also give you some false alarms.

**Document Viruses**

A special class of viruses—called macro viruses or Visual Basic Viruses—attack only Word and Excel documents. If you're using Word 6, you may notice that all of your files are being saved as templates instead of documents and that some options are missing from the menus. Your solution: Don't open Word again, and then contact Microsoft for a special anti-virus tool. If you can live without the documents, you can throw away all infected documents and the Normal template from Word's Templates folder. Then start up, and you'll be okay until the next infection.

One rampant virus at the time of writing has to do with the Mac OS: the QuickTime AutoStart virus. To avoid it, open your control panels and choose the QuickTime Settings control panel. Choose **AutoPlay** from the pull-down menu and make sure that both of these options are *not* checked. The virus exploits the autoplay feature and spreads when it is run.

Virus software is often available in downloadable "demo" form on the Internet. Try the popular Mac shareware sites like **http://www.download.com** and **http://www.macdownload.com** on the Web.

# Stepping into Conflicts

When two applications—or an application and a System extension or part of the Mac OS—don't get along, you've got a conflict. The key to resolving conflict is communication. Because you don't know whether your Mac is from Mars or Venus, though, you're going to have to find some other way to facilitate this communication.

One way is to listen to your applications when they yell things like "Read Me!" at you. You'll find these *readme* files, documentation, and release notes have been included with most of the applications you've installed on your Mac. Check the folder in which the application is installed. Read those files if you're experiencing conflicts. Often you'll find that a conflict is already a known issue.

For instance, my current version of Netscape Navigator features a file called "Known Incompatibilities" in its folder. There I find that Navigator is incompatible with certain versions of Connectix Speed Doubler, among other programs and extensions.

You should also check the product support sections of the application developer's Web site or call their Customer Support lines and ask them about a possible conflict. They probably know what people complain about most often and may have tested for incompatibilities with something else you're running.

**Extension Lists**

Remember the Apple System Profiler discussed in Chapter 25, "Apple Extras?" That's a great tool for dealing with customer support representatives who insist on knowing absolutely everything about your Mac.

## Test for Extension Conflicts

If communication isn't working, you may need to test for the conflict on your own. In relationships, this is the equivalent of sidling up to your significant other and saying, "Is something wrong? Are you sure? Sure? Sure? Sure?" With your Mac, you'll have to do that same thing if you're testing for an extension conflict.

An extension conflict occurs when the combination of a particular extension and a particular application—or another extension—causes your Mac to crash or freeze. This tends to happen with third-party, non-Apple extensions, although it can also happen between any extension and any application. It can also be tough to troubleshoot, because you've likely got quite a few extensions and quite a few applications. Right?

Testing for an extension conflict is a tedious process at best. The first thing you need to do is get an idea *when* the crash or freeze happens; for instance, does it recur when you choose the Save command in your application? Does it happen when you drag some text or when you access a new document? Figure out what application is affected and when it happens. This will help you test for a conflict.

You'll find it's easiest to use the Extensions Manager control panel to help you along. Here's how it's done:

1. Open the Extensions Manager by selecting the **Apple** menu, **Control Panels**, and **Extensions Manager**.

2. From the **Select Set** menu, choose **Mac OS 8.5 All**. This chooses only the extensions that originally come with a full installation of the Mac OS.

3. Click **Restart**. After the Mac restarts, test to see if the error continues to present itself. (You'll test by trying to make the crash or freeze occur in the problem application.) If it does, you either have a conflict between an application and Mac OS 8.5 (especially if a particular application is the problem) or you have a problem with corruption or bugs. Armed with this knowledge, you should probably contact the application developer or try a different application.

4. If you're not having trouble anymore, you may very well have a conflict with your extensions. In the Extensions Manager again, choose **View**, **as Folders** and click the **Name** column to sort the list alphabetically. After all, that's the order in which your Extensions load.

*The Extensions Manager is a handy tool for fighting extension conflicts.*

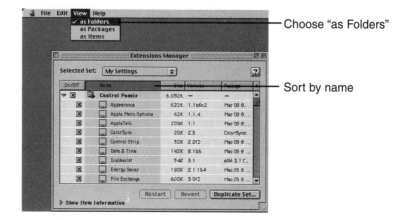

Choose "as Folders"

Sort by name

5. Now head down to the Extensions folder and click a few of the Extensions to add them to the startup process. (The first time you do this, you'll be asked to create a new extensions set—go ahead and do that, giving it a new name.) Once you've added three to five extensions in alphabetical order, click **Restart**.

6. Again, test for the conflict. If things are working fine, head back to step 5 and add a few more extensions.

7. If the conflict does recur, stop what you're doing, go back, and re-disable the last batch of extensions you enabled. (You might find a pen and notepad handy at this point if you're the sort who, like me, is apt to forget a thought midway through.) Now, enable the first of those extensions and **Restart.**

8. If the conflict doesn't occur, go back, enable the next extension, and restart again. Repeat until the conflict does occur. Now you know the extension that is causing the conflict. Or, at least, you know one of them. That's right…it's not quite over.

9. In the Extensions Manager again, pull down the **Select Set menu** menu and choose **Mac OS 8.5 All** again. Now enable the problem extension (you'll need to create yet another extension set). Restart.

10. Test to see if the conflict problem recurs. If it does, you've likely identified the extension or the application that are in conflict. At this point, you'll need to either upgrade one or the other—or decide which is more important and let the other one go. If the conflict doesn't recur, you're still caught in this list of steps!

11. With the Mac OS 8.5 All extensions and the problem extension enabled, you'll start the conflict test again, a few more extensions at a time. The only difference is you're testing them against both the Mac OS extension and the problem extension this time. Once the problem recurs, you'll follow the same procedure (steps 7 through 10) to see if the new problem extension and the old problem extension—together—can help you re-create the problem. If they do, you know the conflict is between the two of them or the application.

Whew. That's quite a listing, but it's quite a problem.

It's not often that it'll actually take you longer to accomplish something than it took me to write about it; in this case, though, that's a safe bet. Any extension conflict can take a while to get all the way through. That's one reason I've heard some wise Mac folk say you should avoid third-party extensions whenever possible.

## Resolving the Conflict

What do you do once you identify the conflict? If you've gotten through all this testing and identified the conflict, you can head to customer service and ask for advice, look around for updates, or toss everything that's giving you a headache and buy all new stuff. Toss in a new Mac while you're at it!

**Order Up!**

Actually, if you've identified a conflict between two different extensions, there may be one solution other than tossing them out. They may be conflicting only because of the *order* in which they're being loaded. Try this: Take the extension that's being loaded second—because it's further down in the alphabet—and edit that extension's name. (You'll have to head to the Extensions folder in the System Folder to do this.) All you need to do is put a space in front of its current name, and that will put it at the top of the alphabetical list. Now it's loading before the other extension. Restart. Test the two of them with just the Mac OS All extensions enabled and see if the problem recurs. If it doesn't, re-enable all your extensions, restart, and test again. You may have solved the problem!

Seriously, you'll often need an update for one or another of the extensions or applications in conflict, or you'll need to find a replacement that doesn't offer the same problems. It's possible, though, that the customer service folks at the various developers don't actually know this is a problem—or they might be testing for the problem in an ongoing way and your report may be helpful. You should, in any case, feel justified in discussing the matter with the vendors in question. You've already done a fine job of troubleshooting—now it's their turn to help out a bit.

# Use the Internet

These days, the Internet can help solve a lot of your troubleshooting dilemmas. (Unless your problem is that you can't get on the Internet, at which point the Internet becomes the proverbial hill-that-needs-to-be-taken or the belltower-that-must-stop-ringing, depending on your perspective.) You'll find that most software authors and publishers have information on their Web sites about troubleshooting, conflicts, updates, and other things that can affect their products. Hopefully, they also offer an e-mail address or online chat for customer service resolution.

You'll also find some other resources pretty useful for dealing with Mac OS problems; specifically, you'll probably really appreciate some of the resources at the Apple Support Web site (**http://www.apple.com/support/**). The resources there include information on Apple products, software updates, and fixes for Apple software (including the Mac OS) and news, identified problems, and so on.

One resource you may really find helpful is the Tech Info Library—a portion of the Apple Support site that's actually used by Apple's own support representatives to help you figure out problems. The Tech Info Library is searchable, allowing you to find information on specific issues affecting your Mac.

When searching, each term should be separated by a comma. If you have two words that are part of the same term (like "Mac OS"), you can use commas to separate those two words from other terms. Once you've entered the terms in the **Search for:** entry box to help you narrow things down, choose a topic area from the **Topics** menu and choose how you want the responses sorted. Then click the **Search** button.

After a few seconds, you'll see a listing of possible answers to your question. Click the hyperlinks to read the full article. If you don't see what you're looking for, return to the main page and try a broader search—use fewer keywords ("Mac OS 8.5" instead of "Mac OS 8.5, conflict, bug") or search in more topic areas. Hopefully, you'll find the answer to what you're looking for.

Or try some of the other Web sites out there that cover Mac problems. Some popular sites for troubleshooting information include:

➤ **http://www.macfixit.com/**—Ted Landau's site for updates to his book *Sad Macs, Bombs and other Disasters*

➤ **http://www.macintouch.com/**—Ric Ford's look at the world of Mac and Mac problems

➤ **http://www.macweek.com/**—News and information from *MacWeek.com* magazine

➤ **http://www.softwatcher.com/mac.html**—Tracks changes and updates to Mac software

➤ **http://www.versiontracker.com/**—A similar service, tracks updates to Mac programs

➤ **http://www.mac-upgrade.com/**—At the humble suggestion of your author, check out my own site for updating and troubleshooting help

# The Least You Need to Know

There are four different types of software failures you'll encounter—error messages, crashes, hangs, and freezes—and each of them can mean something slightly different. To begin with, you'll want to recover from these errors. If they continue to occur, however, you'll want to begin to look deeper and find out why they're happening.

In fact, there are three major reasons that trouble occurs: conflicts, corruptions, and critters (the best name I have for "bugs" that starts with a "c"). Each of these needs to be examined separately to see if it's causing the problem. Fortunately, there are usually some signs.

Bugs are often handled by upgrading the applications that's exhibiting the behavior; corruption can be solved by tossing out the data file that's corrupt or using a disk tool to fix the files. Corruption can also be the result of viruses, which can sometimes be rooted out and fixed with virus protection programs.

Conflicts are more complicated. You'll have to test very carefully for extension conflicts, and then look to the software vendor (or your wallet, if you decide to get different software) to resolve the problem.

Need a little more help? Head out onto the Web. These days, there are a ton of sites dedicated to helping the wayward Mac troubleshooter.

# Chapter 28

# The Macintosh Maintenance Routine

## In This Chapter

➤ Why a Mac Slows Down

➤ Working with Hard Drives

➤ Backing Up Your Files

Hopefully, you won't ever need to worry about Sad Macs, bombs, and freezes. But even if your Mac doesn't meet with catastrophic problems, there are some things you should know about prevention that can keep your Mac clicking along nicely. This will not only keep your Mac running along at a good clip, but it could also prevent bigger, more costly and more time-consuming problems. Keep to your maintenance regime, and you'll have a much better chance of computing along reasonably trouble-free for a long time.

The catch? For best results, you may need to buy a program other than the Mac OS. While the Mac OS has some built-in maintenance tools, Norton Utilities, TechTool Pro, and some other software packages do an even better job.

Even if you don't have one of these programs, though, there's still quite a lot you can do to keep your Mac running smoothly.

# Why Is My Mac Slowing Down?

Your Mac has an internal filing system—how it keeps track of your folders and icons. This is the nitty-gritty, technical, behind-the-scenes way that your Mac deals with data. What Mac does is keep a database of information about all the files you save and where it put them on the hard drive. Sometimes, if this filing system gets confused, it can slow down your Mac.

**Plain Icons**

The Desktop database is where icons and other information about your programs are stored. If you suddenly start to see different or generic icons for your applications or documents, you know your Desktop database is messed up.

This database, called the **desktop database**, is a little like a city map for your Mac's hard drive. Whenever you double-click an icon, Mac looks up that file's location in the Desktop database and tells the hard drive where to find it. The hard drive finds the data on its disks and sends it back to Mac's RAM so you can use it.

## Your Desktop Database Is Too Full

The most common cause of a Macintosh slow-down is a bloated desktop database. Over time, the Desktop database gets used a lot. Files get added and deleted, icons and other information get shuffled around, and the Desktop database keeps getting bigger. Eventually, every time you double-click an icon, it has to search a large file (that map of your hard drive) to find the information—thus slowing down your Mac. The Desktop database can also slow down startups and shutdowns.

**Rebuild More**

TechTool Lite, a freeware program from Micromat (**http://www.micromat.com/**), can be used to rebuild the desktop database completely; the program automatically cleans up the original files and replaces them. It does this without requiring the keyboard shortcut at startup; you just choose to rebuild the desktop from within the program.

To fix this problem, you have to tell your Mac to rebuild its desktop database. You do this by restarting your Mac and holding down **Option+⌘** all the way through the **Welcome to Mac OS** screen until Mac asks you if you want to rebuild the desktop database. Click **OK**, and it will re-create the desktop database by taking a quick look at the hard drive to see where everything is, storing the correct information, and doing away with old or bad Desktop data.

## Your Files May Be Fragmenting

When your Mac saves a file to the hard drive, it does its best to save that file *contiguously*, or all in one spot. If it can, it will find a large enough space on the hard drive to simply drop the whole file in so that, when you double-click on that file's icon, it just has to look in one place, and it can quickly send the file to RAM. It's a little like laying ceramic tile on a floor. You lay one row of tiles all in a neat, straight line. Then you lay another row right next to it, and so on, until you cover the floor. That's what Mac tries to do with files on your hard drive.

Unfortunately, every time you delete a file, you're picking up one of those tiles—leaving a small hole in your neat little system. Over time, a Mac's hard drive looks less like a tile bathroom floor and more like an old tile mosaic—with little holes where files used to be.

Now when your Mac goes to save a file, it tries to fill in these gaps. If the gap is too small for your file, the file has to be split up and put in two or more of these gaps. Suddenly, you're saving files that are **fragmented** or spread out all over the hard drive.

You'll need a special utility program to defragment your Mac's hard drive like Norton Utilities (**http://www.norton.com**). What this program does is determine the best way to pick up your file fragments and lay them back down in a contiguous pattern. Not only does this keep your Mac moving quickly, it also makes your files less likely to be corrupted.

## Preventive Care for Your Mac

To defragment files and do a number of other things to keep your Macintosh healthy, it's a good idea to buy a copy of Norton Utilities or one of the disk fixing applications from Alsoft (**http://www.alsoft.com**) or Micromat to take care of these little ailments. Generally, these software products are actually packages of smaller programs, each with a particular task.

Together with tools built into the Mac OS, you can come up with a maintenance plan for your Mac. One hint: If you use a personal information manager (a calendar or to-do list application) you might want to program a weekly reminder to help you remember to perform these maintenance tasks. Even better, most maintenance tasks can be done with third-party software that helps you automate the task completely.

**Backup First**

This is another time when it's a good idea to have a backup of any important files on your Mac's hard drive. Usually, the utility program will defragment your drive with no trouble. But if something bad does happen during the defragmenting process, you could lose valuable data. After all, your entire hard drive is being re-arranged by the defragmenting program. So make sure you have a good backup before running one of these programs. Of course, you have a good backup anyway, right?

Here's what you should do and when:

➤ Back up your data at least weekly, more often if possible. You may find a program like Retrospect (**http://www.retrospect.com/**) helps you automate this task. See Chapter 6, "Saving Stuff," for more details on backing up your data. Use at least three different disks or tapes and rotate them with every backup. That way you'll have a second backup if you find that one of your backup disks is bad.

➤ Check for viruses weekly (especially if you often use the Internet, a local network, or floppy disks). See Chapter 27, "Fixing Mac Errors," for more on detecting and dealing with viruses.

➤ Rebuild the desktop database file and run Disk First Aid once a month. This should keep the database from getting too corrupted while catching problems with the disk's files before they become more serious.

➤ Once every month or six weeks (more often in a business situation), create an *archive* of your data—a permanent backup of your data that you can refer to if newer backup disks or tapes go bad. You might even want to store the archive in a safe deposit box or elsewhere away from your Mac in case of disaster.

➤ Defragment your hard drive every three to six months. This should keep your Mac's hard drive running smoothly and quickly, while offering less of an opportunity for errors or corruption to creep into the file system.

## Optimize Your Hard Drive

Although it's not required, optimizing can go hand in hand with defragmenting. Many of the applications designed to defragment your hard drive will also optimize the drive if you choose to have it done.

When a utility like Norton's Speed Disk optimizes your drive, it's actually putting your files in order on the hard drive so that they are (1) more readily available to your Mac and (2) less likely to become fragmented. For instance, by putting all your applications in one place (because you're less likely to delete applications), a program can make fragmentation less likely.

## Fix Your Files

Another advantage of many of the "disk doctor" programs is they offer you the chance to recover individual files that have been affected by corruption, trouble with the desktop database, or similar problems. These files may be causing crashes discussed in Chapter 27, or you may simply no longer be able to use the data stored in that file.

If that's the case, turn to a disk doctor program. You can begin by running Disk First Aid; in fact, a regular Disk First Aid regimen might stop these problems before they start. If you still have trouble, use a disk doctor program to attempt to recover the files.

## Recover Files You've Trashed

Ever feel like picking up everything in your office or living room and just tossing it all in the dumpster? This happens to a lot of Mac users with their files. One day you wake up, look at your Macintosh HD window, and realize you've used up gigabytes on your hard drive. You go completely nuts deleting things.

**CanOpener**

You may also have luck with another Mac application, Abbott System's CanOpener (**http://www.abbottsys.com/**). This program is specifically designed to extract text and other data from corrupt, broken, or otherwise inaccessible files.

Then you realize you've thrown away your presentation to the Board. Uh, oh.

With just you and Mac, there's no way to get that file back. But some clever utility programs, including TrashBack that comes with Norton Utilities and some of the other disk management programs, enable you to recover files you've thrown away. For best results, you'll need to have TrashBack running *before* you accidentally throw something away, as a preventative measure. That way it can track deleted files.

The trick is that when you Empty Trash in the Finder, files in the Trash are not actually deleted from your hard drive. Instead, your Mac just makes a mental note to itself that it's now okay to overwrite that file with the next one that comes along. So, for a while anyway, the file is still there on the hard drive. With the right utility, you can get it back. After a certain amount of time, though (if the file has been overwritten by newly saved files, for instance), a file will be lost forever. If you need to recover a file that's been thrown away, hurry.

## The Least You Need to Know

There are a few different problems or issues that can cause your Mac to slow down over time, including file fragmentation and a bloated desktop database. Addressing both of these should be incorporated into a regular regimen of preventative maintenance for your Mac.

Using a regular schedule and some commonly available disk fixing tools, you should back up your Mac, run virus checkers, defragment the drive, and rebuild the desktop on a regular basis. You'll also find that tools like Disk First Aid can go a long way to solving problems before they get out of hand.

Once trouble does strike, Disk First Aid, Norton Utilities, and other software add-ons may prove useful. You can recover files, fix disks, and even get back files you've previously thrown out.

# Index

**353**

**357**

**365**

## X - Y - Z

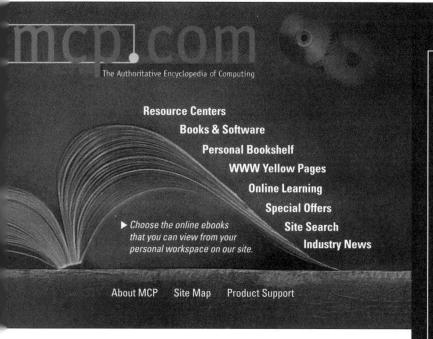